MOTHERS
AND DIVORCE

MOTHERS AND DIVORCE

LEGAL, ECONOMIC, AND SOCIAL DILEMMAS

Terry Arendell

Foreword by
Arlie Russell Hochschild

UNIVERSITY OF CALIFORNIA PRESS

Berkeley   Los Angeles   London

University of California Press
Berkeley and Los Angeles, California

University of California Press, Ltd.
London, England

© 1986 by
The Regents of the University of California

Library of Congress Cataloging-in-Publication Data

Arendell, Terry.
    Mothers and divorce.

    Bibliography: p.
    Includes index.
    1. Divorced mothers—Legal status, laws, etc.—United
States.   2. Divorce—Law and legislation—United States.
3. Marital property—United States.   4. Divorced
mothers—United States—Economic conditions.
5. Divorced mothers—United States—Social conditions.
I. Title.
KF535.A84   1987   346.7301′66   86-6959
                      347.306166
ISBN 0-520-05708-2 (alk. paper)

Printed in the United States of America

1   2   3   4   5   6   7   8   9

To Herbert Blumer,
in appreciation of his lifelong commitment
to the study of human group life

Contents

Foreword

Many well-intentioned self-help books on divorce cheerfully direct the divorcée to a fresh start, a creative new life-style, and new vistas of self-development. "Divorce may be hard," these books imply, "but a sunny disposition will make things right." However, the sixty divorced mothers in Terry Arendell's sensitive portrait were more preoccupied with paying for food and shelter than with a "creative new life-style." The problem of the divorced woman is not her personal attitude, Arendell argues, but her position in a larger economic arrangement between the sexes. Yet just this arrangement is hidden from view by popular notions about divorce.

In certain popular films (such as *An Unmarried Woman* and *Hannah and Her Sisters*) the heroine safely remarries, so that we never actually see how divorce affects the class position of women who remain single. Like popular literature on divorce, these films suggest that the trauma of divorce is basically psychological, that it is similar for men and women, and that it is temporary.

Contrary to popular assumptions, Arendell's book shows that for women, the central trauma of divorce is basically economic. It is much worse for women than for men. And the trauma is often permanent. Divorce usually pushes women down the class ladder— sometimes way down. It is not simply that women drop down a social class as they experience the psychological trauma of divorce. The class drop *is* the trauma.

The frightening truth is that once pushed down the class ladder, many divorced women and their children stay down—because many women find it extremely hard to find jobs that pay adequately, because they are the sole parent to their children, and because many do not remarry. Indeed, one out of three divorced mothers never remarries. Most divorced women remain unmarried much longer than divorced men, and many women remarry only to divorce again. If current trends continue, half of the young women who marry today will eventually divorce. In this sense, the divorced woman's story is becoming the married woman's cautionary tale: "If it happened to her, it could happen to me." For the stably married, divorce happens to "other people." But covertly, ubiquitously, other people's divorces influence one's own marriage. Since most women have more to lose economically through divorce, women have more at stake in marriage. In this sense, divorce acts as a control on married women.

Scholarly studies on divorce, social class, and gender seem to fall into two camps. In one, we find statistical studies on the feminization of poverty, such as "Women, Work, and Welfare: The Feminization of Poverty," by Diane Pearce. These studies focus on an empirical and implicitly structural trend in our society toward female impoverishment, but they do not connect that trend to the everyday lives of real women. In the other camp, we find psychological works, such as *Going It Alone,* by Robert Weiss, or *Surviving the Breakup,* by Judith Wallerstein and Joan Kelly. These studies treat the everyday problems of real women and children, but they detach those problems from overall architecture of gender relations. Between these two camps, we find Lenore Weitzman's *The Divorce Revolution,* which focuses on the legal aspect of no-fault divorce and its economic consequences, and which, because of its approach, forms a nice complement to Arendell's book. Arendell combines the virtues of both camps.

Using divorce as a mirror for marriage, Arendell exposes a key dilemma—for women, a crisis—in the economic relations between men and women. Simply stated, that crisis is this: women still do the unpaid work of rearing children. Since the mid nineteenth century, most American women above the poorest class were economically supported through traditional marriage in order to care for home and children. In a chill economic light, traditional marriage is what the economist Heidi Hartmann calls a "mechanism of redistribution." Men support women to rear children and care for the home. Most men could get the money to support women by earning wages in a workplace that presumed male workers would redistribute part of their wages to women. In the late nineteenth and early twentieth centuries, unions fought for higher "family wages" for men on the grounds that men needed more money to support the women who reared their children. Since this "redistribution" was assumed to occur, it seemed reasonable to many that men should get first crack at better paying jobs, and even earn more than women for the same work.

Virtually all high paying jobs did indeed become male. For many generations women were denied access to high wage jobs on the grounds that they "didn't need the money," or that they would take time off to care for their families. Many women, like those who speak through this book, stayed home to raise their children. Many others took time off, or accepted lower wages in the belief that they would be compensated financially by a "redistribution" of the male "family wage." Thus, the economy placed men and women in separate and radically unequal class positions, with only marriage to equalize them. Conversely, marriage became the main way a woman could avoid or escape the lower class station to which most female work otherwise assigned her. In sum, marriage came to protect women from a class division between the sexes built in to the outside economy.

The position of women in the economy has changed little: today women earn fifty-nine cents for every dollar a man earns for full-time work. A female college graduate earns less than a male high-school dropout.

But divorce has begun to rupture the redistribution of wages that once made economic inequity seem fair. Many divorced men still earn a "family wage" but do not redistribute it to their children or the ex-wife who still cares for them. Today, Arendell indicates, men tend to consider the "family wage" their own property, to spend on themselves or on the second family they begin or acquire when they remarry.

Of course, not all men earn more than women, and not all of them refuse support to their children. But Arendell's data form a distressing fit with findings from other studies that show that the vast majority of divorced men neither financially support nor directly care for their children after divorce.

This predominant male response to divorce has wiped out many gains of the women's movement. A newer, more pervasive, more impersonal form of oppression is partly replacing an older, more personal form. In the older form of oppression, men dominated women within marriage: in the newer form, they dominate women outside it. In the older form of female oppression, a woman was forced to obey an overbearing husband in the privacy of an unjust marriage. In the newer form, the working single mother is economically abandoned by her former husband and ignored by society at large. In the older form, women were socially limited to the home but economically maintained there. In the newer form, women do the work of a housewife and mother but are not paid for it.

Three factors—the belief that child care is female work, the lack of ex-husbands' support, and an economy where men outearn women—increasingly divide the sexes into separate social classes. This class separation between men and their ex-wives and children is new, and it is growing.

Terry Arendell gives this "new" oppression a human face. With a brilliant capacity to keep on listening and empathizing, Arendell invites us into the kitchen and the living room for intimate talks about things that matter to single mothers—the discouragements of long work days and poor pay, the loneliness of being single, the pain of watching a child's induction into poverty, and sometimes the surprise discovery of the courage to face it all. Anyone concerned with social justice in America should be touched and convinced that something must be done. One way to start is by reading this book—and passing it on.

Arlie Russell Hochschild

Acknowledgments

I first began the research for this book as part of my doctoral studies in the Department of Sociology at the University of California, Berkeley. I am grateful to the faculty members and friends there who encouraged me in many ways. I particularly appreciate the efforts of my dissertation committee members: Arlie Hochschild, Herbert Blumer, and Neil Smelser in the Department of Sociology, and Michael Rogin in the Department of History. I would also like to thank Jean Margolis, the Placement Advisor in the Department of Sociology, for her unfailing support and interest over several years.

I first became interested in the formal sociological study of the American family and changing gender roles in a graduate seminar conducted by Arlie Hochschild. It is entirely appropriate that the Foreword to this book should be written by her, for she has been intimately involved with it since it began as a dissertation research topic; she ardently supported my efforts to revise an unwieldy manuscript into a concise book, and she offered valuable comments and insights on countless successive drafts. It is a great joy for me to be able to acknowledge here, in print, how much my life has been enriched by her dedication to scholarship, her skill as an inspiring teacher, and her warm friendship.

My deepest appreciation also goes to Herbert Blumer. He was instrumental in my attending U.C. Berkeley in the first place, and he encouraged my interest in doing qualitative research, both through the example of his own scholarly work and through his personal interest in this project.

A two-year postdoctoral training fellowship in Social Gerontology at the University of California, San Francisco, sponsored by the National Institute for Aging, provided me the time I needed to complete this book and enabled me to pursue an interest that emerged during my research—a study of gender differences in family relations and economic status during mid-life and old age, as well as family transitions over the life course. I am pleased to acknowledge specifically the support and interest of two faculty members at U.C. San Francisco who have played a central role in my postdoctoral training: Carroll Estes, Professor and Chairperson of the Department of Social and Behavioral Sciences and Director of the Institute for Health and Aging, and Margaret Clark, Professor of Medical Anthropology.

My editors at the University of California Press—Naomi Schneider and Barbara Ras—have been wonderfully helpful and patient. And I will always be grateful to Gene Tanke. In the four months we worked together, he gave me a crash course in how to write with the reader's needs always in mind; his suggestions large and small, and his tenacious and subtle editing, improved this book in more ways than I can acknowledge here.

I thank my son Rob for his patience and general good humor, and, as he once put it, for conceding some of his time with me to the word processor. Being one of his parents has been a genuine pleasure and surely one of the most comprehensive of learning experiences.

Finally, I must thank the women who participated in this study and generously shared their personal stories with me. This book is about them, and they made it possible. I sincerely hope that they found some benefit in helping me, and that they will be encouraged by the publication of this book.

1

Popular Assumptions, Personal Experience

Divorce, once a relatively rare event described in negative and stigmatizing stereotypes, has now become commonplace. Between 1970 and 1980, the divorce rate more than doubled, and more than a million divorces occur every year. (See Appendix B, Tables 1 and 2.) Researchers with the U.S. Bureau of the Census estimate that 49 percent of all married men and women will divorce.[1] The continuing high divorce rate may well be the most dramatic change in family life in twentieth-century America.

One major effect of the continued high divorce rate has been the dramatic growth of families headed by mothers. (See Appendix B, Table 3.) The most systematic and comprehensive data available on changing family life, the University of Michigan's Panel Study of Income Dynamics (a nationally representative survey of five thousand families), found that after only seven years, over a third of the families being surveyed had a different person as head-of-household and that divorce was *the* major factor in family headship change.[2] Today over six million families with children are headed by a single mother. The number of children who live with a single mother who is either divorced or separated is nearly ten million. In fact, approximately one in six children lives with a single parent as a result of divorce or marital separation; and more than 95 percent of these children live with their mothers.[3] (See Appendix B, Table 4.)

Directly related to the dramatic increase in female-headed households has been the impoverishment of women.* Numerous studies

---

*I have deliberately avoided the phrase "the feminization of poverty" coined by

have concluded that women, together with their children, are being pushed into poverty while men are moving into higher income brackets. (See Appendix B, Tables 5 and 6.) In 1981 the National Advisory Council on Economic Opportunity reported: "All other things being equal, if the proportion of the poor who are in female-headed families were to increase at the same rate as it did from 1967 to 1977, the poverty population would be composed solely of women and their children by about the year 2000."[4] In 1983 over 40 percent of all female-headed families were below the poverty level ($10,178 for a family of four), and many more of these families were living marginally close to it.[5]

The impoverishment of women has been given increasing attention by the media, state and federal agencies, and independent policy-making bodies. For example, the state of California held comprehensive task force sessions in 1984 aimed at examining this social and economic trend.[6] Nevertheless, the trend shows no signs of abating, and no substantial programs have been implemented to weaken or eliminate the factors that support it.

One primary factor in the increased impoverishment of women and their children is divorce. In other words, the rise in both the total number and the relative proportion of poor women is directly related to the high divorce rate. More specifically, the increase of poverty among women is related to the *way* divorce occurs and thus to its consequences. Equal numbers of men and women divorce, but it is women who are made poor as a result of divorce.

Divorce does indeed affect women and men differently: for women the standard of living declines, and for men it rises.[7] Studies show that men recover economically and in fact improve their financial condition after divorce. For example, Lenore Weitzman's 1981 California study shows that after divorce women experience a 73 percent loss in their former standard of living, and men experience a 42 percent improvement in their standard of life.[8] Further, women generally experience no appreciable economic recovery from divorce unless they remarry.[9]

Pearce (1979), because, although it has caught public attention, it is misleading in that it does not suggest that women are actively being pushed into poverty by social forces. Rather, it suggests that women are taking over poverty! The phrase as it is commonly used ignores the fact that both income levels and the rate at which men are actively pushed above poverty continue to vary according to race. The impoverishment of women also varies by race.

Thus the number of women and children living in or near poverty continues to grow, largely as a result of divorce. Since neither the divorce rate nor the ranks of the poor appear likely to decline significantly, we are faced with a problem of major proportions. Millions of Americans confront economic uncertainties and difficulties that limit their access to the necessities of life. Why has our society—and why have we as individuals—remained so unmoved by the plight of divorced women with children? Why have we done so little about it?

These questions are difficult to answer, for three general reasons. First, various commonly held assumptions discount or ignore the economic and social effects of divorce, including the different ways divorce affects men and women. Second, we receive a great deal of our information about divorce in predigested form, as statistical data. But statistics provide only abstract descriptions of who divorces and what happens as a result; they give us no vivid pictures of personal experience. Third, even those of us who have divorced are tempted to see our own experience as idiosyncratic, even unique. We usually fail to recognize the similarities between our situation and that of others.

Throughout this book, reports of personal experience and recent sociological research will be brought to bear on seven popular assumptions about divorce. These assumptions are widely shared and have some limited basis in fact. But they also represent precisely the sort of thinking that must be challenged if we are to reach an honest understanding of divorce. It will be useful to state them briefly at the outset.

Divorce is equally hard on men and women.   Certainly, ending a marriage through divorce is a major life transition for both spouses. As Judith Wallerstein and Joan Kelly have stated: "Divorce is a process which begins with the escalating distress of the marriage, often peaks at the separation and legal filing, and then ushers in several years of transition and disequilibrium before the adults are able to gain, or to regain, a sense of continuity and confidence in their new roles and relations." [10] Researchers have concluded that it takes more than two years for an individual to regain emotional equilibrium after a divorce. [11]

In national studies that examine people's views on life experiences, divorce has consistently been ranked second among forty-two stressful life events. [12] Only the death of a spouse ranks above it for impact, and even that ranking has been challenged: "Despite the perception that death of a loved one should be harder to adjust to than divorce from a previously loved one, data on the physical and mental health status of the widowed and divorced indicate that there is generally more physical and mental health disturbance among the divorced than [among] the widowed." [13] Emotional stress is viewed as a normal part of divorce. It has social legitimacy, and many divorced persons do not hesitate to seek counseling or therapy for help in sorting out their feelings.*

Children of divorced parents are likely to have serious problems. Divorce research has always stressed the psychological effects of divorce and single parenting on children.† In the 1950s and 1960s many researchers argued that divorce and the subsequent mother-headed family fostered juvenile delinquency, homosexuality, and neuroses in children. [14] Although most scholars and clinicians have now abandoned such arguments, they remain embedded in popular notions about the fate of the child from a "broken home." In fact, much contemporary research continues to assume that the female-headed single-parent household is a "deviant pathological" form.‡ Divorce is thought to be harmful to children at least partly because mothers are unable to raise children successfully without a father present in the home.

Reformed divorce laws have given equality to women. It is widely believed that recent legal reforms aimed at eliminating the law's traditional gender bias in divorce have succeeded, so that in theory and in practice, divorce law is now gender-neutral. Indeed, the

---

*The rapid growth of the counseling profession is doubtless due in part to the increase in the divorce rate. Sardoff (1975) found that in no-fault states, the number of available counseling services increased and more people sought counseling.

† According to Goetting (1981), the areas most heavily researched have been delinquent behavior; physical health, especially the incidence of diabetes; cognitive performance and school success; personality traits; ability to form close relationships with others; heterosexual behavior; mental health and psychosomatic illnesses; and adult marriage and sexual behavior, especially among females.

‡ Crossman and Adams (1980:205) provide a review of recent research. The long-held view that the absence of a father adversely affects children has increasingly been challenged. For example, a study of nearly nine hundred school-aged children found that single-parent families were just as effective in rearing children as traditional two-parent families. After controlling for socioeconomic variables and matching groups of

legal process of getting a divorce has now been simplified in all fifty states. For this reason, many people believe that men's and women's options for obtaining divorce are not only equal but also more flexible and varied than they previously were. It is assumed that personal freedoms and individual rights are now given priority over the state's traditional interest in preserving marriage, and that this trend represents a gain in civil liberties for men and women alike.[15]

It is believed that because society places great value on a wife's mothering activities, and because the law recognizes the contributions of each spouse to the marriage and family life as being equal, recognition is given in divorce settlements to men's and women's different family activities. In other words, it is thought that a primary aim of divorce law is to treat a divorcing husband and wife equally, so that they can live in comparable situations after divorce.

Community property laws treat wives and husbands equally. It is commonly thought that in terms of property settlements, divorcing spouses are treated equally in states that legally adhere to community property principles. Divorcing women are believed to be better off in states that follow community property statutes rather than common-law principles. It is also believed that because the traditional biases that favored men in marriage—such as laws that gave them control over their wives' earnings, property, and legal identity—have been diminished, so that women have gained equality with men in settling property matters at the time of divorce.

Divorced fathers pay heavily to support their ex-wives and their children. It is often believed that most divorced fathers continue to share the costs of raising their children, and also that women who really need financial assistance after divorce receive it through spousal support payments. (In California's no-fault divorce statutes of 1970, "spousal support" replaced the familiar term "alimony.") Apparently, some people even believe that the need to make support

---

children in father-present and father-absent families, they found no significant differences between the two groups (Feldman, 1979:453). Another scholar argues: "Studies that adequately control for economic status challenge the popular homily that divorce is disastrous for children. Differences between children from one- and two-parent homes of comparable economic status on school achievement, social adjustment, and delinquency behavior are small or even nonexistent" (Bane, 1976:111).

payments forces many men to increase their earning activities, sometimes so much as to limit their involvement with their children.* Many still believe the stereotype that men "get taken to the cleaners" in divorce, a belief that is fueled by media coverage of wealthy celebrities who divorce and their focus on the huge spousal support demands often made by attorneys for the wife. Justifications for nonpayment of support are also fairly common. Some fathers' rights groups have even argued that men fail to pay support because they are denied access to their children and that they have little involvement with their children after divorce because their former wives prevent it.†

Divorce affords great opportunities for personal growth and development. This assumption has been widely popularized by psychologists and self-improvement groups. Here is a typical expression of it from *Divorce: The New Freedom,* by Esther Fisher: "Divorce is a dynamic process that can precipitate your growing away from childish dependency toward mature independence. . . . Finally, as a mature growing person you no longer believe in magic but in yourself. You recognize life is an endless struggle and accept its challenges. Having found yourself and having become aware of who you are with all your limitations and all your good qualities, you have the strength and judgment to cope with the many problems life presents. You begin to see what lies ahead as a difficult but exciting and romantic adventure which will demand much giving, loving, taking of responsibility, faith, hope, and trust in yourself and in others. You are no longer bored. Instead you discover an exhilarated feeling of being liberated as you become more and more involved with life and the master of your own destiny." [16]

---

*In *Single Father's Handbook: A Guide for Separated and Divorced Fathers,* Richard Gatley and David Koulack (1979:25) write: "The increased financial burdens of separation and divorce, for instance, are normally carried by the children's father. You may be kept too busy trying to meet these obligations to find time for the kids. Even if you don't have to put in overtime or take another job to make ends meet, your job may permit very little free time to be with your children."

†From Gatley and Koulack (1979:26) again: "Alarm about not having the kids, or about having lost them permanently, is an extremely common reaction among separated fathers who have had a sort of reawakened awareness of their children. Often these feelings are accompanied by angry feelings that the children's mother is somehow holding the kids for ransom. If you don't pay her child support or alimony, or be nice to her, you won't be able to have the kids this weekend."

In this view, the divorced man or woman becomes more able to focus on self and to take up the life-style of a single person. Divorce is the path to freedom; the search for self can proceed unchecked by family responsibilities or the expectations or criticisms of a spouse. Divorce offers the space needed to change one's life, possibly with another partner who is believed more able to meet one's present needs. Above all, personal needs and wants are valued. Personal choices can be made and pursued, free of the constraints imposed by an outgrown marriage. In this assumption, men and women are equal players in the search for self and personal growth, and equal in intimate relationships.

Postdivorce problems are only temporary, because most people remarry. It is often assumed that the problems of the single-parent family headed by a mother are temporary and abnormal, and need not be considered seriously since they will be solved as soon as the mother remarries. It is thought that few divorced women, particularly those who are "middle-class" and mothers of minor children, remain unmarried.

I am not suggesting that these are the only assumptions people make about divorce, or that they have been identified through scholarly research. I would argue only that these particular assumptions, though admittedly stated here in somewhat arbitrary ways, can be readily found in today's popular literature and media representations of our culture. Further, as I suggest in analyzing the experiences of sixty divorced women, the widespread indifference to the socioeconomic effects of divorce on women and their children, and the lack of political and social action aimed at helping them, can only be explained by the continued and wide acceptance of such assumptions.

What explains the continued vitality of such assumptions, particularly given the research evidence that contradicts them? Why are these ideas still taken seriously in political debate, implicitly and often explicitly, from the presidential to the precinct level? One answer, I think, is that we are accustomed to looking at divorce (when we look at all) from one of two extreme angles.

At one extreme, we see divorce statistically—in numbers, percentages, and trends. Such abstractions are easy to interpret in ways that reinforce our own values, because they reveal very little about the moral complexity of the personal experiences involved. The dilemmas of real people are hidden behind the "social indicators."

At the other extreme, when divorce does have a familiar face, because of our own experiences or those of someone close to us, we understand it in the same way we understand marriage—as a "personal" and unique experience. In a society that places a high value on individualism, choice, and the privacy of the family, the many kinds of socially common experiences that shape our personal lives go largely unnoticed. (A sobering example is wife beating. It has a long and shocking history, but until the women's movement of the 1970s began to reveal its true extent, its occurrence in American society remained closeted behind popular ideologies about personal and family life.)[17] Facets of the divorce experience that are shared, particularly along gender lines, tend to be ignored. The connection between the personal and the public is not made.

The purpose of this book is to illustrate the inadequacies of many commonly held assumptions about divorce and to provide a focused sociological picture of the real experiences of sixty divorced women with children. The analysis is aimed at understanding how divorced mothers define their own situations and how they respond to them in their daily lives.

The procedures used to select the sixty women, and the research methods used to organize the information they provided, are described at length in Appendix A. The women are further described in Appendix B, Tables 7 through 12. Here, the following few facts will serve to introduce them. They ranged in age from twenty-six to fifty-eight, and between them they had custody of 121 minor children, whose ages ranged from three to eighteen. Each of the women had enjoyed a socioeconomically middle-class life-style during marriage. At the time of the interview, each had been divorced for at least two years, and each had at least one dependent child living with her. None of the women lived with her parents or shared living arrangements with a male friend. In other words, each was a single-parent head-of-household. In the following chapters, these women will speak in their own voices about the legal, economic, parental, and social aspects of their lives as divorced mothers.

2

Experiences
with the Law

Divorce is in part a legal event: laws exist for officially ending the marriage, resolving separation conflicts, determining custody and support of children, and dividing marital property. Thus the personal experience of divorce is colored, often vividly, by contact with the legal system.

Before they faced their own divorces, the sixty women shared certain popular impressions about the legal system and divorce law. They believed that California's no-fault divorce statutes, in effect since 1970, had made divorce much easier to get and had brought greater fairness to divorce by eliminating its obviously adversarial aspects.[1] They believed that the changed divorce laws made women and men equals within family law, and that because California is a community property state the division of property would be fair and just. They assumed a gender-blind system of justice in which their participation in the marriage, whether it involved economic dependency or not, would be considered of comparable worth to the wage earner's activities. They also believed that the legal system, although gender-blind, would recognize their special economic needs as mothers of children and would see that these needs were met by ordering adequate payments of child support and (where necessary) spousal support (alimony). Finally, these women assumed that the lawyers and other legal professionals with whom they would have to deal would operate from a base of shared values, that they would seek justice and protection of clients' rights and exercise professional responsibility toward them.

In this chapter, we look first at what these women had to say about their experiences with legal professionals—mainly private attorneys but also district attorneys and judges. Then we consider their experiences with the law and their assessments of it.

Experiences with Legal Professionals

Although these women had gradually acquired an understanding of the separate and distinct roles assigned to legal professionals in divorce proceedings, they continued to view them as part of a relatively cohesive system; in their eyes, the law and its legal role players were linked in a single organized arrangement. Still, the complaints they voiced in their interviews were derived from personal experiences with individual lawyers, judges, and district attorneys.

Lawyers

Fifty-three women had strong complaints about the lawyers they had hired to represent their interests. None of the women had engaged an attorney until it was clear that divorce was imminent, though eight of them learned later that their husbands had obtained legal advice several months before their separations. Most of them had found their lawyers through referrals from friends or family members—referrals often based only on hearsay. Several had simply picked a telephone number from the yellow pages and called to ask what a particular lawyer would charge.

Most of the women said their attorneys had showed little interest in their present or future problems and had not tried to keep them informed about divorce legalities and the overall legal process. Although they had been sought out as counselors in a personal life crisis, these lawyers soon appeared to be bureaucratic technicians, more concerned with forms, figures, and procedures than with a client's history, fears, or future well-being. This comment was typical:

> He couldn't stay on top of all the paperwork and everything that needed to be produced, and that was all he was concerned about. I'd call him and try to stay on top of things.

Oversights by attorneys provoked a great deal of anger and frustration. Failure to return phone calls, the most frequent complaint, eroded the attorney-client relationship and increased the woman's sense of stress. Often a lawyer's oversight cost the divorcing woman money:

> So I go to work and call my lawyer. I'm livid. I mean I'm screaming and yelling. There's a bench warrant out for my arrest because I didn't show up for court. The lawyer hadn't notified me that I was supposed to be in court. I had to pay him $300 to go down there and represent me, and the judge threw out the warrant [ruling there was insufficient reason for it].

Because one woman's attorney failed to file the papers necessary to get a court hearing, she was left stranded for months:

> I ended up living with my parents because I couldn't get my husband out of the house; I couldn't even get the furniture out of the house until we went to court, because my husband wouldn't let me have it. I left in August, but I didn't get our things until February. I couldn't even get my daughter's clothes.

Legal delays also increased emotional uncertainty and blocked attempts to reorganize one's life. One woman, for example, was forced to live apart from her children while she waited for legal action she had already paid for:

> I left with the understanding from the lawyer that we could get a restraining order in a few days or a few weeks. But it was four months before I got the order that got my husband out of the house and gave me permission to move back in the house with custody of the children. The children were there with him those four months.

Last-minute decision making and hurried procedures kept many women off balance and contributed to their general unease with the entire legal process. For example:

> We were supposed to go to court at ten o'clock. We were to meet in my attorney's office at nine to sign the final agreements. He was late, so I had to sign all those papers in about ten minutes. We ran over to the court. I didn't even know that my divorce became final on that day; I thought I had medical coverage and all the military benefits for another six months. I was so ill-informed that I didn't know what had

happened until I got the papers in the mail! I'm not a stupid person, either. I'm well educated; I've traveled in circles with other well-informed persons. If that can happen to me, imagine what's happening to others.

Attorney's fees posed a major problem for these women. Many of them had no cash available when they needed to hire an attorney to initiate or respond to divorce proceedings. Some borrowed money from friends or family members just to get the legal process started. Several sought help from legal aid groups but were turned away because the "family" income was too large; the regulations did not take account of the fact that most of the family income came from the husbands of these women and was unavailable to them as divorcing wives.[2] Most regarded their legal expenses as exorbitant, considering the effectiveness of the service they received.

Most of the women reported spending several thousand dollars on attorney's fees, and several had bills over $10,000. High legal costs thus contributed greatly to the economic hardship they experienced after divorce. In general, the more community property there was, the higher the legal costs became. Legal fees were often paid out of a woman's share of the community property settlement, which thus reduced her starting capital for life after divorce. In several cases described to me, the court ordered the husband to pay court costs and the wife's attorney's fees. But not all the husbands paid. Five of these women, legally relieved of these expenses because of their relatively poorer economic circumstances, ended up paying them anyway.

What aroused the greatest anger was the common perception that lawyers were profiting at the expense of children, draining away the financial resources needed for their support and care. As one woman put it:

> I feel the parents are paying attorneys a fantastic sum for this kind of work. The money should be going to the children's welfare. This whole business should be taken away from the courts. The sad thing is that the lawyers are eating up the money that rightfully should be used to raise these children.

For most of these women, filing for divorce was only the beginning of a long series of encounters with lawyers, judges, and the law. Their attempts to enforce support orders or visiting rights, to resist challenges to custody, or to modify financial awards led many of them into repeated dealings with the legal system. The role of lawyers in these engagements was assessed with bitterness. Some women said that seeking legal redress guaranteed only one thing—more attorney's fees. Others said that lawyers profited from scheduling repeated court hearings, and that many of these hearings had been made necessary by inadequate or improper agreements written by the lawyers themselves.

Only seven of the sixty women voiced no vehement complaints about their legal experiences. Three of these, who had few material assets and faced no challenge over child custody, did their own divorce paperwork and simply filed it with the courts. Another three worked out agreements with their spouses before hiring attorneys. In their cases, large amounts of property and relatively substantial incomes were at stake; but in each case, both spouses shared a primary concern for the emotional well-being of their children, and prolonged dialogue and debate eventually produced satisfactory general agreements. The other woman with no complaints about her legal experiences had entered law school upon her separation and had completed her divorce with the help of a law school professor who served as her attorney. She acknowledged that in her situation, it was her husband who was at a definite disadvantage.

In three of the sixty cases, the attorneys' potential effectiveness was undermined by spouses who used the legal system as a battleground. Intent on fighting, or unwilling to compromise, they carried on personal vendettas through their lawyers; as they rehearsed old personal grievances and found new ones, the legal costs for both parties rose, and the divorce process was prolonged. One of the women said:

> Then it went from bad to worse. My ex-husband wanted every piece of jewelry he'd ever given me as a gift to be community property. And his attorney was willing to try to get it for him. Finally the judge told my ex-husband and his attorney to get serious.

Several women ignored legal advice when it seemed to conflict with likely paths to reconciliation, which they still hoped for. One of them, for example, said she had received an unfair property settlement because she had followed her heart instead of her attorney.

The stupidest thing I ever did was not to follow my lawyer's advice and file first. After he moved out of the home, my husband moved to Utah, supposedly to fill in there for his company for a short time. He continued to dangle me, saying he just wasn't sure what he wanted to do and that this separation was probably just temporary. The children and I even went to visit him at Christmas; we all had a nice time. My husband and I didn't discuss any of our problems until the day before the kids and I were to leave. And then he said he was still trying to sort it out. I didn't realize that he was being strategic: he filed for divorce in Utah as soon as he met the residency requirements. He'd just been stalling in order to get a better settlement for himself by not being in a community property state.

Other women reported that they had unintentionally reduced their attorneys' overall effectiveness through their own efforts to appear capable. One of them said:

Part of my problem with the legal system was my own fault. I gave the appearance of being knowledgeable. I knew more about buying property and bank accounts than my lawyer did, but I didn't understand all the tax things. And so I was reluctant to ask some of the things I should have asked, and she [the attorney] assumed I knew a lot of things. I wanted to be competent, and I thought it was really important to have some kind of civilized relationship between the lawyers and my husband.

Judges and District Attorneys

Judges, who presided over and ruled on contested cases, were held in general contempt. They were seen as enforcers of inequitable laws and as personally insensitive to the specific problems of divorcing women. This attitude was often expressed in complaints that judges allowed attorneys to indulge in what the women considered insulting, even outrageous, courtroom behavior. For example:

Going to court was the absolute worst. With my husband sitting there listening, I had to go through the whole list of my expenses [since the divorce]. I had very careful records, and they questioned every damned thing. My husband's lawyer contested every cent. And he challenged every cent I gave the kids. He wanted to know how much each was earning working. Never mind that this is an affluent family—or *was!* He wanted to know if these children—and both of them were still under eighteen—were reimbursing me. I asked, "Reimbursing me for what?" "Well, for food and things," he said. We were going to penalize these guys for earning their own spending money? But that judge just sat there and let them carry on like that.

Complaints of gender bias from the bench were common. This one, directed against a family court judge, is representative:

My kids are fourteen, sixteen, and seventeen. They all live here with me. I support them by juggling bills and expenses—and fighting eviction notices. Fun things, right? I get no child support or anything. I did, until a judge saw my ex-husband in court for beating his new wife. The judge didn't want to deal with him anymore, so he just told him to get lost, as if these kids didn't even exist.

District attorneys most often entered the lives of women whose depleted financial resources led them to seek help in collecting delinquent child support payments. Of the sixty women I interviewed, twenty-four received no child support at all, and another thirteen received support only irregularly and in amounts less than the court had ordered. Most of them had been referred to a district attorney by private lawyers who had concluded that the women could not afford to pay for legal services. Many found that because they were not receiving welfare support, they had little chance of getting state assistance in collecting court-ordered child support.* One woman reported:

My lawyer told me to call the D.A.'s office. I did, and they said to call my lawyer because it would take them over a year to get to my case, if

* At the time of the research interviews, in 1983 and early 1984, Title IV-D of the Social Security Act provided funds to states for the enforcement of child support owed to families on welfare. There were, however, no programs that provided incentives to states for assisting nonwelfare families in collecting support. The Parent Locator Service, established by Congress in 1982, enables custodial parents on welfare to gain access to government record-keeping systems in order to track down divorced fathers who are in arrears and to attach their income tax refunds. The Child Support Enforcement Amendments of 1984 have extended the 1982 laws by opening up the IRS's Parent Locator Service to *all* families entitled to unpaid child support. Further changes in the federal law include new incentives for states to collect overdue child support from nonwelfare cases: states are rewarded with a fee of 6 percent of the total payment collected. Nonwelfare mothers, however, must pay a fee to use the Parent Locator Service. For a review of these changes, see Statsky (1984) and the United States Department of Health and Human Services Child Support Enforcement Act of 1984 in *West's California Code* (1985).

they ever did. So there's really nothing that can be done. They can threaten my ex-husband with jail, but what good does that do? When I asked him for the money, he said, "Get an attorney and try to throw me in jail. I'll just go off to New York and you won't ever get anything." He knows I can't afford an attorney again.

Many said that the treatment they received in district attorneys' offices was not only rude and dehumanizing but incompetent. For example:

The D.A.'s office here is a joke. It's incredible, it really is. I think they must train their people in rudeness—and incompetence. At one time, I said I wanted them to go after my ex-husband for nonsupport and back support. They told me they couldn't do it without a signed divorce copy from the judge. I told them they'd had one on file for over two years. Well, they couldn't find it. They said they'd have to send for it, which would take a while. So I offered to go get it myself, get it signed, and hand carry it back to them. I did that, I brought it to their office. I came back a week later, like they said, and they told me they couldn't find it. They act like, "Why are you here, lady? Everybody wants money, so what?" So finally I gave up on them.

Another woman, who was unique because she had some legal training that informed her how the system was supposed to work, described the frustration she experienced:

I'm getting bitter beating my head against the wall, trying to get my ex-husband to make child support payments. I go back and forth through the Uniform Enforcement Act. It's hell trying to get the D.A. to act on my behalf, because I'm not on welfare. They don't care; they just don't care. I took a whole batch of things to them last December: my ex-husband's name, Social Security number, Union ID, place of employment. They said there was nothing they could do. I told them, "Bullshit." They could get him served by someone from the Southern California agencies used by the casinos [where he works], serve him, and get a judgment against his wages.

Several women accepted without protest a husband's failure to make child support payments. Their most typical reason for doing so was an understanding that he was really unable to pay. Pressing him with legal action, they thought, would be counterproductive—and sometimes it was. One woman told this story of how she was unwillingly victimized by the adversarial nature of the legal system:

> It was really sad. My daughter had a medical problem with her feet, and her father and I felt she had to have surgery. So I went to the social services office and asked for help with the medical bills. They said, "Oh certainly, but in order to get that help, you have to declare where their father is." That was fine, I had anticipated that. I told them he had no money, though. They said they wouldn't cause him any problem, but I had to go to the D.A.'s office and declare that he couldn't pay. They insisted I had to file a complaint in order to get some help. [I did that] and the D.A.'s office took off after him and hassled him, even though he wasn't working then. They took him to court even though he didn't have any money. So he just disappeared after that.

To discover how lawyers might react to reports like these, I talked with five attorneys who had some family law practice. They all defended their colleagues by explaining that clients frequently create difficulties and fail to understand the complexities of the law and the divorce process. They said that divorcing people, especially women, are usually anxious and fearful, and they often want their attorneys to provide personal and marital counseling along with the legal work lawyers are paid to do. They said that clients create delays and unnecessary work by fighting with the other spouse and by being less than fully honest with the attorney. They added that clients frequently fail to pay their bills on time and sometimes prolong the entire process by changing their minds and seeking reconciliation. All five of them said, in one way or another, that "judges have heard it all before, and they have usually made their decision from reading the case before the trial." They also said that district attorneys' offices are deluged with work, and that the divorced women who seek out their services and press for immediate help are generally uninformed about their specific legal needs.

As clients, inexperienced and caught up in a highly emotional process, the women's perspectives naturally differed from those of their attorneys. Some of them feared for their very survival: threats and even attacks had been made by over half of these women's divorcing husbands. They were almost completely dependent on their attorneys for advice and the timely completion of proper procedures, and they expected to receive in full the services they paid for. They also expected to be treated fairly and justly by judges and district attorneys and their office personnel. They did not foresee the extensive bureaucracy and indifference that would confront them.*

Experiences with the Law

While getting a divorce, the women became disturbed by the law in three specific areas: child custody, child support, and property settlements. Decisions and actions in each of these areas were vital to the way they would live their lives after divorce. Legal biases and the system's inertia in enforcing even its own orders were particularly frustrating and alarming to them. For some, child custody was the most important issue because their ex-husbands were challenging court orders giving custody to the mothers. But for most, the issues of child support and property settlement were paramount and produced the strongest negative feelings about the law.

Child Custody and Visiting Rights

As is typical throughout the nation, the majority of these California women had sole physical custody of their children, and their former husbands had visiting rights (two women shared parenting so had joint physical and legal custody).† With only three excep-

---

*Louise Halem (1980:287–288) concludes: "[Divorce] law has not demonstrated its capacity to dispense justice in an equitable and benevolent fashion and to mollify the social, psychological, and economic effects of divorce. . . . Because judicial decisions are inconsistent and contradictory not only within and between states but inside the same tribunal, and because lawyers are trained and paid to function as adversaries, the legal system encourages combat, often ignoring individual welfare and needs."

†Many of these women had divorced before passage of the 1979 California law mandating that in the absence of evidence to the contrary, the court is to presume that joint custody is in the best interests of the child. (Of course, modifications of child custody, including a grant of exclusive custody, can be sought in the courts; see California Civil Code, sec. 400.5a, in *West's California Code,* 1983b). The effects of this legal change are as yet unclear, but recent studies suggest that they are minimal. Over 90 percent of the children involved in divorce still go into the mother's (physical) custody by agreement or default, as previously; and there has been no significant increase in the percentage of fathers who ask for or are awarded custody of children (Weitzman and Dixon, 1979; U.S. Bureau of the Census, 1983c; Weitzman, 1985).

tions, this custody arrangement was agreed upon by both spouses outside the legal divorce process. All but two of the women had done most of the parenting and child care work during marriage, and divorce did not change this fact.[3] Many of the women believed that joint custody could not work because the former spouses were bound to have basic value differences and conflicts, especially over parenting.

Three of the women had sole physical custody of their children but shared legal custody with their former husbands. They were basically hostile to this arrangement, for it left their former husbands with considerable power over their lives and the lives of their children. Indeed, two of the three fathers in question did not even pay their child support, but they continued to harass their former spouses about child-rearing methods, ways of spending money, and social activities.* Without the former husband's permission, or a ruling from the court, the mothers could not move out of the locality, even for financial reasons.

Other women had their custody challenged in the courts by vindictive husbands who seemed primarily interested in harassing them. Although they had not been particularly active parents before divorce, these men could afford to pay for expensive court challenges. Louise Halem argues that in the presence of no-fault divorce statutes, child custody challenges can become a substitute means of assigning guilt and blame. Noting "the legislature's decision to preserve adversary practices and moralistic considerations of transgression in custody suits," she quotes law professor Michael Wheeler: "Much of what the legislature has accomplished in barring fault as a factor in divorce was undone in allowing it to be considered without limitations in custody questions."[4]

One woman's former husband, after obtaining joint legal custody of their daughter, moved to a midwestern state and challenged his ex-wife in court for physical custody of the child in alternate years. The mother explained why she was resisting this challenge:

---

* Visitation cannot be refused a divorced father because he does not pay his court-ordered child support (California Civil Code, sec. 4321, in *West's California Annotated Codes,* 1983a). For a discussion of joint custody and its complicated legal, social, and family issues, see Bruch (1978) and Bodenheimer (1978). For a positive assessment of joint custody, based on middle-class and upper-middle-class cases, see Ware (1982).

My daughter's aware that her father is fighting for custody in alternate years. And he wasn't even interested in her before the divorce. She'll ask me sometimes where she'll be living next year. Then she sets it aside and doesn't want to talk about it. He keeps telling everybody that she'll be there with him. I think we're going about it the wrong way. I think this kid, at five years old, needs more security than that. She shouldn't be worrying about where she'll be next year and with which parent. She's been in the same preschool for almost three years. Even when we've moved, I've made sure that some things stayed stable for her.

Child Support

Attempts to collect child support payments were what most often took these women back to lawyers and the courts after divorce. Several who were owed child support had not returned to court only because they lacked the money. In their search for help, they found a two-tiered system for the collection of child support: one level for mothers receiving welfare payments and another level for all others. In theory, district attorneys could seek enforcement of any court order; in practice, however, public funds were available to enforce only the collection of support owed to women who were receiving public assistance. Only three of the mothers I interviewed were receiving welfare, and their ex-husbands were not paying child support. The others, because they were not receiving welfare, ultimately had to seek legal and judicial enforcement of child support payments on their own, by hiring and paying private attorneys.*

Thirty-six of these women, a full 60 percent, had sought enforcement of child support payments through the legal process at least once. Almost all had learned from experience how costly the process of trying to collect child support could be:

When he was here a couple of weeks ago, I told my ex-husband I needed the money. He told me to take it up with my attorney. He knows what that costs me, and when I reminded him, he told me, "That's your problem, not mine." He's got me. I can't afford to have

*Child support is collected administratively through governmental agencies in several nations, notably Sweden, France, West Germany, Israel, Austria, Denmark, Norway, and Poland. For discussions of child support collection in other societies, see Kamerman and Kahn (1983); Hahlo (1983); Garfinkel and Sorensen (1982).

my attorney do it. It costs me $110 an hour for an attorney. To try to get two months' support, it costs me $175, a whole month's child support. That's just for me to call the attorney and for him to write a letter and get a copy sent to me. I can only afford to pay him $75 a month, and his bill keeps getting higher. I'm having a hard time with it.

We've got a court order for child support. Last year, when I knew my ex-husband had a job and where, I tried to go through my attorney to get enforcement. But all that happened was that I got stuck with court costs and attorney's fees, and I didn't get any money in return. I did have a lien on his paycheck once. I got like two hundred dollars that way, and he promptly got fired. That's the only thing I ever got from him. It just didn't pay off.

By pleading reduced income or increased expenses, several fathers succeeded in getting the court to reduce the amount of their support payments. The ex-wife of one of them said:

Now that his income is back up, they should raise the child support back up. But he's got himself all these debts from his traveling around the world to scuba dive, so I don't know what will happen. His argument always is that my parents have money. So what? I'm not dependent on my parents. And this is his child, too.

More commonly, the divorced fathers did not bother to go to court but simply began paying less, thus forcing the custodial mother to decide whether to initiate legal action. Here is what a woman with four children told me about her continuing struggle to get child support:

My ex-husband earns $36,000 a year as a contractor plus whatever he earns as co-owner of the business. The court order is for him to pay me $550 a month child support. Now he's reduced the child support to $400 and says he's going to reduce it again. He just doesn't know how to handle money and says he has none. But he earns $3,000 a month. Even counting taxes and all, $550 out of it for these four children is not all that much. I called my lawyer, but he said if I take it to court, there's a chance I won't get it, that the judge might change the order to suit my ex-husband. And the lawyer told me it would cost me a lot to go to court. I can't win—you just can't win.

In practice, then, the former husbands of these women had enormous discretion in deciding whether to pay child support at all, and if so, when and how much.* These women's experiences with family law convinced them that its theories of equity are seldom applied in real life.[5]

Another major problem with child support was the low amount usually ordered.† Few of the mothers were given support awards large enough to meet half of a child's living expenses, and most awards were *far* lower.[6] Some child support awards were set low by judges because husbands were able to show low incomes at the time of divorce. To avoid being ordered to pay more appropriate amounts, these men filed for divorce during a temporary work layoff, or voluntarily took a significant reduction in the number of hours they worked per week, or even quit their jobs temporarily. One man successfully showed a notable decrease in income by closing his Northern California professional practice and moving to another state, where he opened a new office. One mother, whose ex-husband quit his high-income work altogether at the time of divorce, said this:

> The support was scaled to what he was earning at the time of the ruling, so I'm now at the bottom of the scale for support. I imagine that's the reason he isn't working. I imagine that after December, when the alimony [portion of the family support] ends, he'll begin to work again. But the present support is like $1,500 a month less than [it would have been] if he'd been working at a position comparable to his previous one. It's curious that he wouldn't be working—this is a guy who was making several hundred thousand dollars a year.

Only five of the sixty women had automatic cost-of-living clauses in their support agreements, and even they had to seek court enforcement of payment. One mother, who had been divorced for nearly nine years, spoke of how her ex-husband had paid child support regularly but had not increased it despite the inflation of the 1970s and despite the fact that his annual income was over $30,000:

---

* No relationship has been found between the ability to pay child support and compliance with child support orders. Furthermore, David Chambers's Michigan study found no significant differences between racial or occupational groupings in rate of child support compliance (Chambers, 1979; Weitzman, 1981a, 1985).

† Census data show that in 1981, divorced fathers paid an average of $2,220 per year in child support, a decrease of about 16 percent in real dollars since 1978, when the average annual payment was $1,951 (U.S. Bureau of the Census, 1983c). Effective July 1, 1985, California implemented the Agnos Child Support Standards Act of 1984 (California Civil Code, secs. 4720 and 4727, in *West's California Code*, 1985). The

I went back to attorneys twice to try to get increases. Child support at $75 a month just seemed ridiculous. It was awful, with the inflation, and I wanted a cost-of-living clause. But these lawyers—*men* lawyers, though maybe I shouldn't say that so strongly—they advised against it. They told me I should be glad I was getting anything. But $75 doesn't even buy a pair of jeans, a shirt, and a pair of shoes for that girl.

Some agreements provided for the sharing of certain major expenses, such as orthodontic treatment, but none of the support agreements given to these sixty women acknowledged that children's expenses—for food, clothing, and activities—were likely to increase as the children grew older.[7]

> There's no cost-of-living clause. Not only that, my kid gets more expensive. He can still get half price on some things, but now he's wearing men's clothes. And things cost more in men's sizes. Do you know how often he grows out of shoes now?

Unless they could afford to have attorneys serve as intermediaries, these women had to deal directly with their former spouses when trying to obtain child support. Issues of child-rearing costs were thus kept open between them and their ex-husbands, adding stress and conflict. The economic dependency of these women, and their lack of power to enforce support payments except through the legal process, allowed their ex-husbands to continue to exert control over their lives. They found themselves vulnerable and on the defensive as a result of the discretionary powers allowed divorced fathers. For example:

> When we left the court after the divorce, my ex-husband told me he would never pay support. At the time, he was ordered to pay only $50 alimony and $50 child support. When the back support got to about $6,000, I sued for it. So he did what he said he'd do—he challenged

---

objective of this legislation is to promote equitable and adequate child support. One test for adequacy is that no child should be awarded support in an amount less than what would be paid by the Aid to Families with Dependent Children program. The court's role in determining child support awards will be much more active, and the standards for support levels will be specified by law. At this writing, the effect of the Agnos Act is not yet clear; nor is it clear whether other states will follow California's efforts to remedy the inequities of supporting children after divorce.

me for custody. To satisfy the court requirements [for a custody chal-
lenge], we had two very expensive psychological workups. I retained
custody, but I still don't get the support.

Anger about the nonpayment of child support was matched only
by anger about the issue of eighteen-year-olds. According to California law, the noncustodial parent has no continuing financial obligation for a child once he or she turns eighteen, because that is the
legal age of majority (as it is in most states). Nor is there a legal obligation (for either parent) to contribute to the child's further schooling. Although children are viewed as being legally adult and self-
sufficient at age eighteen, for most mothers and their children, the
reality is quite different, as these comments make clear:

> My daughter will turn eighteen early in her senior year of high school.
> She'll still be in high school that whole year. I tried to get it estab-
> lished that I would get support for her until she's through with her se-
> nior year. The lawyer said I couldn't do that. I asked him why. He said
> because legally a person at eighteen is an adult. I said I didn't care. I
> wanted support for that kid until she's out of high school. I'm cer-
> tainly not going to throw her out of the house. Is she expected to sup-
> port herself at eighteen while she's in high school?

> What happens when a child is eighteen? Why is it that he's supposed
> to be grown up at eighteen? And why doesn't his father have a respon-
> sibility to help him through school? Times have changed—young
> people aren't independent at eighteen. Say you have an eighteen-year-
> old, and you lose your child support. Because there's no money, that
> child will have to live at home, and instead of going to Stanford,
> where he will probably qualify, or any place else, he'll go to junior
> college. He'll still live at home. And it costs there, too—books, fees,
> transportation. So if you're the kind of student that has to work in the
> first place, you're likely to give up. It's not realistic to think that all
> eighteen-year-olds can find jobs and get themselves through school. I
> think it's really important, and will be even more important later on,
> that they get training. And I don't see why all the responsibility should
> be put on the mothers. If you weren't divorced, the father would be
> willing to help put his children through school. Why do his obliga-
> tions to his child stop just because he isn't living with the child's
> mother?

During marriage, these women had shared with their husbands
middle-class aspirations for their children, including plans to help fi-

nance college educations. They were surprised and angry when their former husbands abandoned this commitment to their children, and they were dismayed when the law apparently justified it. One woman said:

> When I asked my attorney about my son's college expenses, he told me it was between my son and his father, that I shouldn't get into the middle of it. That's an absurd way of thinking. We're all involved in this, not just my son and his father. When I told a family friend who had been close to both my husband and me, he wrote my husband a letter. He said, "My daughter is thirty, and my responsibility didn't end when she was eighteen. Yours doesn't end at eighteen either." But the lawyer was worthless.

Another woman, a homemaker for thirty years whose family income had been over $5,000 a month before divorce, had this to say:

> I have a boy who is not being educated because his father will not pay. In the state of California, a father's obligations to a child end at the age of eighteen. The other children all had an education. They all helped out some, but it was understood that their schooling was our responsibility. Now it's one hassle after another whether this boy will get any help or not. He's been accepted [at a college]. But I have no money to finance it, and he doesn't qualify for financial aid because his father makes too much money.

Aware that their former husbands had wide discretion about whether to abide by court orders, these women blamed unfair laws for maintaining an inequitable system, despite the public claims that significant reforms had brought about equality.[8] Their knowledge that these absent fathers had higher incomes, the economic freedom to indulge in leisure, travel, and entertainment, and the resources to support new families was a painful reminder of personal inequities maintained and supported by the law:

> First, I'm the one who has to be responsible in the relationship. I have these two kids that I have to care for. And whether he's paying child support or not, I've got to find a way to take care of them. And yet he's perfectly free to go out and get another woman pregnant without taking care of the two children he already has. I'm the only one who is socially *or* legally responsible. And second, when I was a welfare recipient, I was facing all this stuff going on in Sacramento, the possibility of having to work off part or all of my grant in order to continue

getting it. What I want to know is why can't *he* be put into a workfare program? If he's not making enough money to pay child support on his job, then he has a hell of a lot more time than I have. I've got twenty-four-hour responsibility for two preschool children. Why can't he be the target for harassment? . . . It all seems to be at a man's discretion. The law simply allows fathers to do what they want and when they want.

One way of reversing the situation was frequently suggested:

I really think if the judge sets an amount for monthly child support, it should be taken automatically—deducted from the paycheck, just like taxes. It would save the state money, for heaven's sake. It's a court order. Why isn't it enforced?

In discussing why lawyers and legislators do not promote such measures, most gave a version of this view:

It's simple: it's a man's world, and they use that old boys' club of theirs to protect each other. Let's just put an end to that.

Property Settlements

Property settlements were the other area of substantive law that aroused great anger among these women. They were especially infuriated by the disposition of the family home and by the calculation of earnings and income potentials. The resolution of both issues, of course, depends upon how community property is legally defined—a question that continues to be debated by legal scholars. Carol Bruch, for example, notes: "The most pressing need in California divorce reform is to find a way to distribute more fairly the true community wealth of former spouses." [9]

Because these sixty women were living in California at the time of divorce and their marital property was defined there, a full appreciation of their divorce experiences requires some understanding of community property statutes, particularly as they compare with the common-law principles followed in other states.* This is not the place for a thorough discussion of laws governing marital property and its division, and other scholars, notably Lenore Weitzman and

---

*Besides California, seven states—Arizona, Washington, Idaho, Nevada, New Mexico, Texas, and Louisiana—adhere to community property principles.

Louise Halem, have already provided comprehensive treatments of the subject.[10] The following brief description is offered as the minimum necessary for understanding the specific experiences of the sixty women interviewed for this study.

Although the community property system, with roots in the civil codes of Spain and France, was widespread during the early history of the United States, it was eventually displaced by the English common-law system in all but eight states. Under community property statutes spouses are legally equals. Marriage itself is recognized, at least partially and theoretically, as a socioeconomic unit in which the spouses are copartners in a joint enterprise. In principle, the contributions of the homemaker are supposed to have equal status with those of the wage earner. Legal title to ownership of property acquired during the marriage is generally irrelevant. Only property obtained before marriage, along with certain gifts, inheritances, and property received in exchange after marriage, is defined as separate property.[11] All other property is considered community property.

Despite the advantages they provide to divorcing women, community property statutes have weaknesses. How to define what is separate and what is community property remains a matter for debate. Material property acquired during the marriage—such as a house, a car, and furniture—is readily acknowledged to be community property. But less tangible acquisitions of the marriage—such as advanced education, professional degrees and licenses, career development, and postdivorce earnings that result from joint marital efforts—remain largely outside the definition of community property. Where these are recognized within the law as being potentially property of the marriage, the definitions of ownership remain ambiguous and unwieldy to implement. Because women typically forgo these less tangible acquisitions in order to support husbands and maintain a family life, it is women who are harmed by the law's failure to specifically recognize these assets as marital property. Legal critics have thus argued that supposed statutory safeguards to spousal equality are ineffective. For example: "[Community property statutes] do not secure equality of result between husbands and wives in relation to their interests in community property. To say, as courts and legislatures persist in doing, that the wife, during marriage, has a 'present,' 'existing' and 'equal' interest in the community with her husband is hypocrisy."[12]

Common-law marital property statutes, a carryover from English common law, exist in forty-two states and the District of Columbia. Generally, the primary dictate of these statutes has been that in deciding who gets marital property, the divorce court must decide "equitably." In their decisions about what is equitable, however, these trial courts have traditionally accepted legal definitions of property drawn from the ancient common-law tradition. In that tradition, property rights were based on legal title to ownership, and ownership was vested solely in the husband because he was generally the wage earner and thus considered directly responsible for acquiring all property. Upon marriage, a woman's legal identity was merged with that of her husband, so that a wife's earnings were traditionally viewed as legally belonging to the husband. Divorce courts had no jurisdiction to divide any property legally held in the husband's name, and wives had no legal right to property acquired during the marriage, even if they had helped acquire it. Divorced wives had the legal right to some support, but the amount was at the discretion of the trial judge. In practice, it was usually whatever "bed and board" the husband was willing to provide.[13]

In recent years, changes have been made in all the common-law states so that wives can hold property and convey it without the husband's permission. Most states have modified their divorce law policies in various ways to recognize the fact that the common-law tradition represents an "antiquated social philosophy" that has caused major inequities.[14] To enable their courts to rule equitably at the time of divorce, most states have given them the power to change the title of ownership in property when it appears that property listed only in the husband's name actually belongs to the marital community. Recently, several states have also specified that divorce trial courts must recognize the homemaker's efforts as "contributing to the marriage" equally, provided both spouses have met their agreed-upon responsibilities satisfactorily. Some states even accept the presumption that the spousal contributions are equal unless proved otherwise.[15]

Although common-law states began to adopt some community property concepts of equitable distribution in the 1930s, the real movement in that direction has come since 1970. Most of these states have now adopted the approach of the Uniform Marriage and Divorce Act, which requires some form of equitable distribution. According to legal scholars, adoption of this act will move common-law states more closely to the approach taken by community property states.[16] Even so, significant biases persist. Norma Harwood describes the process: "One or more of the following frequently occurs in the trial court: income-producing property is granted to the husband; the husband is granted all the property and is permitted to pay off the wife's interest in prolonged installments, thereby using future deflated dollars, and the wife is forced to spend these property pay-off dollars for daily living due to her low income level and/or inadequate alimony award; pension plan contributions and the future benefits remain the husband's, and the value is not included in marital assets; and business interests simply remain the husband's. When one realistically looks at what has been acquired during the marriage, the wife's property award may be as little as 10 percent." [17]

With the exception of the law student and another woman with some legal schooling, all the women in this study learned about definitions of community property through their own divorce experiences. They found that real property and material liabilities and assets acquired during the marriage *were* legally recognized as community property. They were tangible items, owned jointly by the wife and husband; children had no claim to the community property. However, educational achievements, earning abilities, or career development were not viewed as community property even though they had been acquired through joint efforts.[18] Legally, these women's efforts to enhance their family's economic well-being by supporting their husband's development did not count at the time of divorce. Various scholars have noted the complexity of the issues involved in redefining community property and the need to develop more precise guidelines. One of them, Grier Raggio, concludes: "The continued evolution of the case law will tend to diminish the uncertainty and to narrow somewhat the broad scope which now exists in most jurisdictions for exercise of judicial discretion" in determining marital property and methods for property valuation.[19]

Many of these women were given an option to remain in the family home with the children. In order to stay, however, each had to pay her divorcing husband his equity share in the house. Only two of the women were able to meet this requirement by exchanging one asset for another, such as their share of the husband's pension and retirement savings for his share of the home. The seventeen women who were forced to sell the family home in order to reach a community property settlement and the twenty-three who still faced losing the home in order to complete the divorce settlement were generally bitter. The home was usually their only asset with substantial monetary value. More important, losing it meant that children had to leave friends, schools, established babysitting arrangements, and familiar routines and neighborhoods. Loss of the family home, or the continuing threat of its loss, thus caused psychological as well as economic trauma and added greatly to the stress of divorce.

None of the women could purchase a home of comparable value; interest rates had gone up considerably since their family homes had been purchased, and payments on another home were likely to be much higher. For example:

> When we were married, we lived in a four-bedroom, two-bath house which suited us well with three kids. Now my kids and I've got three bedrooms and one small bath. . . . This is low-income housing, but it's share ownership, and I put a lot into it to own a share. I couldn't go out and buy another house. I don't make enough to qualify for anything. And since the child support is inconsistently paid, I can't depend on that.

Renting a new place to live cost some women more than the mortgage payments on the family home; it also meant that capital gains taxes had to be paid on profits from the sale of the home. Some of the women had to use their share of the home equity to meet monthly living expenses. Their former husbands, because they retained their earnings and did not have financial responsibility for the children, were able to reinvest their shares as they wished. A woman who continued to resist selling the family home explained:

> If I have to sell my house to get my ex-husband his $25,000 [share], my share of the property's value starts being whittled away by my daughter's college expenses. His share will start building right away. He doesn't need it. Mine will dwindle down because we'll have rent and all those expenses and her college, too. It's his daughter, too— why is it my share of the community property that gets depleted while his grows through investments or whatever?

Some of the women with teenaged children were granted a divorce that allowed the settlement of the community property issues to be postponed until their youngest child turned eighteen, an option

provided by California law. Because most had been divorced for
three to six years when I talked to them, the time for settlement was
approaching. None of them had been able to gain financial security
yet, and all were worried about the future. Those who had been married longer generally had relatively low mortgage payments, but they
also had larger buy-out amounts, which created a typical dilemma:

> I pay $165 a month. I could afford to live here the rest of my life. I
> can't afford to live anywhere else. If I had the money, I'm telling you
> right now, I'd buy him out today just to keep this house. But I don't
> have $28,000. I have enough saved to cover us for one month in case I
> get sick or something. One month—that's a drop in the bucket com-
> pared to $28,000. But I won't be able to buy anything else—I wouldn't
> be able to make the payments. It's a real dilemma. And it just gets
> worse.

Women who remained in homes that were still jointly owned suffered additional inequities, which were obscured by a legal balance
sheet that showed only an equal division of property:

> We're maintaining this house, the kids and me. My daughter and I
> have been painting the outside. The paint and materials cost me a for-
> tune. I maintain the pool, the plumbing, you name it. But I don't get
> any credit for that at all. My attorney told me that if I lived some-
> where else, I'd still have these costs. He said that actually I owe my
> ex-husband the difference between what I pay on this house and what
> it could rent for. Nobody cares that our daughter and son live here,
> too. He told me that normal upkeep, like painting, was my problem,
> not a joint problem. I told him that in that case I shouldn't do a thing,
> because the house will just rise in value if I do. Then it would cost me
> twice—not only labor and materials, but the increased amount I'd
> have to pay my ex-husband because I've increased the value of the
> house.

Another woman told a uniquely different story in regard to the
family home. Like the others, she had little cash available to her after
divorce. But according to the tenets of the Islamic religion she shared
with her husband, the home itself belonged to her and her children
upon divorce. Had her husband decided to ignore these tenets, the
law would have upheld him, ruling that the house was indeed community property. But he did not, and the couple handled their own
settlement and came to terms outside the legal process.

For the older divorced women in particular, financial futures looked frighteningly uncertain because they had no claim to a return on their investment in a married future. Three such women were denied legal rights to future benefits based on their husbands' employment—a military retirement fund in one case and railroad pensions in the two others. All three women had been married at least twelve years, so the values of these pensions were substantial.[20] One said:

> His Social Security and the railroad retirement can't be touched as community property. I'd love to take this all the way to the Supreme Court or the president. I don't want his retirement money; I really don't. I want my house, and although his retirement isn't considered community property, the house is. My lawyer can't even find out how much retirement money there is. Even half of the retirement would more than pay the equity I'm supposed to pay him. When that man retires, he'll make more than $1,000 a month just from the pension. When I retire, I'll get a total of $35 a month. That's real scary down the line. So I try to remember that I'm not there yet and try not to worry. I didn't even think of these kinds of things before. I was a married women with a husband who made good money and had a large retirement fund.

Not one of these women received a sum designated specifically as a retirement fund, even though they were losing access to future pension income through the divorce. None of their lawyers suggested the possibility of seeking the husband's agreement to setting up a separate retirement fund for the wife out of the community property prior to its division. Particularly for the older divorced women, financial futures looked fearfully uncertain.

Children's Interests

Legal definitions of community property caused the greatest anger and frustration in the area of the children's interests. The women insisted over and over again that lawyers, judges, and the law itself did not recognize an obvious fact: that they, as custodial parents, were representing not only themselves but also—and even primarily—their children, whose interests would be powerfully affected by the divorce settlement. This woman, for example, tried repeatedly to have her child's material interests in the family home considered in the divorce settlement:

Why do children lose their individual status and become merged with their mothers just because parents divorce? When we were going to sell the house, I asked why we couldn't divide it into thirds. Whatever I would get from the sale of the house would be used to support our child. I would have used it to be sure that he was taken care of in the way we had planned to care for him. Instead of my son's education and expenses coming out of my half or my ex-husband's half, why couldn't it come out of his [my son's] third? Why don't children count in the settlement? Can anyone really believe that child support covers the costs of raising children?

Children were not recognized in law as participants in the marital community. They were treated separately from it, and given support awards as dependents, by lawyers and judges who knew from experience that such support awards are widely ignored by men and very difficult for women to enforce. Indeed, a majority of the women saw an institutionalized disregard for children in all divorce laws and procedures. The law's failure to protect children's rights was thus a common focus of their anger:

I think a lot of it boils down to children's rights. Nobody is fighting for the children. Nobody cares. People automatically assume, when you say "support," that it goes to the woman and not to the children. But it doesn't. I think men need to be made aware of this; they need to be educated. There's a whole bunch of us out here who are not getting any support: not financially, not emotionally.

Spousal Support

Only six of the women—all of them divorced after marriages of fifteen years or longer—received spousal support awards.* One of them received an award for life or until she should remarry; the others were given awards of specific and short duration.[21] Legally, spousal support is awarded to a wife only in view of her individual financial need after divorce. Her need, and her chances of gaining economic self-sufficiency—not her past contributions to the

---

*Spousal support or alimony is awarded in less than 17 percent of all divorce cases, and it is actually received in less than 6 percent of them. Even women who have been married more than twenty years are awarded spousal support in less than 15 percent of all cases (U.S. Bureau of the Census, 1985; Weitzman, 1981b, 1985).

family's economic status—are the only factors considered.[22] All six women awarded spousal support said they felt oppressed by the limits these awards placed on their efforts to improve their lives: if they were to remarry or personally earn more than a very small amount, regardless of their long-term prospects, they would lose all financial help from their former husbands. Their ex-husbands, however, could remarry at will and still lose nothing of what they had taken out of their marriages. In fact, if the ex-husband's expenses rose, he could petition the court to lower the amount of spousal support he owed. The former husbands of all six women had already succeeded in doing that.

Earnings and Income

Most of these women viewed their husbands' earnings and earning ability as rightfully being a community property issue. Many of these middle-class husbands, who held professional, managerial, or technical positions, had pursued educations or developed careers with direct help from their wives. Most often, the women had interrupted their own educations to assist their husbands, by taking a job or by assuming complete responsibility for managing the home and children. During marriage, these efforts and their potential outcomes had been viewed as fully shared. At the time of divorce, recognition of this shared effort ceased. A woman who had handled her husband's business accounts and entertained his business clients at home, often at parties for fifty or more, had this to say:

> It's very interesting how men say, "Oh yes, we're equal partners." Then suddenly [when they decide to divorce] it's all their money— they're the only ones who've done anything at all. I really resent it. They say, "Were you out there every day on the line working your tail off? Oh no." And yet for years I heard my husband telling me, "It's so important for you to stay home and be with our sons. They're really important. And I need you to entertain and be there when I need you. I need your help in building this career." Then suddenly none of that counts anymore. It's terribly inequitable. It's not fair, the way men walk away with all the earning potential, without the kids, and then pay a minor amount of support. My ex-husband has had literally everything he could want, and my kids have had to scrape and do without a lot of things.

All these women argued that divorce law ignores the situational and economic differences between spouses and that by trying to treat spouses as equals, the law actually increases inequality between women and their ex-husbands. They found that age, marketable skills, paid work experience, and child care responsibilities were for the most part legally ignored at the time of divorce.[23] As one of the women said:

Legally you deal with property as a separate issue and divide it in half. I was furious. For the last fifteen years, except for the first three when I also worked, my job in the household has been the maintenance of this property. And I maintained it. I'm a carpenter. I built the deck. I built the fence. I've done all the remodeling, except that I hired someone to do some of the kitchen work. And I sewed. I made our clothes. It wasn't like I was some little lady sitting on a cushion being fed bonbons. I was working! And I was raising children! I did the whole thing, and I worked hard. And my husband loved it. Then to suddenly talk about property! We didn't split *his* job in half, or *his* benefits. Not at all! Property is only something they can attach a specific value to and split in half. I'm convinced that the divorce laws have to be changed.

3

Downward Mobility

These women had assumed that after divorce they would somehow be able to maintain a middle-class life-style for themselves and their children. Those in their twenties and thirties had been confident that they could establish themselves as capable employees and find positions that would provide sufficient incomes. Most of the older women, who had been out of the work force longer, had been less confident about their earning abilities, but they had assumed that the difference between the former family income and their own earnings would be adequately compensated for by court-ordered child support and spousal support payments. In fact, virtually all of the women had assumed that family management and parenting efforts, which had kept most of them from pursuing employment and career development while they were married, would be socially valued and legally recognized in their divorce settlements. What had worried them most was not economic difficulty but the possible psychological effects of divorce on themselves and their children. Still, they had believed that they would probably recover from the emotional trauma of divorcing in a matter of months and would then be able to reorganize their lives successfully.

Drastically Reduced Incomes

But even the women who had worried most about how they would manage financially without their husbands' incomes had not imagined the kind of hardship they would face after divorce. All but two of the sixty women had to cope with a substantial loss of family income. Indeed, 90 percent of them (fifty-six out of sixty) found that divorce immediately pushed them below the poverty line, or close to it. As wives and mothers, they had been largely dependent on their husbands, who had supplied the family's primary income.* Without that source of income, they suffered a drastic reduction in standard of living—an experience not shared by their ex-husbands.[1] Like women generally, they were "declassed" by divorce.

The economic decline experienced by these sixty women, all of whom remained single parents, was not temporary.[2] With caution and careful spending, most could meet their essential monthly expenses. But few had any extra money for dealing with emergencies or unexpected demands, and some continued to fall further behind, unable even to pay their monthly bills. One of them, divorced for nearly eight years, described her experience this way:

> I've been living hand to mouth all these years, ever since the divorce. I have no savings account. The notion of having one is as foreign to me as insurance—there's no way I can afford insurance. I have an old pickup that I don't drive very often. In the summertime I don't wear nylons to work because I can cut costs there. Together the kids and I have had to struggle and struggle. Supposedly struggle builds character. Well, some things simply aren't character building. There have been times when we've scoured the shag rug to see if we could find a coin to come up with enough to buy milk so we could have cold cereal for dinner. That's not character building.

Although they had been living for a median period of over four years as divorced single parents, only *nine* of these sixty women had managed to halt the economic fall prompted by divorce; four of these nine had even managed to reestablish a standard of living close to what they had had while married. Thus the remaining majority—fifty-one women—had experienced no economic recovery. Few had any savings, and most lived from paycheck to paycheck in a state of constant uncertainty. One of them, a woman in her late forties and divorced more than four years, told me:

*According to Lee Rainwater (1984) and the U.S. Bureau of the Census (1985), the earnings of working married wives contribute only 22 percent of the average family's total income. For this reason, poverty, which occurs in only one of nineteen husband-wife families and in only one of nine families maintained by a single father, afflicts almost one of every three families headed by a woman.

I can't go on like this. There's no way. I can manage for another year, maybe a year and a half, but no more. I don't have the stamina. It's not that I don't have a job. My problem is money, plain and simple. That's all that counts in this situation.

This group of recently divorced mothers was by no means unique. All female-headed households experience high rates of economic hardship, and the gap in median income between female-headed families and other types of families has actually widened between 1960 and 1983.* Part of the reason is obvious: certain fixed costs of maintaining a family—such as utility bills and home mortgages or rent—do not change when the family size declines by one, and many other expenses, such as food and clothing, do not change significantly. Additionally, in most cases when the mother obtained employment, it provided a low income that was substantially reduced by new expenses, such as the costs of transportation and child care.†

These women understood how their economic dependency in marriage had contributed to their present economic situation. One of them, who had been married nearly twenty years before divorcing, said:

Money does wonders in any situation. I'm sure women with more education and better jobs don't have situations quite as desperate as mine. But I quit school when I married and stayed home to raise my children.

Unfortunately, they arrived at such understanding the hard way, through experience. Before divorcing, they had expected to receive "reasonable" child support and had thought they could probably find

---

*Between 1960 and 1983, the median income of female-headed families with no husband present dropped by the following percentages: from 61 to 57 percent of the median income of male-headed families with no wife present, from 43 to 41 percent of the median income of married couples, and from 51 to 38 percent of the median income of married-couple families in which the wife was also employed. In 1983, the median income for female-headed families was $11,484; for male-headed families with no wife present, $20,140; for married-couple families, $26,019; and for married couples in which the wife was employed, $30,340 (U.S. Bureau of the Census, 1985).

†From his Michigan study, David Chambers (1979) concludes that the custodial parent needs 80 percent of the predivorce income to maintain the family's standard of living. The total income of most family units of divorced women and children falls below 50 percent of their former family income. Sweden, in fact, has determined that single-parent families actually need more income than others and provides cash supports that give them incomes comparable to those of two-parent families (Cassetty, 1983a).

jobs that paid "reasonable" wages. They had only the vaguest understanding of other women's divorce experiences. Thus two of them
said:

> Friends of mine had ended up divorced with children, and they would
> tell me some of these things. But I had no empathy at all. I might say,
> "Gee, that doesn't seem fair" or "Gee, that's too bad." But it never
> *really* hit me how serious it is until it happened to me. So I think there
> must be a lot of people out there who don't have the foggiest idea what
> it feels like.

> I had no idea how *much* money it takes. You don't have the [husband's]
> income, but you still have your family. There's the rub.

Their experiences led them to conclude that in America today, divorced women generally must accept a reduced standard of living.
And as women with children, they were keenly aware that only remarriage could offer a quick escape from economic hardship.* A
mother of three told me:

> I have this really close friend. She was a neighbor and often kept my
> daughter until I got home from school. She and her husband had two
> darling little kids. One day he just up and left. Surprised us all—he
> married his secretary eventually. My friend hadn't worked before, so I
> helped her get some typing skills. She worked for two weeks and said,
> "No more." She called me and said, "Well, I'm not going through
> what you did. I'm getting married." That was like a slap in the face.
> Gosh, did I look that bad? I started to doubt myself. Was I doing that
> bad a job? Should I have gone the marriage route? Gone out and got-
> ten a job and then married somebody? I still wonder about that.
> Things would have been a lot easier financially. The kids would have
> had a father. And I would have done what society looks at favorably. I
> don't know. I still don't know what to do.

Economically these women lost their middle-class status, but socially their expectations of themselves and their children remained
the same. They still identified with the middle class, but their low

---

*Research supports the commonsense belief that the surest way to reverse the
economic decline resulting from divorce is to remarry (Sawhill, 1976; Duncan and
Morgan, 1974, 1979; Johnson and Minton, 1982). Do women remarry because they
conclude, pragmatically, that being a single woman is too costly, for themselves and
perhaps also for their children? Would fewer women remarry if they could successfully
support themselves? The answers to such questions will have interesting political
implications.

incomes prevented them from participating in middle-class activities. This contradiction created many dilemmas and conflicts:

> I went to a CETA workshop, and I started crying when all they talked about was how to get a job. A woman came after me in the hallway, and I just bawled. I'd been searching for a job for months, I had a degree and teaching credential, and here I was being told how to fill out a stupid job application. And I had three kids at home that I didn't know how I was going to feed that week and a lovely home I couldn't afford.

> I moved here after the divorce because the school had a particularly good program for gifted children. Kids were classed by ability and not just by grade level. So my kid was in a really good spot for what he needed. I didn't realize at the time that I was the only single parent in that group. One reason those kids can achieve at that level is because they have a very stable home life, two parents to work with every child on the enrichment and the projects and the homework. I hate to say this, but it's all socioeconomic. Every kid in there belonged to a high socioeconomic group. Oh, they can rationalize that it's not really like that, but it's completely WASPish, all two-parent families where the mothers don't work. Mothers are available to take kids to music lessons, soccer lessons, gymnastic lessons, and all of that whenever it's needed. I had to take my son out of that class. I couldn't keep up the level of activity required of the kids and the parents. The gap was growing greater and greater. If I'd lived like this a long time, I might have known how to cope, but this was all new. And it all came down to money.

The women resented their precarious positions all the more because they knew that their former husbands had experienced no loss in class status or standard of living and could have eased their struggles to support the children:

> Five hundred dollars here or there—or taking over the orthodontist's bills—anything like that would have meant a lot. I don't see why this kid should have to live with jaw and tooth problems because I got a divorce. His jaw had to be totally realigned, so it wasn't just cosmetic. His father could easily have paid that monthly [orthodontist] bill and deducted it. That would have made a tremendous difference. But he wouldn't. By making me suffer, he made his child suffer too.

When the children retained some access to middle-class activities through involvement with their fathers, their mothers had ambivalent feelings. They were grateful that their children were not neglected by their fathers and could enjoy some enriching and entertaining activities with them; but they found their former husbands' greater financial resources a painful reminder of how little they themselves could provide. One woman, who had to let her child get free meals through the subsidized school lunch program, despite her many efforts to make more money, told me this:

> His father seldom buys him anything. But his stepmother sometimes does. She can give him all these nice things. She's given him nice books, a stereo headset. I have no idea what her motivation is, but it's a very funny feeling to know that I can't go and buy my son something he would love to have, but this perfect stranger can. And how will that affect my son ultimately? He must know how difficult things are here, and that I'm not deliberately depriving him. But it's kind of ironic—I helped establish that standard of living, but I end up with none of it, and she has full access to it.

Expenses and Economizing

Living with a reduced budget was a constant challenge to most of these women because they had no cushion to fall back on if expenses exceeded their incomes. Their savings were depleted soon after they divorced; only twelve of the sixty women I talked to had enough money in savings to cover a full month's expenses. Most said they had radically cut back their spending.[3] The major expenses after divorce were housing, food, and utilities. The women with young children also had substantial child care expenses, and several had unusually high medical bills that were not covered by health insurance.

Within a short time after their divorces, more than one-third of the women—sixteen women living in homes they owned and seven living in rented places—had to move to different housing with their children in order to reduce their expenses. Two of the women had moved more than four times in the first two years after their divorces, always for financial reasons.[4] During marriage, forty-nine of the sixty women had lived in homes owned with their husbands. After divorce, only nine of them retained ownership of the family home. Of these nine, six were able to acquire ownership by buying out their husbands as part of the community property settlement (five of them only because they were able to get financial assistance from their parents); two retained the home by exchanging other community assets for it; and one received the home according to the dictates of the religion she and her husband shared.

Home ownership brought with it many expenses besides mortgage payments. Several women neglected upkeep and repairs for lack of money. A woman who was in her fifties reported this common dilemma:

> I owe $16,000 on this house. I could get about $135,000 for it, so I have a large equity. But it would have taken all of that to get that condominium I looked at, and my payments would still have been about $400 a month. I don't know how I'll be able to keep up the house, financially or physically. The house needs painting, and I can't keep up the yard work. I'd like to move. I'd like a fresh start. But the kids don't want to move, and I can't imagine how I'll handle all of this once they're gone. When the alimony [spousal support] stops, there'll be no way I can manage a move. I'm stuck here now. The mortgage is really low and the interest is only 5 percent.

Two of the mothers reduced expenses by moving their children from private to public schools. Two others were able to keep their children in private schools only after administrators waived the tuition fees. Seven mothers received financial assistance for preschoolers' child care costs, five from private and two from public agencies. One of these women, who worked full-time, had this to say about her expenses:

> I'm buying this house. I pay $330 a month for it. Child care for my two kids runs to almost $500 a month. Since I bring home only a little more than $900, there's no way I could make it without the child care assistance. There'd be nothing left.

About half of these women had economic situations so dire that careful budgeting was not enough, and they continued to fall further behind economically. Those living close to the margin managed by paying some bills one month and others the next. Their indebtedness increased, and opportunities for reversing the situation did not appear:

> I'm so far in debt. Yes indeed. I keep thinking, why should I worry about the bills? I'll never get out of debt! All I can do is juggle. With-

out my charge cards, my kids would be bare-assed naked. And school is coming up again. What am I going to do for school clothes? And they've all grown fast this year. . . . I probably owe $3,000 on charge cards, and I still owe rent—I haven't paid this month or last. The landlord I have has been very understanding. He's let us go along as best he can. We've been here four years, and he knows what I'm going through. Over the years, he's given me several eviction notices, but this last time he hired a lawyer and everything. I decided I'd just pitch my tent on the capitol mall in Sacramento and say, "Here I am." I've written my congressman again, because I qualify for subsidized housing. But it'll take forever to get any action on that.

For many, however, even the persistent realities of economic hardship could not extinguish middle-class hopes:

My husband liked really good food and always bought lots and the best. So when he left, it was really hard to cut the kids back. They were used to all that good eating. Now there's often no food in the house, and everybody gets really grouchy when there's no food around. . . . I think I've cut back mostly on activities. I don't go to movies anymore with friends. We've lost $150 a month now because my husband reduced the support. It gets cut from activities—we've stopped doing everything that costs, and there's nowhere else to cut. My phone is shut off. I pay all the bills first and then see what there is for food. . . . I grew up playing the violin, and I'd wanted my kids to have music lessons—piano would be wonderful for them. And my older two kids are very artistic. But lessons are out of the question.

Obtaining credit had been a real problem for many, for the reasons given by this woman, who had worked during the marriage while her husband attended school:

My kids and I were very poor those first years after the divorce. I had taken care of our finances during marriage. But I didn't have accounts in my own name, so I couldn't get credit. I got a job as soon as I could. I was getting $65 a month for child support and paying $175 a month for rent. Between the rent and the child care and the driving to work, I was absolutely broke. I really didn't have enough to live on. I had no benefits either, with my first job. I was living dangerously, and with children. I could barely pay the basic bills. There wasn't enough money for food lots of times. I cried many times because there wasn't enough money. I couldn't get any credit. [When I was married] my husband could get any credit he wanted, but it was on the basis of *my* job, which had the higher income. He couldn't even keep his check-book balanced, but now I'm the one who can't get credit! It was a hard lesson to learn. Now whenever I get a chance, I tell women to start getting a credit rating.

The woman who told me this, incidentally, had managed to overcome initial impoverishment and gain a middle-class income from her job.

Some women regarded personal possessions such as jewelry, fur-niture, and cars as things they might sell to meet emergencies or ris-ing indebtedness:

> I sold jewelry to have my surgery, to pay for the part that wasn't cov-ered. I still have some silver, and I have some good furniture, which could probably bring something. That's probably what I'd do in an emergency, sell those things. What else do people do?

Teenaged children helped by earning money through odd jobs and babysitting. Older teenagers changed their college plans, and several entered community colleges instead of universities. One woman's daughter was already in the Navy, pursuing her schooling in lan-guages and working as a translator, and the daughter of another was considering military service as a way of saving money for a college education.

Most women compared their own hardship and forced economiz-ing to the economic freedom enjoyed by their ex-husbands. For example:

> I know my ex-husband goes somewhere almost every weekend, and he usually takes a friend along. I wonder how he can do that. How can he go somewhere every weekend? The only way I could do that is find a rich man! I couldn't possibly work enough hours to pay for that much stuff. I'd be doing well to finance a [twenty-mile] trip to San Francisco!

There were some exceptions to the general pattern of economic decline. Nine of the sixty women had regained some latitude for dis-cretionary spending, though only three of them had managed this economic reversal without help. These nine were a distinct subgroup; the others did not share their higher standards of living or their feel-ings and approaches to the future. Still, only two of these nine women had not experienced a major decline in income immediately upon divorcing (or separating). One had been living on welfare because her husband's excessive drinking and erratic behavior had prevented him from holding a job; she found employment immediately after separating from him. The other one had been the primary family wage earner during her marriage.* Four of the women whose incomes had dropped significantly had managed to stop and even reverse the economic decline very soon after divorce because they were granted temporary spousal support awards and acquired some money and assets from their community property settlement; two of them, who had been divorced after more than twenty years of marriage, also received substantial amounts of money from their parents. Although these four did not experience the degree of hardship shared by the others, they did not fully recover their formerly high income levels and therefore also had to alter their life-styles. As one of them said:

> Essentially, I took an $80,000 drop in annual income. And I had to borrow again last year. This year I finally sold the house, and that was really the only way I've made it. My change in life-style has been *tremendous*. Just my heating and electricity bill for our home was $350 a month. We just barely got by on $2,000 a month. I stopped buying household things; I stopped buying clothes for myself. And I rented out a room in the house. It was a huge house, and that helped out. I let the cleaning woman and the gardener go. I didn't paint. I let the property taxes go until I sold the house and paid them then. I quit taking trips. This house I'm in now has much lower operating expenses. My son doesn't have the same things he'd had. His grandparents buy most of his shoes and clothes now. He used to have lots and lots, so it's been a change for him.

Of the other five women who succeeded in improving their economic situations after a few years, three did so entirely through their own work efforts, and the other two managed with help from their former husbands—one took in the child for more than a year while his ex-wife worked at several jobs, and the other accepted a shared parenting arrangement.

---

*A recent study by Lee Rainwater (1984:84) shows how economic dependency in a previous marriage makes it difficult for a woman to recover economically from divorce: "By the fourth year that they headed their own families, women who had regular work experience before becoming female heads had family incomes equal to 80 percent of their average family income while a wife. Women who had not worked at all had incomes slightly less than half that of their last married years."

Emotional Responses to Economic Loss

None of the nine women who had experienced substantial economic recovery reported suffering serious emotional changes. Forty-four of the others, however, spoke of frequent struggles with depression and despair. Every one of them attributed these intense feelings, which often seemed overwhelming, directly to the financial hardships that followed divorce. This woman spoke for many others in describing the effects that economic loss had had on her:

> I think about money a great deal. It's amazing. I used to get so bored by people who could only talk about money. Now it's all I think about. It's a perpetual thought, how to get money—not to invest, or to save, but just to live. The interesting thing is that you develop a poverty mentality. That intrigues me. I would never have thought that could happen. But if I had had money, several times in the last year I would have fought what was happening to me in a way I no longer think of fighting. You tend to accept what's coming because there's so much you *have* to accept. You get so you accept everything that comes your way. For example, I accepted at first what I was told about treating this cancer on my face: that the only surgery possible would leave my face disfigured with one side paralyzed. I knew it would ruin any possibility of my teaching if they did that to my face, but I would have just accepted it if a friend hadn't gotten me to go to someone else for consultation. I wouldn't have done that on my own. That's not how I would have behaved at other times in my life. I think it must happen to a lot of divorced women. It was only this year that I realized how strange this has become. I'm educated, I've come through a wealthy phase of my life, and now here I am, being shuttled around and not even fighting. It continues to fascinate me. After a while, you develop a begging mentality in which you'd like to squeeze money out of anybody. I guess I'm somewhere in the realm of poverty. I know there are poorer people, but I'm pretty well down near the bottom. If I were to lose this job—which is always possible, there's no security to it—I'd be finished. Finished. I'd lose the house. I'd lose everything. There's no way I could survive.

The first year of divorce was traumatic for most, especially because legal uncertainties were mixed with other fears. A vicious circle was common: anxieties brought sleepless nights, and fatigue made the anxieties sharper. Although economic hardship remained, by the end of the first year most of the women had learned to control some of the anxiety surrounding it.*

Depression overtook a majority of these women at some time or other. Their feelings of despair over financial troubles were worsened by concerns for their children. One of them said:

> I thought about running away, but who would I have turned my kids over to? I also thought about suicide—especially when the youngest was still a baby and I had so much trouble with child care and it cost me so much. I kept thinking that if I were gone, it would take a major burden off of everybody.

In fact, such despair was a common experience: twenty-six of the sixty women volunteered that they had contemplated suicide at some time after divorce. They mentioned various contributing factors, such as emotional harassment from their husbands and uncertainty about their own abilities and identities, but all said that economic hardship was *the* primary stress that pushed them to the point of desperation.

One mother gave a very detailed account of her experience with suicidal depression, which occurred at a time when she had been barely managing for several months. She would drag herself to work and then collapse in bed when she got home. When she would get out of bed, she told me, the sight of her ten-year-old son sitting in front of the television set, alone in a cold room and eating cold cereal, would send her back to bed, where her exhaustion and despair would be exacerbated by hours of crying. She went on:

> I came home to an empty house that night—it was February. I had gotten my son's father to take him that weekend so I could go to my class—the one about learning to live as a single person again. I'd hoped that by getting some encouragement, I'd be able to pull myself out of this and find a way to make a better living. About eleven o'clock, I just decided this was no way to live. I couldn't take care of this child. I'd gone to Big Brothers, and they wouldn't take him be-

---

*Various studies argue that the first year or so after divorce is the most stressful and traumatic (Hetherington, Cox, and Cox, 1976; Wallerstein and Kelly, 1979, 1980; Weiss, 1979a, 1979b). Additionally, both Pett (1982) and Buehler and Hogan (1980) found that financial concerns were among the factors that limited divorced mothers' emotional recovery from divorce. None of these studies, however, attempts to distinguish the effects of economic uncertainty from more generalized separation emotions.

cause he had a father. But his father wasn't seeing him. Family Services weren't any help. The woman there did try to help, I think. She cared. But she'd been married more than twenty-five years and just didn't understand. All I could do in the fifty-minute appointment with her was cry. My attorney wasn't giving me any help or getting me any money. My mother was mad at me—she said it was my fault for leaving my husband.

I just couldn't see it ever being any different, so I decided to kill myself. I'm sure that's not a unique thing. It was the most logical thing in the world. I knew exactly how I was going to do it. I was going to fill the bathtub with warm water and cut my wrists. It would be fine then—that thought was the only thing that made me feel any better. Nothing was as bad as the thought of getting up the next day. So I called my son's father—he was going to bring him back the next day—and I asked him if he thought he could take care of him. I didn't think I gave any evidence [of my feelings] or anything—it wasn't a desperate call for help, or a threatening call, or anything like that, because I'd already made up my mind. I just didn't want him to bring my son in here and find me like that. I wanted him to make some kind of arrangements to take care of him. He didn't say anything on the phone, but in about twenty minutes the doorbell rang. Two young men in blue uniforms were standing there. They wanted to take me to an emergency room. It was a crisis place, they said. They were young and scared themselves and acted like they didn't know what to do.

I guess the shock of realizing how far I'd gone was enough to snap me out of it. I'd spent those twenty minutes [after the phone call] piddling around taking care of some last-minute things, tidying up and so on. It seems that once I made the decision, it gave me such inner peace, such a perfect reconciliation. It seemed the most logical, practical thing in the world. Then their coming stopped me from doing it. I didn't go with them, but they gave me a phone number and told me there were people there who would come and get me anytime.

I've only recently put into perspective what happened. It wasn't so much my inability to cope as it was the convergence of everything in my situation. That person at Family Services did help, actually, when she pointed out that some people who've never had trouble dealing with anything don't know what else to do when they feel like they can't cope. That fit. I'd never had a crisis I couldn't deal with in some way. I'd gotten myself into bad situations before, but I could always see cause-and-effect relationships, and I'd always felt like I could make some changes right away that would change things in my life. In this case, I couldn't figure anything out. I don't even know how to tell you what I thought.

This woman had been divorced before and had not suffered depression; but she had had no child then, no one else for whom she was responsible.

These women who were new to poverty had no ideas about how to cope in their new situations, and they found little help in the society at large. Some of the most desperate were unable to afford professional counseling. One of them said:

> At one point during the eviction, I was getting hysterical. I needed help. So I called a program called Women's Stress. Good thing I wasn't really suicidal, because they kept me on hold a long time. They said, "Well, this program is just for women with an alcohol or drug problem. Does that fit you?" I said, "No, but if I don't get help, it will." They said they'd send me a pamphlet, which they did. It cost twenty-five dollars to join. I never did find any help.

The worst personal pain these women suffered came from observing the effects of sudden economic hardship on their children. Here is one woman's poignant account:

> I had $950 a month, and the house payment was $760, so there was hardly anything left over. So there we were: my son qualified for free lunches at school. We'd been living on over $4,000 a month, and there we were. That's so humiliating. What that does to the self-esteem of even a child is absolutely unbelievable. And it isn't hidden; everybody knows the situation. They knew at his school that he was the kid with the free lunch coupons. . . . My son is real tall and growing. I really didn't have any money to buy him clothes, and attorneys don't think school clothes are essential. So he was wearing these sweatshirts that were too small for him. Then one day he didn't want to go to school because the kids had been calling him Frankenstein because his arms and legs were hanging out of his clothes—they were too short. That does terrible things to a kid, it really does. We just weren't equipped to cope with it.

But the need to cut costs—on food, clothing, and activities for the children—was not the only source of pain. Most of the mothers reported that their parenting approaches changed and that their emotions became more volatile, and even unstable, in periods of great financial stress. Mothers who went to work full-time resented the inevitable loss of involvement in their children's lives:

> I wish I could get over the resentment. [In the first years after the divorce] I spent half the time blaming myself and the other half blaming their father. Because I was so preoccupied, I missed some really good years with them, doing things I'd looked forward to and wanted to do. Those years are gone now.

Some of the mothers also thought the experience of economic hardship after divorce might eventually affect the society at large, as more and more women and children come to share it.[5] For example:

> It's not just the mother [who's affected]. It's a whole generation of kids who don't even know how to use a knife and a fork, who don't sit at a table to eat, who don't know how to make conversation with people of different ages. There are so many awful possibilities, and it's a whole society that's affected. I'm not talking about people who have lived for years in poverty. We planned and lived one way with no idea of the other reality. Then this harsh reality hits, and everything becomes a question of survival. I think it must be different if that's all you've experienced. At least then your plans fit your possibilities—that sort of thing. You can't spend your whole day trying to survive and then care anything about what's going on in the world around you. You really can't. . . . Maybe it's going to take 50 percent of the population to be in this shape before we get change. But some of us have to be salvaged, just so we can fight. We can't all be so oppressed by trying to survive that we can't do anything at all.

Although their despair was worsened by concern for their children, it was the children who gave these women their strongest incentive to continue the struggle:

> Sure, I think about suicide. And I'm a smart lady who's been creative and able to do some things to change our situation. But I'm tired— *tired.* And it's real hard. What keeps me alive is my kid. I may be boxed in, but if I give up, what will happen to her? She doesn't deserve that.

Most of these women also admitted to having lost a sense of the future. A fifty-year-old woman, who said she wondered if she would someday become a bag lady, told me:

> That's what I started to say at the beginning—*I don't have a future.* I can sit around and cry about that for a while, but then I have to move on and ask, what am I going to do about it? And there's not much I can

do. What career can I start at my age? How do I retrieve all those
years spent managing a family?

And another somewhat younger woman said:

The worst poverty is the poverty of the spirit that sets in when you've
been economically poor too long, and it gets to the point where you
can't see things turning around.

To avoid this sense of hopelessness, a majority of the sixty women
tried not to think about the future and made only short-term plans:

I learned very quickly that I couldn't think too far into the future or I'd
drive myself crazy. The future became, "What will I do next month?"
I learned I had to go day to day and just do the best I could. That's
been my major technique for coping, and I learned it right away. I've
built up some retirement and Social Security through work, thank
heavens. But I have to live right now. I just can't think about the future.
The worst that can happen is that the state will take care of me, and
I'll end up in a crappy old folks' home. But I don't think about that.

Ten of the sixty women—a unique subgroup—said they had not
experienced serious depression or despair after divorce. But the reasons they gave simply reemphasize the central importance of economic loss in the lives of divorced women. Four of these ten had
various sources of income that protected them from poverty and enabled them to work actively toward improving their situation. Two of
them were using income from the divorce property settlement to attend graduate school, and they hoped to regain their former standard
of living by pursuing professional careers. Two were receiving financial support from their parents while they sought employment and
planned for the possible sale of their homes as part of the property
settlement. The remaining six said they were generally optimistic *in
spite of* their poor economic positions. Like the others, they found
the financial hardships imposed by divorce surprising and difficult to
handle; they simply found these hardships easier to cope with than
the despair they had known in their marriages.

In summary, these women discovered that the most important
change brought about by divorce was an immediate economic decline, which for most of them had not been reversible. Despite their
economizing efforts and dramatically altered life-styles, many of

them continued to lose ground financially. In addition, economic circumstances had a powerful effect on their emotional lives. Only a very few escaped feelings of despair and hopelessness. Most found that economic uncertainties fostered depression, discouragement, and despair, and nearly all said they had endured periods of intense anxiety over the inadequacy of their income and its effects on the well-being of their children. Most of them felt trapped in their present circumstances and said they had no sense of the future.

4

Sources of Income

Few of these women had anticipated the economic realities that would face them after divorce: they had taken for granted that they would be able to maintain their middle-class life-styles for themselves and their children by combining wages with child support. Because they were relatively well educated and middle-class, they had believed that those who are willing to work can always get ahead, and they had expected to find jobs that would provide an adequate income for their families. They had assumed that their former husbands would contribute to the costs of raising their children after divorce—if not generously, at least according to what the court ordered. However, although they had some general ideas about how they would manage financially after divorce, few had seriously anticipated the economic effects of divorce; they had expected to be successful at finding paid work and becoming independent. Likewise, although some had worried about how working full-time would affect their children, nearly all had expected to find ways to manage the conflicting demands of working and parenting.

These women had three possible sources of income: employment, welfare, and "private transfers"—that is, child support and spousal support from ex-husbands, and gifts and loans from relatives, usually parents.* Many of the women had income from their employment only. But even most of those who had several sources of income

---

*The sources of income to mother-headed families in which the mother is age twenty-five or over are as follows: earnings, 70 percent; Social Security, 7.3 percent; public assistance, 10.6 percent; dividends, interest, and rent, 4.3 percent; and alimony and child support, 8.0 percent (U.S. Bureau of the Census, 1980).

remained economically depressed.[1] The United States, unlike most other industrial nations (except Japan), offers no financial support program to shield families and children against serious economic hardship.[2] And so the women who received no assistance from their ex-husbands or families were essentially on their own, regardless of their circumstances.*

Employment

Earned income was the primary source of money for these women.[3] All but three were employed or looking for work at the time of the interview: fifty-five had jobs and two were looking for work after having lost their jobs when their employers went out of business. The other three unemployed women were attending school full-time. Thus finding a job was the most common response to divorce.† For all of them, the loss of class status and extensive financial hardship that followed divorce occurred despite their wage-earning efforts.

Because only twelve of these sixty women were holding jobs at the time of their divorce, finding work was a first priority for most of them. (Several, anticipating the need, had found jobs in the months just before the actual separation.) Those who were working part-time shifted to full-time work. One woman quit her job to return immediately to school, and several others found better paying jobs soon after separation. Several women later left their jobs when they found ways to attend school.

Entry into the labor force was traumatic, especially for the women who had not worked for wages during marriage.[4] Because no financial assistance (other than welfare) was available to them, they had to find work almost immediately. There was not time to come to terms

---

*Most advanced industrial nations provide a family or children's allowance that is aimed particularly at helping low-income, mother-headed families. For discussions of these programs, see Kamerman (1978, 1984); Keniston (1978); Adams and Winston (1980). According to Rainwater (1984:78), virtually all Swedish and 85 percent of British families headed by a single mother who has earned income receive government income subsidies.

† Some 75 percent of divorced mothers are employed, over 88 percent of them full-time. Proportionately, divorced mothers are the largest group of employed women (U.S. Bureau of the Census, 1984). Yet Schorr (1981:102) concludes that female single parents "hold the most miserable jobs in every Western economy."

with the emotional experience of divorce; the legal process, the shift to single parenting, and new fears about finances all occurred while they were making the adjustment to full-time work.[5]

Several women who had been out of the workplace for some years began their job search by using vocational testing and school programs to assess their abilities and skills. Four women found work through their parents. Six others, like this one, found jobs through leads given by friends:

> Once my friends started giving me some help, it wasn't all that hard. I hadn't worked in fifteen years. My degree was in history, so I didn't even consider trying to find a job in that field. My friends raised my hopes a lot and talked me into getting something better than what I was expecting. Thank heavens. I might be working at Jack-in-the-Box. A divorced friend of mine is working at McDonald's.

Kinds of Employment and Wages

Their pressing need for immediate employment limited these women's options: their years spent outside the employment sector, gender and age discrimination, parenting responsibilities, and economic necessity combined to prevent them from finding congenial work at decent wages. Even women with marketable training and education took whatever work they could find, despite relatively low wages.

> It was outrageous, just terrible, when I went back to work. I'd gotten a second degree in land management, so I tried looking for employment in my field. I tried and tried and simply couldn't get anything. Finally, after my husband left and I'd gone a month without work, I knew I had to get something. So I took a clerical job. The pay was $780 a month. I have a better job there now, as an administrative assistant in a small office, but a "career path" just doesn't exist for me.

The majority found "pink-collar" jobs—positions in the relatively few job categories that are occupied largely by women and offer low wages and few opportunities.[6] In fact, nearly two-thirds of these women did clerical work. Five held higher-level positions such as executive secretary and administrative assistant. Others worked as bookkeepers, salesclerks, and waitresses. One woman worked as a telephone operator, another rented cars for an agency, two taught school, and one directed a day-care program. Three others worked in their areas of advanced education, as a lawyer, a counselor, and a nutritionist; three taught college courses part-time. One woman had a job doing manual labor. Being underemployed was common: nearly a third of the women doing clerical work had college degrees, as did the one blue-collar worker.[7] One woman earned over $2,000 a month and another less than $600, but these extremes were the exception. The majority had net incomes of between $800 and $1,200 a month, or $9,600 to $14,400 a year. This range was not unusually low: among heads-of-household in 1983, the median income for women was $11,484. It was $26,019 for men.[8] (See Appendix B, Tables 13 and 14.)

The two women who were unemployed at the time of the interview were looking for work.[9] Both were desperate for employment, especially because neither was receiving any child support or significant financial help from other family members. One of them said:

> You get so depressed when you can't find a job. I'm getting unemployment benefits, but they're about to run out. Right now I'm caught in the state's holdup of the unemployment checks. I've already borrowed from my fifteen-year-old son, and if the [state] check doesn't come today, I'll have to borrow again to buy groceries. I've had a terrible time finding a job. The jobs that I seem to qualify for are paying $4 an hour. I didn't know many jobs are so low paid. I don't see how they can expect anyone to live on that kind of pay. I went to a large company yesterday, an insurance and credit company. They offer $4 an hour and say that the job hours are flexible, between six and eight a day. By doing that, they don't have to provide employee benefits. Still, they told me they had over two hundred applications.

Wage discrimination in the job market came as a surprise to most of these women when they began looking for work; their previous reliance on their husbands' earnings had shielded them from this fact of American life.[10] They considered themselves penalized for the time they had spent raising children and managing their family lives; they could not find jobs that offered a "family wage" because they were considered "reentry" women, individual candidates for work in a labor market structured to meet the needs of male family heads. Almost all of them—fifty-three women out of sixty—felt strongly that they had suffered gender-based discrimination of various kinds.

One woman, who had worked as a temporary clerical worker in a large architectural firm in San Francisco, had this to say about wage discrimination:

> The two owners each get $300,000 a year, and the ten architects each earn $200,000 a year. Each of the two draftsmen earn $50,000 a year. But the two clerical workers *together* earn $25,000. The office is fully computerized and done on word processing. You can't take a person off the street and send her to work in this office. It's not a matter of typing a little letter and answering the phone. It's a very sophisticated, complicated job—and I have a hard time believing it's worth only one-fourth as much as a draftsman's job. This office couldn't be run without those women. Everybody, including those two females, thinks that's okay. But it's only because they are women. As long as you're stuck in that kind of thing, as long as everybody thinks it's okay, nothing ever changes. And it's not okay. I don't know what it takes, either. If the quality of life for a female depends on a man, you're right back where you started. If I do manage to get on my feet economically, I don't ever want to be in that position again, where the quality of my life depends on a man.

Another woman, who found a clerical job in a large auto parts dealership, said this:

> There are a lot of us women out here, and we need some attention. I work full-time and bring home less than $10,000 a year, and four of us have to eat on that amount of money. We're not getting equal pay with the guys, even for the same work. And the union isn't even fighting for us. The guys work outside, so they get more than double what we get inside.

Another woman, who worked as a secretary at a large hospital, believed that she experienced discrimination because she was female rather than because she was black.

> I want to ask my boss, "Did you ever see the movie *Nine to Five?* As a female, I've been discriminated against on the job in a lot of ways. I get paid less because I'm a woman. I also feel there's discrimination against me because I'm a mother. We women are fussed at when we need to take our kids to the doctor or when we need time off to study. I've run into that a lot. Some flunky guy's doing some little job and getting more money than me. Men also get better treatment if they're out sick. If a woman is out sick, they think she has the cramps or a

headache! It's the guys who give us a headache—I can live with the cramps! These guys just knock me for a loop. The treatment is different, and they don't give us a reason. I'm in a management position. But most bosses still look at women as their mothers, their wives, their sisters, or their lovers. They *never* look at us as their equals. We're always somebody in a personal relationship. Someday I'm going into politics and fight this. Women's jobs need to be improved, and we need comparable pay.

These women began their lives as divorced mothers during times of high national inflation, relatively high unemployment, and underemployment. Unemployment, inadequate wages, and dead-end jobs were obstacles they could not overcome by their own efforts. One woman, for example, spent the first years after her divorce completing her college education and getting a teaching credential, only to find that the demand for teachers had decreased dramatically while she was in school:

So, after I finished college, I couldn't get a teaching job. Who expected the market to change so drastically? The only way to get a teaching job then was to substitute for a year. I found a district that said I was likely to get on eventually. But one hundred people were ahead of me on the substitute list, and a hundred were behind. So you can see that I couldn't support three children on that hope. Even if I could work every day as a substitute, there were no guarantees or job benefits. I graduated in June, and by October I knew I had to have a secure full-time job. And once you're in a job, you can't take time off to look for work. I'm still paying on student loans. I took out one of those loans on which you don't have to pay the full amount back if you teach. Am I over all the disappointment? Probably deep down, I'm mad as hell. There was so much effort and so many hopes.

Those women who allowed themselves to ponder the future expressed anxiety about how vulnerable they were to disability or illness. Their employment earnings, on which they were acutely dependent, were inadequately protected—or not covered at all—by insurance policies or pensions. A woman who still owed her husband more than $20,000 on her purchase of his share of the family home, and who was supporting herself and her children entirely on wages just above the poverty level, told this story:

Because of my job waitressing, I'm having trouble with my wrist. I have to wear a brace all the time except when I'm at work. If I have to give up that work, I don't know what I'll do. I wouldn't be able to use the wrist even to type. My boss has said if I have any more trouble with it, I'm out the door. I'm on borrowed time now. And that's scary. Disability payments [from the state] would be $100 a week. So I don't use my wrist any time except when I'm working; I keep it in this brace. The doctor says either something will happen or it won't. The injury happened at work, and the doctor says for me not to let them intimidate me, that I have protections. But what would I do? Hire an attorney? With what?

Their dependency on regular paychecks also made these women afraid to assert their rights and make wage demands.* They felt trapped and relatively powerless to alter their employment conditions or futures. This comment was typical:

I'm an intelligent woman who's done various jobs. And I have quite a bit of education. But I'm too fearful to hold out for the kind of money I think I should get. I'm too desperate for income to do that. And although my employer doesn't dare say it out loud, I'm supposed to be grateful.

Age discrimination was an additional obstacle for some.[11] All the women over forty-two said they had difficulty finding work because of their age. Most of them had spent more years raising children and had been away from employment longer than the younger divorced women. One woman, nearly fifty, said:

I've quit putting dates on my résumés, to try to stop the age discrimination. Even giving the years I graduated gives me away, so I've taken all dates off except the dates of jobs I've had since the divorce. There are some career possibilities now if I can just find ways to tap into them. I feel frustrated by the financial constraints and by having been

---

*Only the four women who did not fall near the poverty level at the time of divorce, because they had several sources of income, did not feel trapped in their particular positions. Only one of them worked full-time, and the other three had part-time employment, two of them in teaching. Two attended graduate school, and one was developing a private consulting business. Having some money to back them while they sought to become economically self-sufficient gave them some flexibility in the wage market and more options in shaping their futures.

out of the workplace for so many years. Nobody puts any value on those twenty-five years, no matter what kinds of things I did. But it doesn't matter—the page is turned now.

Even a woman who had a position as an administrative assistant, and earned a higher income than most, often worked at two jobs to make ends meet. And like others, she believed that the labor market is "stacked" against women in many ways:

Isn't it odd that the people with the high incomes—*men*—get the expense accounts and don't pay for their lunches and don't even pay for their gas? And that the rest of us—*women*—have to pay for everything and don't earn enough even to do any of that? Getting out and working has paid off for me. But I believe there are some women who nearly kill themselves working, and it doesn't pay off for them. I'll tell you what really burns me the most. It's what I call the "old boys' club." Mediocrity is so accepted there. They watch out for each other. They get jobs for their friends who are no more qualified than the man in the moon, but they hang on to those jobs because they're the right gender. All the time they're protecting each other, they deny there's any advantage. And often we women are doing the work some man is taking credit for. We're computerizing our department right now. Our boss struts around and takes all the credit, but he doesn't even know what's going on.

Three women complained of overt sexual harassment on the job.[12] Two were clerical workers, and the third worked as a manual laborer in a workplace that employed only two women. The woman doing manual labor, who had moved herself out of poverty by working double shifts that totaled sixty-five hours a week, reported this experience:

There's a problem at work, too—you're supposed to fit into their sexual fantasies or something. I say, "Hey, I work here because I have a kid to support, a kid whose father doesn't support him. Don't think for a second I want to be here." But they think you want to be there with them, and that you're supposed to listen to whatever they have to say. They feel free to say anything. It's incredible what some of these guys will say—and try. I still can't believe it. There's a senior guy who thinks he's my pimp or something. One time I walked up to him and told him to cut it out, I'd had enough. In the two years I've been there, I've gone out with only one guy who works there. That's it. These guys don't know any limits. It's been one long struggle.

A woman with a college degree, employed as an office worker, summed up the overall employment situation facing women:

> I think the most important thing is to get comparable wages. And of course that means a whole restructuring of the workplace. It will require that women be able to get jobs and take jobs that aren't open to them now. Women's jobs—if we're going to keep women in these traditional kinds of work—have to be given some decision-making power. The whole workplace has to be reexamined. And we need to redefine the relationship between family and work. I'm reluctant to talk about these things, because they're never going to happen. The [inequities] are so entrenched in this system that the changes won't happen.

Work and Family Conflicts

Conflicts between work and parenting were frequent in these women's lives. Each was a full-time job, demanding large amounts of time and energy, and coordinating the two satisfactorily was seldom possible. For example:

> I was working nights when I first started here. I hadn't had a choice about when I worked. I had low seniority, so I was assigned nights. Also, you get paid more for night work. But that didn't work at all. I thought it would, but kids were going to my house to party because there was no parent there. I got a hysterical call one night. My daughter's boyfriend and another guy had gotten into a fight and knocked a hole in the wall. So that was that. I told the guys at work that either they put me on days or I'd have to find another job. [Now that I work days] my teenage daughter will come home late and be asleep when I leave for work. I'll come home from work at about half past four in the afternoon and she's already gone. I leave at seven in the morning, so in the summers I don't see my kids at all in the mornings.

Children's illnesses created major problems for these single working mothers. Child care facilities are not prepared to deal with sick children, and most employers do not consider a day spent caring for sick children a legitimate absence from work.

> It's a big problem when they're sick. They can't go to school or to day care if their temperature is even a degree above normal. I stay home with them as much as I can. Last year they changed the policy at work

so that out of the twelve days [allowed for sick leave] only five can be used for family reasons. That policy only considers men who work and have wives to stay home. It surely doesn't take into account mothers who work. With three children, five days off for illness is nothing. And doctor's and dentist's appointments are supposed to be taken out of that. Just everywhere you turn, it's a man's world, it really is.

The limited availability of child care restricted employment possibilities. Jobs requiring irregular work hours posed particular difficulties, and most single mothers felt they could not accept them:

I have training as a respiratory therapist, but I can't work like that. I like the hospital work, but it's real hard with two young kids. The hours can be real bad. Child care is usually only available from seven in the morning to six in the evening or so. I can't get overnight child care that I can afford.

Flexible working hours were not available to most of these women.[13] In fact, only one had been given a choice about the hour at which she started her working day. Many began and ended their workdays worrying about the well-being of their school-aged children who were being left on their own before and after school.

Several women found that working full-time was too taxing when their children were very young. They reduced their workdays and made extraordinary efforts to coordinate parenting and earning money. Reducing the workday to meet family needs, of course, meant reducing their earnings. For many of them, an acceptable coordination of work and family depended on whether their children could reach them at work by telephone:

My girls can call me at work. They call about anything and everything. The department I worked in before didn't allow that. It was awful, and I transferred as soon as I could. The kids need the security of knowing that I'm available to them. If they haven't called me within five minutes or so after they should be home from school, I'm calling them!

Work had powerful effects on parenting styles: many of the women reported that fatigue, stress, task overload, and competing demands made them inattentive and irritable parents. Both of the women who had dramatically reversed their after-divorce economic decline said they had done so at the expense of successful parenting. One of them told me:

I realize that what I gave up in the trade-off was the mothering. Coming home, I'd get one foot into the garage, and my kids would be on me right away. I felt like I was being torn apart. I'd been pulled at by people all day, like a veritable computer giving out facts. Then I'd come home and be pulled at again. So I'd retreat or collapse in tears. I just always made sure there were babysitters there. I didn't have all that much flexibility. I had work to do at night and appointments to go to. I was out there selling—that was my job, I had to. I chose not to be a victim; I fought it all along. But whether it's worked out, I don't know. Look at how my children have been neglected all these years.

Such feelings were not confined to the mothers with the most demanding work schedules. Virtually all of those who had full-time jobs felt that divorce had pushed them out of their primary occupation of parenting and that their children's needs were generally being slighted in order to meet the demands of outside employment. The basic position was this:

The main anger I have is about the children. They lost a father and then a mother, because I'm not home most of the time now. I'm working. Before I was either home with them or available. But if we're to survive, I have to work.

When they tried to be both provider and parent, these women found that there was no one left to perform the domestic services they had provided as wives. What they needed to ease the strain of doubled responsibilities was someone in the home to do part of the work of "a traditional housewife"—washing dishes, doing laundry, shopping for groceries, caring for children, and so on. But only one woman had any household help, and that was provided in conjunction with a boarding and child care arrangement. Lack of money severely limited these women's options. The most overburdened were those who had preschool children or three or more children and those who tried to supplement their incomes by taking second jobs or renting household space to boarders.

Supplementing Incomes

Taking a second job was the most common method for adding to the family income. Thirty-three of the women interviewed had tried "moonlighting" to supplement their earnings. All of them said that this further reduced the time they had left for nurturing and caring for their children. Renting out a room was the second most common method. Nine of the women had taken in a roommate at one time or another since the divorce.* One of them, who had increased her income enough after nearly nine years to make a down payment on a home, spoke of the advantages:

> Having a roommate is one of those tricks in getting through life. It helps me out financially. It's a sacrifice to have someone live in my home, but it helps me get what I want. It's not like being in college. I look for someone who's very independent and who moves in with me maybe to save money and have some company, but doesn't want a smothering kind of relationship. The roommate has to be able to get along with my son.

But there were disadvantages, too. Having a roommate could increase one's responsibilities for managing the household, for sharing and coordinating activities, and for mediating differences between additional people and the children; and these could add to emotional strain. Thus the women's low status in the labor market led them into moonlighting or taking in a boarder, low-status strategies that added work and responsibilities to their already overburdened lives.

Child Care and Work

A major cost for many of these employed mothers was child care.[14] Preschool children presented the greatest problem; none of these mothers had been willing to leave a child of six or younger alone. All the mothers with children of elementary school age also had to find, retain, and pay for child care. They had to find child care for the hours before and after school, on school vacation days, during summer vacation, and for days when a child was sick. In their neighborhoods, latchkey programs (organized and supervised before-school and after-school child care for children of working parents,

---

*None of the women interviewed had a male roommate. Because of the possible confusion between male roommates and live-in companions or lovers, who would probably contribute financially in more ways than by paying a fixed monthly rental fee, only women who were clearly the head of the household were interviewed for this study.

often sponsored by school districts, city governments, or associations such as the YMCA) were not available; babysitting was difficult to find, and the cost of it on a regular basis was prohibitive. One mother who began working full-time when her children were ten and twelve years old reported this experience:

> I didn't have any child care. I just couldn't afford it. We were living on $600 a month. The school is only two blocks from here. I'd come home and there would be food all over and things scattered everywhere. It was awful. They'd be here four or five hours by themselves, and the house would be totaled. [Before I had to take a job] I'd always picked up after them. It took them a full year even to begin to learn how to pick up after themselves with no supervision. I take responsibility for all of that—the disaster *and* the change! We all learned, and they did get better. I never quit worrying about them, though. It's much easier now that they're older.

Mothers trying to work overtime or attend school in the evening ran into special difficulties. This mother of two young children had income only from welfare.

> I go to school right now only in the evenings. That way I can be with the kids during the day. I used to take both my kids to the college child care, but since my oldest started kindergarten, it's gotten too complicated. She has to be at school in the middle of the day for four hours. I have to be here to walk her to school and then meet her when she's done for the day. Since I gave my car up, because I couldn't afford to keep it running, I have to take the bus to my classes. I tried going to day classes after she started school, but most of the time either I was late to my class or was late to meet her, and she'd be very upset— she's only five. It was just too much. So I have a babysitter come here at night. I pay her $100 to $120 a month. It's a major expense. It's all I do—eat, pay the bills, and pay the babysitter. I don't like it either. Babysitters don't care the same way as parents.

Child care was a major monthly expense. On the average, full-time child care cost these women over $250 a month per child. Five mothers of young children had child care subsidies from private organizations to which they had been directed by personnel at their children's day-care centers. Without that assistance, they simply could not have afforded to continue working. One of them explained:

When I first started working, I was trying to pay the whole $450 a month for child care—it was awful. My ex-husband had agreed to pay that amount, that was to be the child support. I counted on him to do it, but he never even paid for one month. I was getting so far behind. [Now] my child care is paid for by an organization. That's how I manage to be able to have child care for both children. I now pay a parent fee, because my pay has increased somewhat, but it's only twelve dollars a month.

The cost of child care was the greatest burden to women with children of preschool age. Because their marriages had been relatively short, most had no home equity or savings with which to supplement their wages; in addition, the divorced fathers of preschool children had often left their communities and refused to pay child support. Confronted with the major new expenses of child care, most mothers of younger children had only one resource—their own earnings, which were low. Among the nine women who escaped a fall into poverty or recovered economically from divorce, not one had a child of preschool age.

Feeling guilt about having to leave their children in someone else's care while they worked was a common experience for these women, especially those with younger children. Their feelings of guilt and worry, however, could be eased by two things: child care arrangements that were satisfactory to both the mother and the child and continuity of the caretaker. One mother explained:

Without child care—good child care—I don't see how single parents can work. The first requirement is the children. At first a girlfriend of mine took care of my kids, and it was a nightmare. I was involved then in on-the-job training, and it was stressful—it was like I'd gone back to school to learn everything. Then I was juggling the children. They were very unhappy. I found myself sitting here trying to work and then suddenly worrying about them. With the woman now, I don't worry. She takes care of about twelve children at her place. Sometimes I'll wonder what they're doing, and if I'm in the area, I can stop by and see. But it's not the same kind of anguish I had before. The kids are happy and well cared for. They just love it there, and that makes it real easy for me to go to work.

Maintaining continuity in child care arrangements was often difficult, especially when money was short. For this woman, who had supported her children alone and never escaped poverty, child care arrangements and expenses were sources of despair:

> I hired babysitters for child care. I needed someone to come here when I had the baby and the two other children were not yet in school. It was awful—just horrendous. I had five babysitters in one year. But you do what you have to do. I just worked with unsatisfactory baby-sitters. Some people wouldn't do that. I had a job I thought I had to hold on to. But it was awful. I don't know how any of us has survived, to tell you the truth.

One mother shared custody with her former husband, and together they worked out child care for their two elementary-school-aged girls. As she reported, even with two parents available, the arrangements were complicated:

> Needless to say, I sometimes feel overloaded. Now we have summer to deal with, and the tension level goes up a bit around that. We were just discussing what to do over dinner last night. There's part of a week coming up where there's nothing planned for the girls. I asked their father if he'd go by the city recreation department and see if we can enroll them in a one-week day camp, from nine to half past three. Thank God for their father's schedule. If he were in a job that required a normal presence, like mine does, this would never work—we'd have to use sitters. . . . If the camp session is filled, I can take off a couple of days next week, and he could take the kids the other two days. But hopefully, they can go to the day camp. If so, he'll arrange to pick them up each day when they get done. Friday they'll take off for a one-week Girl Scout camp, which is their first overnight experience. They'll be at the same camp and in different groups. They're really looking forward to that. After that, they're back for five days, and then they go back east for an extended visit with their grandparents. Their father will be with them the first part, and I'll be there later. Then there will be two more weeks until school starts, and we'll have to figure that out somehow. Maybe they'll like the day camp and can do that for those two weeks. Or if it's a terrible experience and they abso-lutely refuse to go back, we'll have to play it by ear and work it out. Somehow it always does seem to work out. But it's very tiring, even with this smooth relationship between us.

Despite the evident complexity of coordinating work and child care, this woman was far better off than the others. Because she could share parenting and its costs and had an adequate income herself, she had more options and greater resources for getting adequate supervision for her children. The other mothers of young children could only dream of such luxury.

Benefits of Working

Along with frustration, stress, and fatigue, work brought certain secondary benefits, which helped offset regrets about the amount of time spent away from children, even for the women with the most oppressive jobs. Most of the benefits they mentioned came not from the particular job but from the social act of working: contact with other people, time out from family duties, health and retirement programs, and heightened self-esteem and personal growth.

Not surprisingly, the greatest benefit was the most tangible one: earned income. Even though their earnings were inadequate to support a family, more than 90 percent of these women depended heavily on their earnings for family support. In that situation, any paycheck is a reward, as this woman made clear:

> My life has changed since I got back to work [after several months of unemployment]. I feel better. By God, I can support us. I can pay the bills and feel good about myself. It was a long dry spell. We're still living just month to month, and no savings are being put aside. But hopefully that will turn around. I have a lot of plans. I don't know how things will actually evolve, but things do evolve.

After depending on welfare, one woman found a relatively high paying job. It was demanding physical work, requiring much overtime and changing of shifts. But despite her fatigue and her resentment about the sexual harassment she experienced at the work site, she valued the economic payoff of her job:

> For Christmas I bought both of us skis and equipment, and we went up to ski for two days. My son looked at me and said, "Mom, look at all these other people who've just started skiing." I said, "No, *we've* just started. They've been doing it for years." He knows what it's like to be poor, and he's really pitched in. He knows what I've done is unique— that's what he told my girlfriend.

More than 20 percent of these sixty women had earnings that did not much exceed the amounts available from welfare when child care and transportation costs related to their employment were figured.

But work gave them a sense of purpose and some reason to hope that their economic circumstances might improve in time:

> I never considered not working. At least I feel better this way. If I'd been home all the time, I'd have gone nuts, absolutely nuts. So it seemed like I was in better financial shape because I was working rather than just being on welfare—though actually I didn't bring in any more money by working. It would have been easier if I could have worked only part-time.

Not all financial benefits appeared directly in paychecks. Employment brought health insurance to many women who otherwise could not have afforded it, and several women contributed to employee pension and retirement programs. However, none had a job that provided an expense account or a car, and none received child care benefits. One woman received occasional travel options from her travel agency work.

Social contacts with other adults were valued by-products of working; friendships and support systems often developed with work associates. A mother of two preschoolers, for example, had little social life outside work. Although her earnings were near the poverty level, she said her work had helped her realize that she could survive and raise her children alone:

> I have a great time at work. There is so much love lavished on me there, and at the beginning, I didn't know how to take it. My co-workers think I'm good at what I do, and I enjoy it. I've learned a lot about people and openness working there. I've really grown from knowing them. They've invited me and my kids to their homes, and they welcome us. It's really my only social outlet.

Although they resented their low wages, their lack of future prospects, and the difficulties they experienced in trying to be both parents and providers, none of these women wanted to be totally free of employment. What most of them did want were alternatives to the regular work week that would help them handle their dual work loads. As one of them put it:

> If only women could get good jobs and child care, they could support themselves and their children. Some help is also needed so mothers with very young children can work only part-time. I think it's much better generally to give kinds of support other than welfare. Jobs are much more important. We just need a decent income.

In summary, these women described the jobs on which they had to depend for a family income as generally unsatisfactory. They said that low earnings, few flexible scheduling options, lack of job security, and poor prospects for improved pay and working conditions were the chief causes of their dissatisfaction. They were underpaid and undervalued workers, primarily because they were women doing "women's work." But their heavy dependence on personal earnings kept them from demanding better pay or challenging the inequities.

Public Assistance

The only source of public cash assistance available to these divorced mothers was the federal welfare program, Aid to Families with Dependent Children. Their children, unlike those in families that had lost support from a male head-of-household through death or unemployment, did not qualify for benefits as dependents under Social Security or unemployment compensation.* Although the women themselves had lost their primary positions as housewives, they did not qualify for any kind of worker's compensation. To qualify for welfare assistance, families had to be below the poverty level and have limited assets.

At the time of the interviews, only three of these sixty women were receiving any welfare. All three had children under the age of six and were attending college, preparing themselves for careers (two were undergraduates, and one was a graduate student). They had received public assistance for between two and three years and had not received any child or spousal support.[15] However, many more had previously used some form of welfare support for short periods: seventeen had received cash assistance, and three had used food stamps (prior to the 1981 changes that prevented the working poor from receiving any aid). Thus twenty-three of these sixty women had used

---

*Welfare amounts are substantially less than amounts from Social Security or unemployment: in 1982, the national average to recipients of Aid to Families with Dependent Children was $106 per individual and $310 per family. Nearly 60 percent of all AFDC families had three or more family members dependent on this amount. The 1981 California average family amount was $416. In contrast, Social Security benefits in 1982 to a child whose father was deceased were $285 per month, and the benefit to the widowed mother was $303.

some component of the welfare program at one time or another since divorcing. (Only one woman had received any welfare before divorce, and she did not receive any afterward.) The use of public assistance by these women was typically short-term and prompted by desperate circumstances; and only four of them had depended on it as their primary source of income.* Only one of these four had received any child support—a total of only $50 a month for two daughters. Three women had attended and completed college, and one had depended on welfare checks until both her children were past two years of age. Two of the three who completed school found work in their fields, preschool education and law; the other took a job as a skilled laborer.

Three women used welfare immediately after their husbands left the home, for an average of five months. They gave it up as soon as they found employment, even though the jobs they took paid wages below the poverty level and they were receiving no child support. Another three used public assistance in brief periods of unemployment between jobs. The other women who used welfare checks, food stamps, or Medi-Cal did so before 1981 to supplement their inadequate earnings. The only one who continued to use any public assistance after that year was a woman who used Medi-Cal coverage to pay for treatment of her chronically ill child. The others lost supplemental assistance in 1981 when welfare changes ended their eligibility for supplemental assistance as "working poor." [16] Here are two of their comments on that change:

> I had welfare help for almost three years while I worked, raised my kids, and tried to get my life in order. Things got much worse for us when Reagan came into power and changed the welfare rules. I lost

*Other researchers have confirmed these characteristics of welfare use. Rein and Rainwater (1977:6, 8) found that "only slightly over 20 percent of those on welfare at any one particular time are members of the welfare class" and that "the other 80 percent have short or medium-term welfare careers." They add that the welfare system "seems to serve primarily as a way society copes with two of its problems—family disruption and the inadequacy of the labor market." Another study found that only 2 percent of AFDC recipients received 50 percent or more of their total incomes from welfare for eight or more of the ten years studied (Corcoran, Duncan, and Hill 1984:245–246). And Masnick and Bane (1980:88) found that "public assistance (mainly Aid to Families with Dependent Children or AFDC) provides about a third of the total income of young single-parent families, but under 10 percent when the single-parent head is over 25."

the support we had then. So things are really much worse now. We have less money and the kids are more expensive.

I was getting some supplemental welfare support in addition to my full-time job. I work for the state. I've been there full-time since 1977. My wages were really low, I had no child support, and I was paying a babysitter full-time, so I qualified for the help. I got food stamps, Medi-Cal. And I hated it. I could write a whole book on that. And I was employed full-time the whole time. There are lots of women in that position who don't want to publicize it. Welfare alone isn't enough to live on. Neither are our wages. Now I'm in worse shape than then. With the changes Reagan made two years ago, I don't qualify for anything.

All the women who had experiences with the welfare program and its personnel said they had been harassed, intimidated, humiliated, and stigmatized. Having already lost their middle-class status through divorce, they found that the treatment they were given when they sought public assistance added insult to injury. The woman with the full-time state job continued:

Talk about being on welfare and working—it's worse than just being on welfare. You're working all day. The welfare office isn't open at night, neither is the food stamp place, so I had to use vacation time to do that kind of business. I'd take a vacation day to go to the D.A.'s office or to the yearly review for welfare. Sometimes I'd get to the food stamp place just about five o'clock, and they'd shut the door in my face and refuse to let me in. I'd tell them I got there from work as soon as I could. There would still be a bunch of people in there, but they wouldn't let me in. It was a Monday one time, and I needed the food stamps then. The guy said, "Well, you don't work on Saturday, do ya?" So I ended up waiting the whole week. It's almost a full-time job just to deal with them. And there's the stigma of welfare. People would be so nasty in the grocery stores. They didn't know I worked all day. They didn't know I paid for all but $24 of those food stamps. And it's a terrible invasion of privacy. One time they sent two men out here to my home because there was a computer foul-up. Those two had the nerve to stand there and condescendingly tell me how *they* had to *work* for what they got, how they had to stick to a budget. By anybody's standards, even with working and welfare help, I was falling far below the poverty line. And these two guys had no idea what it's like to support children on this amount of money. Do you think *they* pay their child support?

These women turned to welfare in desperation, often only to have their fears increased. For example, when one of them first went to a welfare office, looking for information and assistance, she was completely broke and living with the fear that her estranged husband might carry out his threats to kidnap their children:

The first time I went to see about getting some help, a worker told me they'd throw my husband in jail [for not paying child support] if I received welfare. I asked her who makes the final decision whether he goes to jail or not. She told me I did. I asked what happens if I don't agree to have him sent to jail. She said they'd take my kids, because legally I was neglecting my children if I didn't throw their father in jail. I got up and ran out of there crying, I was so scared someone would take my kids away. I told my lawyer about it, and he said, "Where are they going to put those children?" That didn't help. I said, "I don't know, but I don't want to lose them." I didn't know better then. I believed the woman was being honest when she said they could take my kids away because I wouldn't sign for my ex-husband to be put in jail. I was crying all the time anyway, so days like that just caused a few extra tears.

Struggles with the bureaucratic structure encouraged some women to leave the welfare program. Many said they wondered if obstacles hadn't been deliberately built into the system in order to discourage its use. One of them was this woman, who had managed to recover economically from divorce after several years, during which she often worked at two jobs:

I did use food stamps for a while, and I certainly got hassled about that. I wondered, "What the hell am I doing this for? What I need is a job so I can pay for food." It wasn't worth the damned hassle to get food stamps. I never want to go back there again—never! They didn't care that I had a baby—that was *my* problem. I can say now that it helped make me strong, but I was in tears then. I hate even to think of what it was like, it was such a struggle. This is the first year I haven't lived in terror about money.

Receiving welfare payments or food stamps also made these women vulnerable to harassment from others. Several reported being insulted by strangers, even in public. Here are two typical examples, the first by a woman who used welfare and food stamps when her daughter's surgery and medical treatments prevented her from working:

From the surgery she'd had, my younger daughter had big bandages on her face and a great big one down the back of her head. She was pallid and puffy from her medication. Obviously she was very sick. I'd gone to the grocery store, and my other daughter was in tow, walking along pushing the cart while I did the monthly shopping with my $90 of food stamps—not a speck of meat in the cart, a box of powdered milk to last us through the month, and so on. But a woman standing in line behind me said, "Aren't you ashamed to use those things? How can you use our good tax money for that sort of thing?" What can you say?

Being on welfare is horrible. People treat you like shit. I've had landlords hang up on me, and I've never damaged anything. I've had nurses and doctors mistreat me and my child. I've had people at the grocery store make outrageous comments when I was using food stamps. I was working hard to get through school and raise a child, but nobody cared.

Welfare assistance was not enough to lift any of the recipient families out of poverty, but any effort to make ends meet by earning small amounts of unreported money could make a mother vulnerable to criminal charges of fraud. However, reporting any extra income jeopardized the next months' assistance.

You can't live on welfare. I don't care who you are. There has to be something else, so you have to look for ways to supplement it—and you don't claim everything you earn. I was dependent on the state for a long time—over two years, until my youngest child was almost two and a half. I was under a lot of stress financially—I'd get sick to my stomach thinking about it. With the rate of inflation and the rising costs of kids, something had to give. I had always done creative things before, like making stuff to sell and that sort of thing, so I just went on doing that. But I always lived in fear of being charged with welfare fraud.

These women also expressed disappointment and bitterness that welfare programs did not help them escape poverty through their own efforts:

I think when a woman has to go on welfare—and it's usually a woman who does—that an effort should be made to help her set her future course. We should have been given lists of resources, schools, and programs. A woman should know some options. In this county now, welfare is sending out notices telling women they should train to be child care workers or gas station attendants. Can you believe it? There's no money in either of those. A woman simply can't earn enough money in a minimum-wage job like that. If she has to pay child care with a minimum-wage job, she simply can't work. Can you imagine them telling a single-parent father to go into a minimum-wage job?

Inadequate though they were, monthly welfare payments were essential to these women. Their fear of being caught with nothing, as they had been when their husbands had left the family, worked to foster a psychological dependency on welfare. All the women who had received a welfare grant said they had feared becoming welfare dependent, despite the reality that they were using welfare only as short-term, emergency support or occasionally to finish occupationally oriented educations.

Women who used any form of welfare assistance shared in society's ambivalence about it: as mothers they were supposed to be engaged in full-time mothering, but as divorced women they were to be self-supporting, even though adequate child care was hard to find and extremely costly:

> I'm told on the one hand that I'm a parasite if I'm on welfare. I'm "a no-good mother." But I'm told on the other hand that if I go to work, I'm abandoning these children and allowing somebody else to raise them—that in the end, all of society's troubles will be my fault because I wasn't there during the "critical" years when my kids needed me at home.

Because the majority of these women were still living from paycheck to paycheck, the possibility of their having to resort to welfare again was very real. So even though they had been stigmatized and humiliated by their experience with it, they believed welfare should remain available for other needy mothers:

> These guys I work with complain all the time about welfare. But I just leave the room. I've been there, and I have totally different views about it. But welfare should be a tool. It should be a resource to help you get self-supporting, and it's not because it doesn't pay enough. I know there are some women in the welfare office dressed to the hilt, and their kids look dirty and ratty, and the boyfriend is sitting in the parking lot in his new Monte Carlo [car]. That's for a few, it's true, but not the majority. The majority are working at what they can. And for

some, that's the caliber of their lives, and they're incapable of anything else. So give it to them. The money that gets dished out for the paperwork annoys me. More of it needs to get to the people who need it. And welfare should help educate people. But I can't believe all the complaining about these programs, considering the way really wasteful government stuff gets ignored.

Support from Ex-Husbands and Parents

Court-ordered support payments from former husbands—child support, spousal support, or family support—contributed by far the smallest amount of income to these women and their children.[17] Outrage was expressed by many women about these low support orders; one of the women said this:

> We wouldn't need welfare if the men were paying their support. I know all kinds of women who are so poor they are hardly surviving. I'm really angry toward men because of this. Don't they know what they're doing? Don't they know this affects their kids? They don't pay, and then they show up and lavish stuff on the kid. Never mind that there's no medical coverage, or the rent is behind and we're threatened with being thrown out on the street. I've seen this over and over. And it makes me see red.

Nevertheless, even a small amount was crucial: almost all the women who received no support were living in poverty or close to it. Twenty-two of the sixty women received child support regularly, and one shared all parenting and child-rearing costs with her ex-husband. Thirteen women received child support occasionally, though not in the full amount, and six had not received payments for three months or more. Among those who received support, the amount for each child ranged from $350 to $50 a month, and the average was $112 a month. Another twenty-four women were not receiving any child support and generally never had. Most of the children who received child support regularly also received other benefits, chiefly medical coverage obtained through the father's employment. Other major expenses, such as orthodontists' bills, were shared by some of the twelve fathers whose divorce agreements included stipulations that such major expenses were to be shared.

Overall, these women received more financial help from their own parents than from their children's fathers. In fact, two-thirds of these sixty women were helped in some way by their parents. A third of them had received significant financial help, and the parents of another third made major contributions by buying children's school clothing, Christmas and birthday gifts, and so on. Here are two typical reports, the first by a woman with four children who was living below the poverty level despite her full-time job:

> My parents have been my biggest support. They've literally saved me many times. It's only because of them that I've made it. Almost every month in most years, they've given me money. They don't expect it back. But they don't have a lot, especially since my mother retired. The only time any of us gets clothes is when they buy them. They paid my car off. They totally give us birthdays and Christmases. I've drained them all these years.

> I don't know what I would have done without my mother all these years since the divorce. On my income, I just haven't had the money to provide my kids with even the things they've needed. She's had a really good job for years, and she's always taking the kids out to buy clothes and things. I don't know what I would have done about my kids' school clothes. I've just never had the money. She never even brings it up. She loves those kids and likes being able to help out. As a matter of fact, she recently bought me a new dress. I've felt terrible, but I don't like to tell her how bad it is because she just worries.

Crises, especially involving homes, were often met only because of family help:

> When the kids told my folks that an eviction notice had been filed and that we were going to court, they sent me money. They sent $1,500 and I paid the landlord [the back rent].

> My father saved the house for me. I had to come up with $3,000. He's retired and has stock and whatnot, but he lives on that. He gave me the money and said it was for me, that I could use it as I wanted. I was five days away from foreclosure on the house.

Two women paid a relatively low rent for homes owned by their parents. Three others lived temporarily with their families immediately after their marital separations. One woman, with her small child, stayed with her parents for almost nine months after her divorce.

Like others, she said that living with parents while being economically dependent on them was not easy:

> It was difficult for my parents. They kept asking me where they went wrong [because of the divorce]. And they were setting curfews on me when I had night classes. They were trying to have some control, and we went through exactly the same thing we went through when I had first gone away to college. They insisted I shouldn't move out when I did. It was more than eight years since I'd first left home, and here we were going through the same stuff.

This woman's parents continued to help her financially even after she had moved out so that she could complete a community college degree.

One woman whose husband was not making support payments got help from members of *his* family:

> They've done special things to help out, mostly the sister I like so much. Another sister, though, took my daughter to Disneyland, which was wonderful. When my son needed corrective shoes, her husband bought them. They called me up one day and said, "Come on, we're going to buy him those shoes." Then she got me to go to these neighbors of theirs who were selling some furniture. It was nice furniture for $100—a couch and two chairs. They asked $25 down and the rest in payments. So I put down the $25. A few days later I was vacuuming the living room, and I thought, "How will I ever pay these people?" So I went over to my sister-in-law's, and before I could tell them, her husband asked, "How much do you owe the neighbors?" I told him it was $75 but that I was returning the stuff. He said, "Oh no, we're going to pay it for you," and I just burst into tears.

Partly out of pride but mostly not to cause worry, many women tried to shield their parents from knowledge of the difficulties they were facing. They were especially reluctant to let them know how pinched they were financially:

> My parents helped out as much as they could. But they're in the construction business, and the last couple of years have been difficult for them. So I haven't told them how awful things have been financially. My father really worries and loses sleep over how I'm doing. On the other hand, they feel just as helpless if they find out I'm holding out on them. I was out of work for six months before they found out about it—a cousin heard and let them know. They called me right away, quite upset.

Several women were angry that former husbands felt absolved of responsibility for the children when grandparents were helping out:

> I have a wonderful family. But my parents still have four children at home and one in college. So it's not like they can be supporting us—they still have other children to support. But my ex-husband keeps telling his lawyers that my parents can support us. Yet why should they? This child isn't theirs.

> His ace in the hole is that he knows my parents will help me. He knows they'll help the kids. And they are. They're financing the kids' [college] schooling—the kids will pay back the money loaned to them, but without interest. But like my oldest son said, "I don't want to have to pay back my grandfather because my father walked out." He's especially aware of it because his father and I had paid for his first two years.

This woman, one of the few whose divorce did not pull her into or near poverty, spoke of renewed reliance on her family's help with a sense of sadness:

> When I was first divorced, an aunt gave me $1,500. I was really touched by that. I needed it desperately right then. I was living hand to mouth, with no backup because we hadn't yet sold the house. But at the same time, it was kind of hard. And then before some of my loans came through, my parents loaned me money. I find it's really hard to be thirty-five years old and have my parents helping me, when I hadn't needed or asked for anything since I graduated from college and got married. It's all those little ways in which you're like a child needing help again. Like my mother calling me all the time and sending checks for my birthday or for Christmas that are far more substantial than before.

This comment suggests some of the cruel ironies these women felt. Many of them had expected to be able to help their own parents after retirement; now they were the ones in need of financial assistance. Those with older children were particularly aware that they could not offer them the benefits their own parents were providing. This dependency was also ironic in light of these women's complicated feelings about their parents. These people who were now helping them survive the economic losses of divorce were the same parents who had raised them to consider marriage, and the economic dependency that went with it, as a primary career.

5

Mothers and Children

Before they divorced, these women shared assumptions common to the middle-class culture around them. They expected that they would be married throughout the years they were raising children, and they believed that the most important tasks that they would have to do in the family while the children were young were those involved in mothering. They believed the familiar rhetoric: our society reveres motherhood and considers the well-being of children a matter of paramount concern. Thus when they first confronted life as divorced women and single parents, they expected to receive strong social support and encouragement for their continued work as mothers. Although they were aware that certain new tasks would arise for them as single mothers, they continued to believe that taking care of their children's emotional and physical needs would be their greatest concern. Finally, many of them believed that parenting would not be much different after divorce because they had already been parenting with little help while married. Indeed, the fact that they had always taken primary responsibility for their children was the major source of continuity between their married and divorced lives. But the transition to becoming a true single parent forced them to cope with many problems they had not anticipated: a serious lack of money, the heavy demands of full-time employment, shaken self-esteem and emotional depression, and a lack of parenting supports.

After divorce, almost all of these sixty women had lived alone with their children, and for most of the first year after divorce, nearly all of them had felt overwhelmed by practical and emotional demands.[1] Most gradually regained some sense of being in control of their lives, but many remained heavily overloaded for years, emotionally as well as logistically. Mothers of preschool-aged children and mothers with three or more children (unless they were older teenagers) were especially overextended. Not surprisingly, the women who were most overburdened were those who had the least money and the least outside support. Those who found it easiest to adjust to single parenting reported the following circumstances: Their children were of elementary school age or older. They received regular financial assistance in supporting their children. They worked fewer hours than the average workweek. And they had parenting help—from their own parents and relatives, or from the children's father. Very few of the women, however, said they had all of these advantages.

Redefining Parent-Child Relationships

After divorce, both mothers and children had to redefine the parent-child relationship. They had to learn to accept such changes as a move away from the family home, the absence of the father, and new child care arrangements. Patterns of communication and behavior had to be changed, and this usually brought many months of emotional upheaval and family turmoil. One mother of four children, whose marriage had been strongly influenced by her husband's heavy drinking and frequent abusive episodes, was able to reconstruct her relations with her children in less than a year:

> My oldest two were really happy when their father left. My oldest son was afraid of him and had been having really severe abdominal cramps for months; my daughter was real quiet and depressed, and she was behind in school. Those two spent most of their time hiding in their rooms. My two little ones had spent a lot of time crying and fussing. We were all relieved when he left, but things were shaky for a while because I didn't know how to maintain any control. We were all so used to being on guard that it took us several months to settle into a new routine. Then it got interesting. Everyone played a role in the system.

Another woman said it took her family nearly two years to reach a balance:

> I had never worked at all, and then suddenly I had to be gone from eight to five every day. And with their father gone at the same time, it

was a real shocker for my kids, who were eight and nine. I mean, their lives changed 100 percent. I think my kids went through a tremendous readjustment, but it took them a couple of years. My son probably went through the worst of it. He cried a lot and acted out. And I felt threatened all the time that their father was going to come and take them away. It was a real mess here for quite a while.

Because most of these women had to find employment immediately, their choices about how to ease the transition to single parenting for the children were sharply limited. Many who tried to remain in the family home, in order to preserve their children's familiar routines, found that even this choice had limiting consequences. One woman, for example, chose to forgo returning to graduate school in order to keep her children in their home. She found a job nearby, doing clerical work:

I decided I wanted my kids to stay in their home and to stay in their neighborhood—it's a marvelous place to live. I didn't want to relocate them, and I also wanted to be available to them as much as possible. It's very upsetting when marriages break up and dad leaves, so I wanted to reduce some of the shock. I don't know how one does that, or if the way I did it works best. Perhaps I just needed it for myself.

All but two of these mothers said that their experiences during and after the divorce had brought them closer to their children. Without a father sharing the parental role in family life, they could be more open and direct with their children. They said there was less sense that two opposed subgroups, adults and children, made up the family. Some mothers deliberately changed patterns of communication with their children. One of them, for example, asked her son to take an interest in her college work:

At the beginning, when he was about eight, I sat him down and said, "You know, I ask you every day what you do in school. So now you should ask me too." At first he'd say, "Well mom, how was your day?" Then his eyes would glaze over! But now, after doing it for a while, he seems to be interested. He knows when I have tests, and he asks how I did. He's not intensely interested, but he does show a bit of interest. I felt like a huge part of my life didn't exist for him, so I wanted him to be more involved.

In the shift to single parenting, these mothers had to redefine their own roles. Because they had married expecting to share the parental role with a spouse, their long-held expectations and time-tested approaches had to be changed. For example:

> It was awfully hard at first, but more and more I've enjoyed being a single parent. In fact, I never saw myself as a natural parent. I didn't even want to have children. That's why we were married for eight years before we had our daughter; I was going to pursue a career. It was my husband who wanted children. He'd say, "Remember now, you're not doing this by yourself." So all right, I had these two children. And when I had them, I got very committed to the idea. If I was going to have those children, I wanted it to be worth it for them. But I never intended to have anything except the traditional family situation, and now their father is simply unavailable to them.

The woman who said this also reported that she made no attempt to hide her financial situation from her children, but deliberately made it a family matter:

> It was the worst when the kids were really young. Now, whenever they give me any of that crap about not having any money, I say, "Now look, you guys, you know what the circumstances are around here." I think they're absolutely fantastic kids. I think they understand, *really* understand, what it is that we're contending with. The thing that's important to them is love and caring and feeling good. So we do things. We go camping, and we have fun. It's not all just hard work.

Although most of the women reconstructed a stable family life within a year, they still had to cope with the problems raised by their children's growth and development over the years, as well as with changes in their own lives, especially the entry or departure of male friends:

> Single parenting is great. But when you do have a problem, then there's no one to turn to. Like now, with my son nearing adolescence, he doesn't like me having relationships with men. He gets really quiet and moody, and I don't want to mess him up—he's got a whole lifetime ahead of him. I'm not sure how to handle it now. I'm not sure what's going on with him about this.

One of the few women who expressed serious regrets about her relationship with her children said she had worked sixty-hour weeks in an effort to be a good provider and had also tried to pursue an active social life, at least in part to escape from unhappiness and stress at home:

Because I was too needy myself, and too self-involved, we spent three years trying to bridge what became a permanent gulf between us. I have a great sadness about the kids and my relationship with them, even though they're nearly grown now. In many ways, they were emotionally neglected. I was under a lot of stress, and they added to it. So they became targets for my outbursts and my anger. That's the worst part of all this, and I wish I could do it over again.

These women had a great deal of themselves invested in their parenting. All of them said they loved their children. Most said they were satisfied with their accomplishments as parents, and many said there were definite advantages to being a single parent. But they reached these positive self-assessments despite many handicaps.

A woman who spoke of feeling abandoned and isolated for years said this:

I think single parenting makes you really strong, very creative and resourceful. You know the saying, "Necessity is the mother of invention"? Well, you find out how strong you really are and just what you can do. It's amazing.

A woman with a preschool child whose only source of income was welfare payments said this:

I really advocate single parenthood—I think it's just great. I'm not sure what the benefits of marriage are—except a steady sex life! That would be a real benefit. But is it worth the expectations and the arguments? The most rewarding thing has been having this wonderfully normal kid. She's sociable and plays well with other kids. Yet here she is in this "abnormal" family situation.

A mother of three children close in age, who had not been able to escape financial difficulties for eight years and often had to rely on her own mother for help, said this:

Actually, I think I'm an exceptionally good mother—though I don't know what the kids would say! But it's been great. I've felt sort of like a pioneer with this single mother thing. And it's been good that my kids go into their friends' homes and see how others live. And their friends love to come here. I have rules—certain things just aren't done here—but we have a fairly popular house, especially now that they're teenagers. The place is always crawling with kids. And I like it. I've loved it, actually—they're so interesting and so much fun.

Mothers assessed their parenting at least partly in terms of their previous family lives. Most of them, like this woman, were satisfied with the overall situation but concerned about the effects of economic hardship and uncertainty:

> It's much easier for me and the kids that I'm a single parent. Poor? Yes.
> More honest? Yes. My daughter really resents being poor, but my son
> doesn't mind so much. Anyway, being poor isn't intrinsic to single par-
> enting; but it does reflect the society and its positions toward women.

There were a few exceptions to this pattern. Five of the women disliked single parenting and were also somewhat negative about parenting in general. It is worth noting that all of them had lived below the poverty level since divorce (despite their employment), all of them had children close in age, and none of them had received emotional or financial support from their children's fathers or from friends and family members. Three of these five women, including this mother whose four children ranged in age from four to sixteen, were bitter about their experiences with motherhood:

> My best advice to everyone is to *not* have kids. You never know if
> you'll end up doing all the work yourself. And my experience while
> married was that I was doing all of it alone anyway. So if you *are*
> going to have kids, you'd better be prepared to do it yourself. I just
> recommend you not have any kids. It's just too hard. I think the kids
> have borne the brunt of a lot of my frustration. Now I know how child
> abuse occurs—it happens when you're trapped. There's just been con-
> stant stress because of being so poor. You're raised to be a nice person,
> and you expect to be nice to your kids. Besides, I didn't know how to
> discipline anyone. So when the kids would do something to irritate
> me, all of a sudden I'd lose control and start yelling and hitting.
> I found out that I had to start taking care of myself, too, because no-
> body else cared. I was an only child, raised in a middle-class family,
> and that's just made this even harder. I always had nice things, every-
> thing I wanted. And I haven't been able to get my own kids anything.
> I mean *nothing*.

The woman who said this made it clear that she had lost hope for a brighter future and had fallen into a state of emotional poverty only after many years of economic hardship.

Almost a fourth of these women said they had worried about the lack of male role models in their children's lives. All of them who said this reported that the father of their children had maintained no contact with them. Two mothers, who were unusual in their concern about maintaining traditional gender role behaviors, criticized single parenting because it could not provide an "authority figure" in the family. Both said they liked mothering but resented the fact that divorce had forced them to adopt "abnormal" sex role behaviors. One of these two explained:

> Of course, I tried to be a father too, which was really tough. I realized only recently that I should stop trying to be a man and stick to being a woman—that's enough. I tried to play the father role—very tough and unyielding, not soft and not nurturing. The mother is the nurturing one, and the father is the authoritarian. There were lots of emotional problems, and when I didn't have the stamina or capacity to treat my kids as the nurturing parent, I'd try to be aggressive and assertive. But no matter how much I might yell or whatever, I couldn't find the authority I thought a father should have. So then I'd try to be the nurturing parent again, and it all got very confusing to my kids.

In my discussions with them, these women emphasized the fact that they were not simply divorced women but divorced women with children—so that divorce was a family affair, with a potentially great impact on the children. Because all of them had been divorced for at least two years, and the median time since divorce was four years, the family relations they described were already occurring in a context of normalcy rather than crisis. For this reason, when I asked them to evaluate the effects of divorce on their children's lives, they spoke with confidence. I asked them to say what their children had been like before and after divorce, in terms of performance and relations with peers and adults, and to compare their own children with others they knew.

Although they expressed concern about their children's long-term development, nearly all of these women considered their children "normal" and said they considered divorce only one event among others in their lives.* As one put it:

*In its issue for December 20, 1984, *USA Today* summarized the key findings of seven national studies of children of divorced parents, sponsored by the National Institute of Mental Health. Two of the findings—that divorce does not harm children and that children who live with divorced mothers actually do better on achievement tests and have fewer school problems than children from two-parent homes—were supported in the assertions of the women I interviewed for this study. Significantly, both

I really believe my children are fine. They both exhibit wonderful senses of humor. They are hell-raisers at times, too, but they seem to be genuinely normal children. They're active and into everything they want to be. They're both terrific in school, academically. One is also gifted artistically, and the other is outgoing and a real social butterfly.

Even mothers who had struggled with great difficulties themselves were pleased with their children's development. For example, one woman, who often held two jobs at once in order to make ends meet, said she had come close to neglecting her son. Finally, at her request, her former husband took the child for a year. Before that year was up, she found a relatively high paying position; her son returned to live with her and began to visit his father regularly. She was delighted with this result:

He's never seemed to have suffered from any of this. He's very well liked in school, he gets along equally well with adults and children, he has a good time, and he's a really likeable boy. I think he's incredibly well adjusted. He's had the best of two worlds, I think. He's got like three sets of grandparents since the remarriage of his father, and we all really care about him. He's a pretty flexible child. I've just been lucky; that's all I can say.

Regular and frequent contacts between children and their fathers, mentioned by the two women just quoted, was a rarity. But most of the women whose children seldom saw their fathers also made very positive assessments. For example:

My son has really blossomed. He was very quiet and introverted before, but now he's really active and does well in school. He's getting average grades, and he's applying himself much more. He's doing

---

my study and the studies summarized by *USA Today* involved children who were not receiving any kind of medical or psychological therapy. The fact that much previous research on children of divorced parents has been based on clinical and therapeutic populations may explain some of the contradictory findings that are plentiful in the literature. For example, Kurdeck and Siesky (1980) conclude in their study of 132 subjects that the majority did not view their parents' divorce as a distressing experience. But Wallerstein and Kelly (1979), using a population engaged in family therapy, found that after five years, 34 percent of the 131 children were doing well, 37 percent were suffering from moderate to severe depression, and 29 percent had resumed appropriate developmental progress but continued to show some adverse effects. Other contemporary studies examining the effects of divorce on children include Kurdeck (1981); Fulton (1979); Raschke and Raschke (1979).

school things, and has a money-making project he's working on. He needs some successes, and he's getting them. And he's resourceful: he got himself a job on his own, sweeping in a store part-time every day.

It was generally agreed that children matured after divorce and acquired greater independence.[2] In response to their changed situations, children assumed more responsibility and became "more grown up." The pleasure the mothers took in this, however, was often tinged with concern that their children were being pushed to grow up too fast:

I was so poor I couldn't afford a babysitter, so my son has been on his own since he was seven or eight. He's eleven now, and he's great. I've come home to find that he's cleaned the whole house and done the laundry so I could have my day off free. And he does really well in school. When we first moved here and I got this job, he started skipping school because I had to leave before he did. So I told him that each of us had a job, and his was to go to school and learn. I told him that if he didn't pull it off, I'd have to quit work to police him, and we'd be back on welfare. That's all it took. He's got a lot of common sense and can read situations, so you don't have to sit down and explain things. He acts a lot older than eleven, really. His friends seem very young to me in comparison. But I try not to treat him like an adult—I don't want him to lose that kid thing. He says he wishes I didn't have to work so much—he really does. Fortunately, he has good friends. But I feel like much of the time his friends' parents are raising him, not me.

Children's Responses to Divorce

Children's negative or regressive responses to divorce were short-term: only a few mothers saw any relationship between divorce and their children's problems. Even the women who reported such problems said there were other causes, and the single cause they all mentioned was a difficult postdivorce relationship between a child and his or her father.*

* Most studies of the children of divorced parents, besides using clinical populations as their subjects, have not used comparison groups of children from traditional two-parent families. Nor have they compared the effects of divorce per se with the effects of other major family and life changes. For example, few studies control for socioeconomic variables, and none attempts to assess the effects on children of downward mobility resulting from divorce. For these reasons, research on the effects of divorce on child development often reinforces popular stereotypes.

Few children were surprised when their parents announced that they were divorcing, but many mothers noted how strong their children's immediate emotional responses were. Some parents did not directly tell their children, believing that they would grasp the situation as time went by and the father did not return. Others brought their older children directly into discussions about dividing property and making new living arrangements.

Several mothers undertook some kind of counseling with their children, hoping to ease their adjustment to the new situation. One reported:

> Though everybody usually goes into therapy, when I filed for divorce, we went into biofeedback. I wanted my kids to know that there was nothing wrong with them. They were powerless to alter the divorce, but they still had power over themselves, and I wanted them to know that. After three months of biofeedback training, the kids began fiddling around—my son was making airplanes, and my daughter was doing her homework. So the counselor said that until the kids were willing to make a contract and participate, he didn't want to see us! The kids were fine. They just didn't want to go anymore because they had other things they wanted to do with their time.

Only one divorcing couple—one of the two couples who chose to co-parent after divorce—went into family counseling together with their children. This mother's report, therefore, was exceptional:

> I insisted that we go see a child psychiatrist. I was afraid their father, because of his tendency to put the best face on everything and avoid problems, would ignore everyone's feelings. I thought maybe the girls really needed to talk to somebody besides us. I wanted them to be taken seriously. Because I moved out and was looking for a place to have them with me, I was worried that the children would think I was leaving them, too. Their father did a wonderful thing: he put our oldest girl in what used to be his study. And he gave her a telephone— it was a family line, but he put an extension in there so she could call me. In the beginning, especially, I think it was really important to her to be able to call me late at night or early in the morning, just to talk and make contact. She doesn't do that so much anymore [since the children spend equal amounts of time with each parent in a shared parenting arrangement]. Now she tends to use it if she's sort of depressed about something her father does! But that's okay. I think there's an advantage to having two parents because the kids can complain and

let off some steam. But my daughter's been real careful about doing that, because she doesn't want either of us to say anything bad about the other. She's very quick to defend. . . . Also, her teacher did a wonderful thing. Before we told our kids about the divorce plans, we went to tell their teachers, so they would know what was happening. Several months later our older girl's teacher said to her, "You're doing so well. Some of the other students are going through divorces in their families, too. Would you be willing to talk with them occasionally?"

Most of the women said they had done little to prepare themselves emotionally for divorce. Most children were cared for and parented during the separation process, but most were also left largely on their own to deal with their emotions.[3] Their mothers—already emotionally depleted from trying to cope with their own feelings as well as with the legal divorce proceedings and the need to find employment—said they were least responsive to their children's emotional needs during the first few months after divorce.

It was the younger children who most often showed signs of distress during the early phases of divorcing. All were old enough to understand that their parents were no longer living together, that their father had left the home, and that their mother was upset. This report was typical:

My daughter was not quite six at the time, and she kind of regressed. She began to suck her thumb again, and she got kind of quiet in her social reactions. However, she's come around. She seems to be much better adjusted now.

Such problems were temporary, however, and diminished steadily as mothers reestablished control over their lives. Teenagers aided their own transitions by seeking support, during the first year, from other adults. This ultimately helped everyone in the family to adjust. Like others, this woman understood that her children had to adjust not only to their father's absence but also to their mother's newly overburdened life:

My kids are good kids. We have a lot of fun, and we're open and talk a lot. They do excellently in school, and they're into good clean activities, so far. I've found that in the high school years, they still need you. The first year after their father left, I was working night and day. If it hadn't been for the family next door, I don't know how my daughter would have come through it. I was working so many hours, and was such an emotional wreck, that I was seldom with her.

Some children felt torn between their parents. Young teenagers, particularly, tried to promote a reconciliation, and when that failed, they often tried to be the emotional caretakers of their absent fathers. Children whose parents had separated and reconciled previously were the most resistant to accepting the parents' separation as certain:

> They knew things weren't okay between us. We didn't even sleep in the same bedroom. So it wasn't a shock to them [when we separated], but they were really depressed at first. They'd go to their father's place, and he'd be putting on this pitiful show, looking sad and carrying on. So they worried about him and were afraid he'd really move to another city.

Family history had a significant effect on children's emotional responses to divorce. For example, children who had witnessed fighting between their parents prior to the divorce showed signs of relief immediately after their parents separated. The children of three of the women who had been physically battered by husbands showed almost immediate improvement in their schoolwork after the parents' separation. One of these women said:

> There had been so much bad stuff going on in the last couple of years before he left that the kids just hoped it was over for good this time. They didn't want the hassles anymore. We had separated a couple of times before that, but each time I had him come back home when I couldn't make it financially. It was funny, because I was projecting my own pain onto the kids. I thought they were feeling as awful as I was. But they weren't! They still had a father—they just didn't have to live with all the hassling. They really didn't feel terrible like I did.

Besides assuming greater responsibility for themselves and developing more mature interpersonal skills, children became more active participants in home life. The mothers who worked full-time increasingly depended on their children for substantial household help, and with only one exception, every mother said she had increased the home responsibilities assigned to the children. Housekeeping standards changed; women who had previously judged their own performance as wives and mothers by the cleanliness and order of their homes found it necessary to reduce their expectations. A woman who had done all the housework and cleaning for her family described how she shared home tasks with her three teenagers:

We have a list of duties and chores. It's a fight to make sure it all gets done, but fortunately it's not terribly important anymore to have an immaculate house. The kids do most of the cooking on the days I work. They're real good cooks and good shoppers, too. Sometimes we all get in there and cook. And let me tell you, there are no sex roles attached to any of the household chores. My son can cook as well as any of us, and my daughters can mow the lawn just as well as he can. I'm not having any of that stuff in this family!

Breaking patterns in which the mother had done nearly all the domestic tasks required effort and organization. Mothers had to determine what was appropriate for their children's ages and daily schedules, then give assignments and monitor their completion. In general, they agreed that the most difficult part of changing family work patterns was to be consistent about their expectations. The only mother who said she did not depend on her teenaged children for household help also noted the effort required:

I think I haven't expected enough from my kids. I was too tired to get them organized and hold them accountable. So they have really been self-centered. I probably contributed to that because I was trying to compensate for a lack of money. Life hasn't been easy for them either, but they could have been more help.

Activities and Schedules

When interviewed, 85 percent of the women said they considered themselves active participants in their children's lives and activities. Their leisure pursuits varied according to personal interests and the age and number of children involved, and preferred activities changed as children grew older. For example:

We can go up to my folks' place on the lake, two hours away from here. We can afford to do that because it only takes gas, and we have to eat anyway. It used to be that if we didn't do that, we'd sit around here and go stark raving mad, and up there we'd play until we were exhausted. The kids still like to go, but now they often have other things they want to do with friends. We've probably been there only six times in the last six months.

But many women said that excessive demands on their time, even more than financial constraints, limited activities with children;

managing child rearing, a job outside the home, and domestic tasks consumed most of their waking hours. They had deep regrets about having to reduce the amount of time they could spend on educational and recreational activities with their children, and many expressed anger at being declassed in this way by divorce. One mother said:

> I went to a thing about six weeks ago, a meeting. The people I'd met there—mothers of children my son is in school with—all went and had coffee afterward. There were about nine of us sitting around the table, and I looked at each one of them and thought, "You know, I'm the only one who can't afford to be here. I'm the only one here who should be working. I'm the only one here who can't really afford to eat lunch here." Everyone else was talking about the music lessons and everything they were doing for their kids. I was the only one who couldn't volunteer for a job during the day. When I looked at them, I thought, "It isn't because they are better than I am, or smarter than I am, or more capable. It's because each of them is married to a man who makes a good income." Do you know what I mean? Their life-styles depend on that man. When I think about single parenting, I can't get past the economics of it. And what's going to happen when there are more and more divorces and fewer and fewer mothers able to ac-tively participate in their kids' lives, their kids' school lives? It's just so sad.

The key to managing single parenting successfully was to be ex-traordinarily well organized. But even the mothers who succeeded in establishing a fixed routine suffered from fatigue and stress. Those with children under the age of eight or nine (and especially if they were preschool children) often suffered from near-chronic fatigue. Getting off to work in the morning required early rising, hurried deal-ings with children, and frequent emotional chaos. The evening hours were a time to prepare meals, do laundry, make shopping trips, and take care of all the business of running a household. One mother— who had children of seven and nine years of age, no family help, and only her earned income for support—described her daily life as follows:

> I start laundry in the morning when we leave and put it in the dryer when I get home. I get up at half past five and go to bed about half past eleven or midnight—always. And I'm used to it. I do houseclean-ing after the kids are in bed, and sometimes I cook then, too. I buy groceries once a week at an all-night market after the children are in

bed. Once in a while we stop for groceries on our way home, but it's already six o'clock then, and the kids are hungry, so we usually try to go straight home. I have a microwave oven, so I cook on weekends and have meals ready for the week. That way when we get home, we can heat up dinner and eat. I never fix just one chicken; I cook two or three. On Sunday we go to church and try to do something together in the afternoon. When I think about it, I can't believe how organized I am, or how we make it work. [But without that organizing] I don't know how we'd get through the evenings in the few hours we have. I don't get sick—there's no time to be sick. It's bad enough when the kids are sick. They don't get sick often, though, so that's a relief.

This mother of two preschoolers said that even though life had become easier as her children had grown older, she still felt chronic fatigue:

It's so much easier now. I don't have to do diapers; I don't have to dress either of the kids. My daughter wasn't even feeding herself when my husband left. And now both kids even help with meals. They may not be the best meals, but we all enjoy doing it. They pick up their toys and things and make their beds. I'm up at half past five. The kids get up at about half past six. Sometimes they have breakfast here; sometimes I pack it and they eat it at school. They get dressed while I pack lunches for all of us. We leave the house at seven o'clock, I drop them off at preschool, and I get to work by twenty past seven. I'm off at four, and I pick them back up, and we come back home. I come home and fix dinner. I usually do a big shopping once a month, on the day after I get paid. On Thursday, I go to the family counselor—that's the day my mom takes the kids for the evening and feeds them. The kids go to bed by half past seven at the latest. I'm usually in bed by nine— I'm beat then. Some nights after dinner I lie down for a minute and then fall sound asleep. So I get up, put the kids to bed, and go back to sleep. The housecleaning usually gets put off, and so does the yard work. I try to do those things on weekends. Fortunately, I don't get sick much. When the kids get sick and I feel like I'm coming down with something, I tell myself I can't afford to get sick—and I don't.

This mother noted that her young son also suffered fatigue, perhaps in part because of their schedule and the large amount of time he was spending at preschool while she worked:

He'd sometimes come home just exhausted and not even want to eat dinner—he'd just lie down and go to sleep. Every time I turned around, he was sleeping. He wasn't eating, and he's a skinny little thing anyway. I took him to the doctor last month, but he checked out okay. The doctor said he was just exhausted. So I've been pushing naps. He'll nap for two hours—that's napping time for little kids, not five-year-olds. But he really seems to need it.

Mothers whose children were older were usually less constrained by their demands and had relatively more free time, as this woman's comments suggest:

> I work from seven to half past three, so I'm up early. Usually my fourteen-year-old gets up about half past five, so that's my alarm clock. I get home about quarter to four and generally start dinner. Lately I've been going to an exercise class in the late afternoon. If the kids haven't finished fixing dinner, then I do it. I'm satisfied with the time I spend with my children. Even when I'm home, they don't want to hang around me—they want to visit their friends and things. That's fine. But I'm usually the one who drives them around to those places. I spend most of the weekend doing grocery shopping and taxiing them to their activities. Recently I had a whole weekend to myself: their dad took them to Los Angeles. It was really nice. I can't remember the last time I had so much free time. I did a major cleaning. It was so good to be all by myself and just clean. Sunday I went to church and did some more things around the house in the afternoon. Usually the kids do most of the cleaning, so it's not done the way I would do it. But at least it gets done.

Virtually all these women said that their efforts to care for their children were not recognized by society, and that the hardship of having to take sole financial responsibility for their children was ignored. They also said that their economic problems, the source of greatest difficulty, were worsened by a lack of parenting supports and social isolation.* The great majority said they were at least initially uncertain about how to function successfully as single parents. Some of these uncertainties were common to all parents regardless of marital status, but some were unique to single mothers: the two-parent,

---

*Other studies have validated this opinion. For example: "In almost every study of female-headed households, women mention their loneliness, isolation, and overwhelming responsibilities" (Wattenberg and Reinhardt, 1979:464). "The fundamental problem in the single parent's situation is the insufficiency of immediately available support. . . . The single parent must make do with the much more limited help available from children, kin, friends, and professional helpers" (Weiss, 1979a:265).

nuclear family model they had been raised to believe in often became irrelevant or counterproductive. In addition, they felt stigmatized— watched and judged harshly by others simply because they were single parents.

Some women reacted to a lack of societal appreciation by discounting their own parenting contribution. Thus one mother of three children, two of whom were almost grown, expressed pride in her ability to manage a family, even under conditions of extreme economic hardship, but she had trouble incorporating successful parenting into her own self-image:

> I lose sight of what I do as a parent, and I'm always embarrassed when people call it to my attention. The society doesn't value parenting, but it's more than that. It's the way people talk about parenting. I've raised some reasonably happy and productive kids, but that won't work on a job résumé.

The majority of these women—and with few exceptions, even those who greatly enjoyed single parenting—said they felt socially isolated and unsupported as parents. These two comments are representative:

> Do you know that I've been away from my kids for one week in eighteen years? That's the only time I've ever been without at least one child in all these years. I've just parented. I've read a lot of books on parenting and child development. I felt responsible for them, but no one else—no one—gave a damn. I was literally alone. My in-laws are back east. I don't have any brothers or sisters. My parents weren't interested in the kids and wouldn't even take them for a weekend. They don't even go to their dad's. It's been really lonely and tough.

> Sometimes I get really tired. And I feel like I'm *alone*. I wish I had someone to share what I am doing with. I've got friends and acquaintances and people to do things with, but it's not the same thing. They don't share my interest in my child.

The most exhausted and emotionally depleted women were those who received no help at all in parenting; their emotional energies were simply drained away, and they had no source of replenishment. Ironically, the women with only one child tended to have the most support; it was the women with several children who received the least amount of assistance from others. Overall, mothers of very young children and mothers of teenagers had the fewest offers of help, partly because the fathers of such children were the least likely to play a significant role in the postdivorce family.

Financial circumstances allowed these women no time away from their children, and the lack of relief from responsibility was wearing. One woman's mother had taken the children one evening a week; but when she died, that respite from daily child care vanished. She said:

> What can I do? Run away from my kids? Hang around drinking in bars? I'd love to leave my kids for a weekend, but I have no desire to leave them altogether. I've put a lot of effort into them and I love them, but I could sure use a break. I'm beginning to get more independence now that they're older.

The degree of isolation and the overwhelming sense of sole responsibility came as a surprise to many mothers. Most had believed that because they had already been the primary parent in marriage, parenting alone would not be particularly stressful. They learned that it was the sense of isolation, not the parenting itself, that was most overwhelming:

> I think what I really missed most was just the sharing of daily ups and downs. I'd never lived alone. Even though I still had kids, it wasn't the same. About six months after my husband left, I got totally hit with this anger about being a single parent. There are times—like when you're having a midnight crisis with the youngest one, and you're still trying to solve something with one of the other kids, and you've already done everything you can think of—when you wish there were another parent around.

Most had come to accept their feelings of loneliness in parenting and had regained a sense of emotional control:

> You get so frustrated and wish you had some help sometimes. You have to be there for the kids all the time. I've had to learn a significant amount of self-control to handle this. I used to cry and scream—I was terrible. But with no one else here to balance this, I've had to learn some self-control.

Where were these women's families? All but two of the sixty women had some contacts with their families, but only three of them received fairly regular assistance from family members. One of these three, a mother of two preschoolers, said that her parents made it possible for her to work full-time and "stay sane":

Mom takes the kids one night a week—feeds them dinner—so I get a break. I pick them up about eight, and it's time for bed. If I want to go out and can't find anyone to sit with them, or if I'm out of money, she'll take them. My dad has done something I really appreciate, too. When the kids are sick and he's home all day, rather than me taking a day or a week off to care for them, he takes them. I just bundle them up and take them over there, and he takes care of them. He takes them to the doctor and the dentist for me, too. When my folks talk about moving out of town, I wonder what I'd do. In that respect, I'm very dependent on them. The kids love their grandparents—both sets of them, actually.

Four other women received help when they were ill or when they requested it, which they occasionally did.[4] Another six believed that help would be forthcoming from their families if they asked for it, which they generally did not do. Former in-laws provided emotional support to three mothers of younger children; all three had initiated such contacts after deciding that it was important for their children to know these relatives. Some of the older women had contacts with their former in-laws but did not perceive them as a source of support in their lives.

Reactions about the lack of family support included anger, resignation, and positive acceptance. Few women had expected such help in raising their children; even those who received substantial financial assistance from their families neither expected nor received other kinds of help. Those who were satisfied with this situation usually placed a high value on keeping their own independence:

I've never had any real help with the kids. No one in the family has ever volunteered to give me a break. None of my single friends rely on their families either for help with children. They want to stay independent, and it's hard to make growth changes when you're involved with parents—there's still the expectation that you'll follow family rules. If you stay somewhat free of parents, it's easier to make friends with other single-parent women and be your own self.

As this woman continued to talk about the lack of supports available to single mothers, however, her perspective shifted:

But I found out that I had to reach out and ask for help. One person took care of my middle son in the afternoons for months and took very little money for it. She liked my son and got along well. One summer my daughter's regular babysitter took her on a family vacation to Canada with them in a motor home. If you take the attitude that these children are not just yours but everybody's, then somehow other people are willing to share. But if you view them as your property and solely your responsibility, then that's what you have. If you take the position that they are a gift and that somebody would really like their company, then people seem to be there! I've had to learn that.

The least overloaded or isolated women were the two who shared parenting with their former husbands. One of them had parented alone for the first two years after her divorce and then began to share parenting with her former husband:

I feel so sorry for the single mothers who get no breaks, who get no support from either a present or an absent father, to take the burden off. I really look forward to my long weekends when the kids aren't with me—even if I do nothing but putter around the house or do normal chores. To have that element out of your life is a very great relief. And their father gets that relief too, so it works both ways. Neither of us has to feel that there's no break. That's really wonderful. And I think—I hope—it enhances parenting. I think how well joint custody works depends on the parents. If they're doing it because they agree that it's going to be good that way, that it's not going to be full of upheavals or traumas for anyone, and that the kids matter—that's the key in fact—it'll work. It's written into our dissolution agreement that our primary concern will always be the well-being of the kids and what's best for them. So far it's worked.

Although co-parenting provided a definite relief from parenting duties, it also required greater efforts at communication with the former spouse, and both women who were engaged in it were quick to acknowledge that co-parenting would probably be unworkable for most divorced parents, who were unlikely to communicate well with each other. Aside from these two, there were only four women whose children's fathers were regularly involved with them in ways that helped. Eight other fathers generally visited their children several times a month, and another seven saw them at least once every six weeks, but these visits did not give mothers any substantial relief from child care or parenting responsibilities. Nor did these fathers typically provide emotional support for parenting.

While discussing their own experiences, over a quarter of the women referred to men who act as single parents. Their cynical and sometimes humorous comments revealed a resentment about their own lonely efforts and society's double standard. For example:

> Most men simply have no concept of what we're up against, even when they're single parents and have custody. Men still have this whole troop of women—mothers, aunts, sisters, friends—to wish them luck and give them household help and child care. And they've got enough money so they can afford to pay for such things if the women around them don't come through. Society at large gives men moral support, but it acts like mothers don't need any. It just galls me.

> It really disgusts me to watch single men who have custody of their children get so much attention. Friends invite them over to dinner. My friends who are couples don't invite me and my children over; they just expect that I can manage. Men have double the income and can afford to pay for all the services they need, but they get treated as if they're wonderful to be doing all this and must be really overloaded. I've never had that kind of support from anyone.

These women felt especially deserted and segregated when they heard frequent cultural messages to the effect that children raised by divorced mothers are likely candidates for delinquency, homosexuality, or abnormal social behavior. Already overburdened with financial and emotional responsibility for their children, they found societal indifference hard enough to tolerate; blanket criticisms based on negative stereotypes outraged them.[5]

> I get really upset and resentful over all the media talk about the negative effects of divorce on children. There's more of it lately than I've seen for quite a while. It just really makes me angry. I resent the tube telling me, and my kids, that "children of divorced parents don't make good peer relationships and do poorly in school, and they're likely to live a life of crime." That's *garbage!* The media ignores the fact that we have crazy people running around who grew up in the so-called normal family. I think the media images are really damaging.

Several of the women said that negative stereotypes produced distrust and lack of acceptance among other mothers, which increased their own social isolation and loneliness:

> The stigma of being a single mother! For example, the friendships that are typically formed in a neighborhood were never really there for me because I was a single parent. I was never really a part of the neigh-

borhood gatherings. My kids never got to see that part of socializing in a neighborhood situation. We were the *different* family. My daughter had a friend whose parents told her not to hang around with my daughter because I was divorced and would be a bad influence. In 1981! I was the oddball, too, because I worked full-time. The other mothers, if they worked at all, worked only part-time. My daughter, though, made friends with some neighborhood women, and she'd come home and rave about how wonderful they were. Like, "She's the mother-type!" Where'd she get that idea—watching "Father Knows Best" or "Leave It to Beaver"? You know, where mother warmly greets everyone as she puts dinner on a beautifully set dinner table, dressed in her heels and pearls?

6

The Role of
Ex-Husbands

These sixty women entered into divorce with two important but conflicting assumptions: that the intimate, personal relationship with the former husband would be ended forever; and that the ex-husband would maintain some sort of relationship with the children. They worried less about their individual loss than about the psychological distress their children would experience because of the father's absence from the home. They shared the popular assumption that divorce usually has serious emotional consequences for children. In this chapter, we examine these two relationships—between the women and their ex-husbands and between the ex-husbands and their children—and discuss the connections between them.

Relations with Former Wives

It came as a surprise to most of these women when divorce did not effectively cut off personal relationships with their ex-husbands. Because all but three of the sixty had sole custody of all their children, they found that they had to redefine an ongoing relationship with the children's father, a task that often caused intense emotional suffering.* For some, this relationship became even more

*Two women shared custody of their children with their ex-husband, and another mother had custody of one child while the father had custody of two.

complex and stressful than it had been during marriage, and most found few constructive social guidelines to help them in dealing with the problem.[1]

Only a minority of the women (eleven out of sixty) said they had fairly positive relations with their ex-husbands. Their relationships, in varying degrees, were adversarial, businesslike, friendly, and sexual, and caused a variety of feelings—affection, indifference, hurt, anger, and hostility. Nearly all the women reported conflicting feelings about their former husbands and said that their postdivorce relationships caused stress and depleted their emotional reserves.

The kind of relationship that existed after divorce was loosely related to earlier experiences in marriage. Thus, women whose marriages had been riddled with conflict and anger tended to have hostile divorce proceedings and no direct relationships with their ex-husbands afterward. Women whose husbands had left them for another woman also tended to have no contact at all, generally because the former husbands refused it. But there were several exceptions to these patterns. One woman whose husband had left her to start a new family, and another whose marriage had been full of conflict, reported having relatively friendly associations with their former spouses. Even the payment or nonpayment of child support or continued joint ownership of a home did not predict or explain the postdivorce association between former marriage partners.

Many women "still felt married," regardless of whether they had any relationship with their former spouses. Divorce could not erase the memory of their married years or negate the presence of their children, who were a constant reminder of shared parenthood. "Feeling married" was reinforced by the fact that these women could not live like single people without children; as single mothers, they had more than their share of family responsibilities. Some of the complexity of postdivorce feelings is suggested by this comment, from a woman who had been the wife of a pastor for twenty years:

> I still feel like I'm married, even though we have no contact. How do I undo those years? And we've got kids. I think it's worse, in many ways, than being a widow. If I had lost a husband through death, the church probably would have been much more supportive. There's a real gap in our culture. People are threatened and really don't want to

deal with pain, so you're left alone to cope with these feelings of grief
and anger and loss. And yes, I am angry. At the same time, it's so
very sad.

Expressions of sadness and sorrow were frequent, even among the
women who had wanted a divorce. Redefining the relationship after
divorce was painful, for it required recognizing the loss of the marriage and the partner and acknowledging the failure of many hopes.
A woman whose decision to divorce three years earlier had been
shared by her husband described how her sense of loss lingered on:

> We've stayed in touch even though he married right after we broke up;
> they have a baby now. I can't say that we're friends, because I don't feel
> the kind of warmth about him I would feel for a friend. But we don't
> fight. It just happened, which is the way I think divorce ought to hap-
> pen. We just didn't have the rapport anymore. And we both saw that
> something was happening that changed the whole relationship. I was
> very emotional about it for some time. We both knew we weren't either
> of us bad people. For two years after the divorce, when he would
> come to the house, I would cry. We wouldn't argue or anything, but I'd
> just feel so sad.

Some women had separated previously from their husbands, only
to reconcile later. For them, finally deciding to divorce was especially difficult, and they struggled to limit the new relationship with
the former spouse. Their postdivorce associations were shaped by a
conflict between the desire to be independent and autonomous and a
sense of continued dependency on each other. One woman told me:

> The first two times we broke up I was angry, and it was hard to know
> for sure what I was doing. This time I'm not angry; I'm calm. So
> there's been no playing around—no sexual intimacy—and I've been
> sure that this is what I want. It wasn't good to have to go through it the
> way we did it. It was too hard on everybody. The kids just didn't know
> what was going on. We were confused; they were confused. There's
> still a tie—we're tied financially. I won't really be divorced, I think,
> until I can break that tie. He's around and still part of my life. I depend
> on him for financial support. And since I have the kids, they need their
> father even if he's not in the home. He's still their father. Whenever I
> have a problem, I call him. I've said, "You come get them before I kill
> them!" He'll come over on Sundays sometimes. If I've had people
> over the night before, he grumbles and wants to know who was here

and what went on. But he doesn't need to know about everything we do. He gets real nice to me when he's involved with a girlfriend. When there's no girlfriend, he's real grouchy. He doesn't admit to it, but I know when he has a girlfriend. I think he feels guilty when he's involved with somebody, and that's why he's so nice then. I think he feels guilty if he's spending money on somebody else while I'm struggling over here, so he just goes out and splurges. This year at Christmas, he went crazy with gifts for us all. I asked him, "Am I dying?"

Over a third of the women had shared some sexual activity with their ex-husbands during the first year after divorce, but only four of them maintained a sexual relationship for longer than that. Each of these four said she had had "a very enjoyable sex life" during marriage and had experienced emotional difficulties in going through with the divorce. One of them said:

One of the things I miss about being married is having a regular sex life. That would be a reason to be married, I think! But to be honest with you, we've continued having a pretty regular sex life even though we're divorced. It's just been so hard to give up. The only difficulty is that we try to keep it from the kids. We've agreed that it would only add to whatever fantasies they might have about us getting back together—and we won't be doing that. I suppose if one of us finds someone else we care about pretty seriously, we'll break off this sex thing. We've tried before! It's probably rather strange, but I know some friends who've had ongoing sexual affairs after their divorces, too.

However, none of the four men involved in these situations paid much attention to their children after divorce. This is an interesting finding, because most fathers who had reasonably harmonious relations with their ex-wives were very actively and regularly involved with their children.

Five women said their ex-husbands were friends with whom they had no sexual activity. The deepest friendship reported to me was between ex-spouses who had decided to share parenting equally after several years of regular visiting by the father. The mother told me:

We can now relate as the parents of our children and as old friends who have a lot of history—we spent more than half of our lives with each other. We have an excellent relationship. He's part of our ongoing family. He's a terrific person—very sweet, caring, and generous.

Generally, women whose former husbands used alcohol or drugs excessively during the marriage had no contact with them. Nevertheless, three of them whose ex-husbands continued to drink excessively after divorce said they did have regular but insignificant contacts with their former spouses, contacts they described as being like meetings with distant relatives.

Most of these women discovered that their relationships with their ex-husbands continued to change after divorce, as various experiences affected their understandings and intentions. The relationships that were most likely to change were those in which no third party had been involved at the time of divorce but the ex-husband later remarried or seriously considered remarriage. One woman who reported having had a highly emotional relationship with her ex-husband said this:

> I never really let go of that man, my past life, until last January. That's when he told me he was getting married. And that's when I knew I was through struggling, hoping he would change, and that things would work out. I was able to start getting on with my life. I started insisting that he had to help support the kids, and I insisted that he at least explore some ways I could keep this house. I started standing up for myself, probably for the first time in my life. I started demanding things for myself.

Although some women described relatively constructive affiliations with their ex-husbands, most had relationships with them that were generally antagonistic. Anger at former husbands was not uncommon, even though the women believed that anger between the divorced parents adversely affected the children.* And even women who felt good about their relationships with their former spouses, as this one said she did, recognized that the link with their children had become the stronger one:

> He gets really mad if I take a particular position with the kids on anything regarding him. . . . I reminded him, "You know, you asked for these children." He answered, "Yes, but only as long as we were in a nuclear family." Good grief, does that mean the children no longer exist?

---

*Wallerstein and Kelly (1980) found that continuing anger between divorced parents was great: four-fifths of the men and a slightly higher proportion of the women had enough anger to add stress to their children's experiences of divorce.

One woman said that after several years of little association with her former husband, she was tentatively constructing a renewed friendship with him. Their meetings elicited powerful feelings:

> When I saw him this week, I realized how hooked on him I still am. We got together to talk about finances and selling the house, and we started to swap teaching stories. That's one of the things I'd been looking forward to doing, even if my teaching is only part-time. We could still swap experiences and what we'd learned from teaching. It was tough. I share creative work with my children, but they haven't lived the twenty-five years that I've lived with him. The only point at which it got emotional was when he was asking me to sort of stand with him against something one of the children wanted. I was having trouble with that, feeling more linked to my children at this point than to him.

Some women, like this one, discovered that mutual dislike did not dissolve after divorce:

> I had thought that once we got a divorce, the pressure would be off. We wouldn't have to spend time disliking each other, and each of us could live our own life. I thought it would be better for our child not to be around people who were always negative with each other. Not much has changed, though. We still actively dislike each other. It's just that the child doesn't have to hear it.

Anger and resentment were generally strongest among the women who had little or no contact with their former spouses. Nearly all of the twenty-six women whose former husbands maintained no association with their children were angry, bitter, and resentful about the absence of a father from their children's lives—emotions that made it even harder for them to cope with the children's own feelings about paternal neglect. Bad feelings were aggravated by a lack of financial assistance: nineteen of these fathers paid no support at all, and six more paid only irregularly.* Indeed, lack of interest in the children seemed directly related to an unwillingness to contribute to their support, even though nonpayment of support did not legally prevent a

---

*Noting the complexity and subtlety of the data on the relationship between support payments and visitation, Chambers (1979:128, 129) states: "For most men, both payments and visitation probably flow from a common source—affection for the child. In some cases, perhaps many, visitation may help induce continued payments by keeping the child's needs vivid in the father's mind. If the latter is the case, policies that encourage visitation may help produce higher collections." Regarding the eighteen Michigan men in his sample who had made frequent court complaints about visi-

father from being involved with his children. A mother of two young children offered this illustration:

> This summer he's living in town again, and he called and said he wanted to see the kids at such and such a time. I told him, "No pay, no see." He got mad and hung up, and that was it. He said, "No big deal—at least I get to keep the money." He's not concerned about the kids.

Women whose husbands left in order to marry new partners had their marriages ended dramatically and conclusively: nearly all of them had no postdivorce association with their former husbands. With one exception, it was the husbands who refused all contact. The following two stories are representative:

> My ex-husband will not speak to me. After all these years of marriage, he will not speak to me, or to the children if I'm present. He says I've been so unreasonable. I guess he wanted me to pat him on the back and tell him anything he wanted was okay. He believes he has been completely misunderstood. If he'd asked me a year ago, I might have been stupid enough to take him back—not whole hog, or tomorrow, but eventually. Now I don't know. My heart still says one thing, but my head says another. Anyway, it'll never happen. He'd never say he's sorry or was mistaken. He'd never ask what happened to us. He'd never ask about the pain he caused so many of us.

> When he left, we still saw each other occasionally. We sort of dated and did family things together. He left in June, and until we went to court in December, we did see each other. By then, I guess, he was so tired of it that he wasn't ugly about it particularly. But he was ugly in court, and he hasn't spoken to me since. We don't talk. He never sets eyes on me, and I haven't met his wife. He will only talk to the kids, and he hangs up if I answer the phone. He won't even say hello to me.

Whether generally friendly or typically hostile, these women's various postdivorce relationships with their former spouses were complex. Most of the women held on to the belief that once their children were grown, their emotional attachment to the ex-husband

---

tation, Chambers says: "[the data] suggest that over the life of the decree, men who fight over visitation are those who are, on the whole, involved with their children, and that involvement is a good sign for high lifetime payments." We need systematic research with noncustodial fathers to determine why some of them pay support and many do not.

would disappear. However, in speculating about their future relationships, three of them entertained thoughts of an eventual reconciliation with their former spouses. Here are two of their comments:

> I think being a single parent is a *drag*. You watch the kids grow up and are satisfied, but it would be nice to have somebody share it with you. When their father calls, we get along great, and so I'll tell him about them. He's in the South. He's not married either. I think I'd go back to him, providing that the problems of the past are really over. He hasn't been involved in drugs for a couple of years now. He's done real well in making the changes it required. I always said that maybe one day we'd meet on the street, and we'd be different people. I was twenty years old when I met him, so that was a long time ago. And it's been over two years since I've even seen him—but we've communicated on the phone once a week. He talks about me coming down there [to see him]. But we wouldn't even know what each other looked like anymore.

> I've heard stories about where this happened. Five years down the road the husband suddenly gets on the phone and wants to talk about old times because "we have so much in common." Next thing you know they're together again. God forbid that should happen! After thirty years [of marriage], who wants to resume that old pattern?

Relations with Children

Like their mothers, children also had complex emotional relationships with the divorced father, even when he did not visit them regularly. The mothers noted that their children's feelings about their fathers often differed significantly from their own, and they regretted that their children were affected by these differences. Somewhat ironically, these mothers did not "feel divorced" from their husbands in the ways they had expected, but they came to believe that their children felt "divorced" in ways they had not expected.[2] Over two-thirds of the absent fathers saw their children less than five times a year, and the mothers of these children found it hard to watch their children struggling to cope with this apparent indifference.*

---

*Carol Bruch (1978:41) argues that it is time for society, parents, and the courts to recognize that fathers have a continuing parental, moral, and economic responsibility for their children, divorced or not: "Children are a joint undertaking: no logic requires that an inevitable consequence of divorce be the replacement of two parents by one."

Three broadly defined types of relationships between divorced fathers and their children were reported: regular visits (including shared parenting), occasional visits, and no contact. There seemed to be no satisfactory general explanation for these differences in contact.[3] There did, however, seem to be a loose correlation between the degree of paternal involvement and the age of the children. Children of elementary school age tended to receive the most attention from their fathers, unless the fathers had remarried; teenagers and very young children generally received the least attention.

Regular Visits and Shared Parenting

Children in twelve of the sixty families had regular visits with their fathers. Two of these fathers had their children for much of the holiday and summer vacation periods, two saw or telephoned their children at least once a week, and eight contacted or visited their children at least three times a month, sometimes for an overnight stay. Four children in two other families (two elementary-school-aged daughters in each) were co-parented: they spent half their time living with one parent and half their time with the other, alternating between two homes. Overall, only 20 percent of the families (and 18 percent of the children) had regular visits from the father or shared parenting.*

Visiting arrangements fell into no clear pattern. Several children saw their fathers according to a fixed schedule, which would be altered only in case of illness. One daughter, for example, had seen her father regularly every Wednesday evening and every other weekend for nearly four years. But other children who saw their fathers frequently had no such routine:

> The kids have had continuing contacts with their father, at their will. They see him at least every other weekend and have phone calls in between—even now, when they are older and busy.

> He sees them whenever he wants to—or whenever they want something from him! It's not really on a regular basis. I couldn't get him to

---

* *USA Today*, December 20, 1984, in summarizing key findings of seven recent National Institute of Mental Health divorce studies, reports: "In a survey of 1,423 kids, 52 percent of those from broken homes [*sic*] hadn't heard from their fathers in the past year; 35.5 percent of those children had no contact for five years."

agree to take them every other weekend. He said, "But I don't know what I'm going to be doing!" I'd like him to have them on a regular basis. I need some space once in a while, and I'd like to know when I could plan on doing some things for myself. He lives only ten minutes away from here, so it's not that far. He just doesn't want to be scheduled. He does call every now and then. I guess the kids see him at least every two weeks, sometimes more. Sometimes he'll just stop by here on Sunday afternoon. And they feel free to call him and ask to see him, too.

Although the second statement suggests a rather limited relationship, the father referred to was in fact more active than most of the other former husbands. For example, when one of his daughters had been ill recently, he had checked on her daily and taken juice to her so that her mother was able to remain at work. And he was looked to by the mother as well as the children for opinions on certain parenting issues:

> The oldest can go to the movies during the day with a guy, but both her dad and I have to meet him first. And she can't date at night or anything yet. Also, she can only go out with someone in her school—and not with someone older. She likes older boys, but we're staying tough on this!

Of course, as the primary parent, this woman did not consult her former husband on all parenting matters. But some issues were understood by all as sufficiently serious to warrant his involvement or opinion. And sometimes when the children did not like one of their mother's decisions, they had sought assistance and intervention from their father.

Another situation in which there was active involvement worked differently. The remarried father lived twenty miles away with his wife and two small boys, but all three adults tried to reinforce the idea that the father's nine-year-old son belonged to both families, even though there was not shared parenting as such:

> During the school year, my son goes down to stay with his father one weekend a month. That way he doesn't lose contact with their family life. His little brothers there are three years and one year old, so he's like a big brother to them—he really loves those boys. And it's nice to have that one weekend a month because I can make plans to go out of town if I want. In the summer, he's mostly over there, and he comes to

stay here on weekends. Last weekend he had some friends over, and they had a barbecue and slept out in the tent; then I took him to a baseball game. I see him, but not a whole lot; we pretty much do our own things over the summer. Actually, I think it's good for him, this arrangement. It gives him some direction and provides some continuity between the two homes. But I have some strong ideas about education and moral standards that I want to impart to him, and I think I can only do that if he's living with me. So I actively chose to be the primary parent.

Another divorced father had fairly frequent contacts with his fourteen-year-old daughter but did little in the way of reliable parenting:

Her father takes her to lunch, maybe several times a month—if he doesn't have a girlfriend at the time. He doesn't see her that often if he has a girlfriend. She never stays over there with him, and he takes no responsibility for her. But she defends him and says he's just too busy to see her—she's doing that kind of stuff.

Two mothers, each with two daughters in elementary school, shared parenting with their ex-husbands. The four children involved spent much more time with their fathers than any of the others surveyed, and their mothers were the least overextended of the sixty women. One of these women, who had shared custody with her former husband since their initial separation, described their relationship this way:

We're both real committed to raising our kids together—in a lot of ways, we had an extraordinary marriage. He only works about twelve days of the month, so he calls me and we work out our schedules with the girls. We've always been quite inventive in thinking of ways to manage this. And we've been able to talk about it and keep it working. That's something: we've both been able to admit our own fears even when we had trouble talking. He was able to say he was afraid that because he's a man, the kids could be taken away from him. I could say that I was afraid they'd be taken away from me because I can't support them like he can. There's a spoken and unspoken commitment to supporting each other as parents.

These two parents, by the way, had devised this joint custody arrangement on their own, before consulting attorneys, and they had continued to have a generally friendly relationship after divorcing.

The other woman who undertook shared parenting did so after three years in which she had custody and her ex-husband made regular visits. She described the close relationship they all had, despite the divorce and the maintaining of two residences:

> I feel very, very fortunate, and that's one of the reasons I wanted to speak out. [My former husband] just returned last night from a four-day trip with the girls, so I invited them to dinner here. The girls are very comfortable with us all sitting down together for dinner. We've constantly kept it in mind that this is what we want to have going on in our lives, so that affects how we deal with each other. Plus we enjoy each other's company. And we frequently do things in a group, too. Sometimes we both go to school functions, and if one of us can't go, the other one will.

In four other families, divorced fathers who did not share in parenting occasionally participated in special occasions or holidays. Such family activities were typically initiated by the children; none of these four families had very young children, and in only one had the father remarried. One of these women told this story:

> We had him here for Father's Day. That was hysterical! I agreed to make a favorite dish he hadn't had in years. It was all okay. My children adore him. He's not a very responsible human being, but they know that, and they can love him as he is. We've done birthdays together, too. We try to be civil. Sometimes it doesn't work, but generally we pull it off. We've had major conflicts over money, though. We do try not to pull the kids into that. Like I said, they adore him.

One case in which a divorced father participated in family events was unusual because he did not see his children regularly: his remarriage immediately after divorcing had set up a tension between himself and the children that had not eased over the years. The mother said:

> Isn't it terrible? The first couple of Christmases my daughter would spend the first couple of hours at my house crying, because the night before she'd been at her father's. It just sort of exaggerated the whole situation. He'd have us over for the Christmas Eve thing, and he sort of let Christmas Day remain at my house. We went to a friend's funeral together—my ex-husband, the children, and me. In financial and medical things and big rituals, we're still involved. When my nineteen-year-old graduated from high school, we went to the ceremony as a family.

Only a few divorced couples, however, managed to get along well enough to join each other for occasional family activities with their children. Most fathers who visited their children regularly either picked them up or had them dropped off at their homes, and then pursued activities with them alone.

Most difficulties raised by visits from absent fathers were tolerated by the mothers, who said they believed the children benefited from such contact. A common complaint was that high tension accompanied a child's return home. For example:

> We always have an hour or more of conflict when my son comes home. He comes in swaggering and really sassy. It must be very hard to go and be with your dad and then come home and be with your mother. It must be a tough transition. He'll come home and push me and push me, until finally I react. Then he bursts out into tears and starts to pull it together. Also, he comes home very tired.

In several families, however, the emotional trauma was so great that the mothers seriously questioned the value of visits from the father. For example, one mother's custody of a preschool child was being challenged by her ex-husband, who wanted custody every other year. He had initiated repeated court hearings contesting their custody, visitation, and support arrangements. She told this story:

> I think my little girl's pretty well adjusted right now, which pleases me. But she asks me repeatedly how long she's going [to be staying with her father]. She says she gets scared at night when she's there. She wants to go for only a week. It was the worst when the court ordered that I had to send her there for four months at a time. Still, the week before she's going to leave to see him, her personality sort of changes, and she's hard to deal with. And that's when I notice her having most of her bad dreams and climbing into bed with me about three in the morning. It's like that a week or so after she's back, too, but then she starts to pull it back together again. I guess that's part of adjusting to going back and forth. But I do worry about the nightmares. She needs and loves her daddy, but I think we all need to keep in mind that she's only a five-year-old.

Another mother who found visitation exhausting for both herself and her young children was relieved that her ex-husband saw his children less frequently than specified by the court agreement. Like the other mothers, she believed that ideally children should have both parents available after divorce, but she considered that impossible in her situation.

> I wish he'd go back east, so I wouldn't have to deal with him. But the kids love him—he takes them out sometimes on Saturdays from nine to three. He fought really hard for joint custody and has all this visitation specified, and then he doesn't see them nearly as much as he could. He could take them overnight, but he doesn't. And he's unreliable—he's often late. He always wants to argue because he blames me for kicking him out; the kids are usually crying before he even gets out of the house with them. And he still threatens me in front of them. I can't keep him away from the kids even when he's been drinking.

Assessments like these were uncommon, however, and reflected extreme circumstances. Most mothers wished their children could see more of their fathers, despite the stresses involved.*

Occasional Visitation

A total of forty-four children, from twenty of the families, had only occasional contacts with their divorced fathers. Specifically, in the preceding year, thirteen fathers had contacted their children between three and five times, and another seven had contacted their children between six and nine times. All the mothers of these children expressed some sort of concern about the father's lack of interest in his children, but their emotional responses varied considerably, as these two examples suggest:

> My ex-husband just doesn't want much contact with his son, and it's very unusual for him to arrange to see him. I didn't think it was good for my son to have essentially no male contacts—he's had very few,

---

*Carol Bruch (1978:25, 41) proposes that judges write into court orders a requirement that fathers make active efforts to have regular visits with their children in order to serve the rights of both the child and the custodial parent. She believes that financial penalties for failure to comply with this requirement, together with better methods of collecting child support, will increase absent fathers' involvement with their children. Calling her proposal "dual parenting," she says: "The availability of dual parenting orders may well result in fewer requests for joint custody, a model that frequently poses more difficulties than it resolves." She continues: "Except in the case of divorced parents, our society has never accepted the proposal that parents should be free to ignore the care or needs of their children simply because it is inconvenient or unpleasant to them as adults. A societal norm that condones total parental freedom for selfish purposes simply because divorce has occurred is far from desirable."

since my father is dead and I have no brothers. So once I called social services and asked if there wasn't anything I could do to make his father have more contact. They told me no, they can't make someone care. But it took me a long time to realize that. And it's my son who loses.

I just hope *I'm* around when these men get old and try to make some contact with their kids, who'll want nothing to do with them by then. And it's really sad to think, "Is that what's going to give me satisfaction?" I hate to think so, but I *would* be satisfied; I really would. In fact, my kids already don't want anything to do with him. They've already written him off in many ways after trying so unsuccessfully to get him interested in them.

Only two of these twenty fathers had seen their children fairly regularly in the first year or so after divorce, and almost all of them had decreased their contacts over time.[4] The reasons for this decrease in paternal involvement included changes in the personal and social lives of the fathers—most notably, remarriage—and the limiting of contacts by older children whose own activities began to conflict with weekend visits.* (In several instances, the family's or the father's change of residence altered the visiting pattern but did not appreciably reduce the total mount of time the father spent with the children. Usually he would see more of them during their school vacations.)

This woman's account of the father's changes in behavior after remarriage was common:

At first, he'd go boating and do all sorts of great things with the kids. Then he remarried. Before that he was a nice guy: when we desperately needed some help, he'd try to see that we got it—like once or twice he helped buy school clothes. Since he's remarried, it's completely different. He won't even talk to me. And I've never caused any trouble. In fact, I was happy about the marriage. My kids always knew their dad loved them whether he was here or not. He used to have them come visit him, but he just has no room for them anymore

---

*The notion that custodial mothers frequently deny their ex-husbands visits with their children found no support among the women interviewed. In any case, the law is clear that only a court ruling, based on strictly defined evidence, can deny the non-custodial parent access to the children after divorce. Neither nonpayment of child support nor the mother's or children's preferences can legally restrict a father's access to his children.

now that he's remarried. It's like the kids don't belong in his life anymore. How sad it is for them. And it's sad for him too—he doesn't
know what he's missed. A couple of months ago I sent him some pictures of our son in his outfit for his first formal dance. He looked so
good, and I was really sad that his dad misses all of that.

Even fathers who had seen their children only occasionally after divorce saw them less after they remarried. Often the remarriage
worked in conjunction with other family dynamics to reduce such
contact. One woman gave this example:

> My children refuse to accept his new wife. It's because of the way it
> was done: he started living with her immediately, as soon as he left
> here. I asked him please not to do that. I said he couldn't raise these
> four children the way he had, lecturing on and on about the old moral
> values and how life ought to be lived, and then leave us and go live
> with her right away. I wanted him to take time to build a new relation-
> ship with the children and slowly introduce her into the picture. He's
> done nothing to help them accept her. He just told them they had to
> accept her as his wife, and then he left it at that. He has no sense about
> working things out. And he expects them to get themselves over there
> to visit him; it's twenty-five miles, but he won't pick them up. I heard
> from friends last Christmas that his wife was telling them I should
> make the kids see more of their father, that he was miserable. But
> neither of them has ever invited the kids over, even for Christmas.
> See, she's doing what I used to do for him. He has no idea how much
> we catered to him and gave him his way. And he expects the children
> to go on doing that now. It's hard for him to understand that they won't
> do it anymore. It's the "Leave It to Beaver" attitude about the family
> [let mother and the kids take care of dad]. I wanted it that way too, but
> I've realized it can't be that way. There are other people in this family
> besides him.

Remarriage of the father often helped stabilize the remaining family unit of mother and children. Several mothers reported that remarriage had made fathers less likely to entertain their visiting children
lavishly. For example, one woman said that her son's resentments
about their life of economic hardship had increased whenever he
would visit his unmarried father, who had a comfortable life-style;
she said she found single parenting much easier after her ex-husband
remarried:

Two years ago, when my son was thirteen, he was really hard to have around. It was the worst time I've had with him. He was really rebellious and obnoxious and acted all the time like he had a big chip on his shoulder. He resented his sister, and he resented being here. He'd gone to his father's at Christmas and was treated like a king. He gained ten pounds he was fed so well! And there was money there, too, so they could go and buy all of these wonderful things. Then his father got married in April, and my son went back to visit him in the summer. I think his father's new wife deliberately made it really rough on him so he wouldn't want to stay there. There was no more royal treatment. After that, I didn't look so bad, and things really eased up around here.

Typically, when fathers decided to visit their children less often or to stop seeing them altogether, they did so unilaterally; and because their participation in the children's lives was not enforceable, mothers who opposed this decision met with frustration and failure. In one exceptional case, however, a divorced father, who had visited his nine-year-old son and seven-year-old daughter regularly, sought his ex-wife's cooperation in reducing his involvement with their children. And when she opposed his plan, he did not go ahead with it on his own but continued to accept the court-ordered schedule while trying to make a new arrangement. His ex-wife explained:

Part of the divorce arrangement was that he was to buy a house with rooms for the children, so they could spend time staying with him. The kids were all very excited. Then he got married in the summer, and that fall the kids were essentially told they were no longer welcome there after school and at other times, even if they had activities in that neighborhood or just wanted to be there. I was very unhappy about that. So we went according to the court-ordered schedule after that: the kids would see him on alternate weekends and on Wednesday nights. He said he'd prefer to have them only one at a time, but I wasn't going to let that happen very easily. He's welcome to have them one at a time in addition to his regular visitation, but I wasn't going to start separating the visitation into one kid at a time—it's not natural. Also, I saw myself as being abused somewhat by that plan.

After several months of disagreement over this matter, this father agreed to meet with a court conciliator. His ex-wife continued:

I had decided that the only issue I would address was why we were there: my concern for the children—they look forward so much to

going to their father's. At first, when he started out, the court conciliator thought he'd said he wanted the children *more*—he couldn't
make the outright statement that he wanted to see them *less* often. But
after ten or fifteen minutes, she got the picture: "Oh, you're saying
you'd like it better if the children saw *less* of you!" "Yes," he said.
When she asked me what my concerns were, I told her that sure, it
affected my time for myself, but that was not my primary concern.
I said I'd talked with the children, and they wanted the visitation to
stay as it was. Then my ex-husband finally said that the communication between him and me was terrible. Well, that's true. It seems to me
that no matter what I say, he takes it as some sort of attack on him.
We'd been there forty-five minutes or so before I finally mentioned
that there was a third person involved—his new wife. At that point,
[the court conciliator] dropped the issue of the two of us seeking
counseling. She talked to him about how the children's perceptions
would be different than his. She had excellent skills and really got a
hold on the situation. And she pointed out that any reduction in his
involvement with the children needed to come from them, not from
him, and suggested that he ought to get counseling with the children—especially with our daughter, since he has particular problems
dealing with her. I felt this was okay, because if nothing else happened, my children would get some sense that they do have some
power in the world.

This woman's experience was unique, not only because she and her
ex-husband were willing to seek outside counsel in resolving differences regarding their children, but also because both of them were
willing to struggle with each other personally in an effort to explain
their different perspectives. But her experience also reveals some of
the complexities that are involved in other postdivorce relationships
between former spouses and their children. Like many couples, this
one experienced great difficulty in breaking their emotional bond,
and this fact caused continuing problems in their relationship with
their children.

No Visitation

The mothers I interviewed provided these aggregate statistics: fifty-three children in the sixty families had not seen or heard from
their fathers for more than a year—fifteen children, from seven families, had not seen their fathers for over a year but had seen them within

the last two years and thirty-eight children, from nineteen families, had neither heard from nor seen their fathers in more than two years. Among the comments made by mothers whose ex-husbands had essentially "divorced" their children were these three:

> My children's father—the airline pilot, mind you, who flies all over the country—sees his children about once every two years. He doesn't even telephone them. Last time they were with their father, my daughter started crying and crying, saying she wanted to get to know him better. My son said he wanted to leave, and their father was squirming. They haven't heard from him since.

> My son's father has no contact with him. He's written me maybe once or twice in these six years. But he's never sent anything—no money, no cards, no gifts.

> He never sees the kids. The first year after he left town he had no contact whatever with them—not even birthday or Christmas cards. No contact whatever. Last year he did remember Christmas and their birthdays with cards, but that's been it.

Fathers who failed to visit their children nonetheless influenced life in the postdivorce family. Images and fantasies about the absent father were common to their children; and the mothers' knowledge of these fantasies led them to wonder if their children were actually carrying more images in secret. Here are two comments by mothers of preschool-aged children:

> They do miss their father, and they do know that he's out there. And they have ideas that their daddy lives in a castle and is a knight in armor. None of it is realistic at all.

> My oldest, who doesn't remember her dad, really dreams about him. It's funny—the parent that doesn't pay attention is the one they want. He hardly realized she existed when he was here—it was all so unconscious. But she talks on and on about things they used to do, which they couldn't possibly have done—she was still just a toddler, and he usually wasn't straight. I worry now about what would happen to them if I should die or something. I read in the paper that legally the father would still have first choice for custody, regardless of what I did. And the kids have this super image of their dad, because they don't know him, and they'd want to go with him.

Feelings of rejection did not always disappear as children grew older. One mother of a teenager reported:

My daughter had all kinds of fantasies about her dad; he didn't make any contact with his children for years. She finally had me track him down through his brother, and she went and stayed with him for three months. She came back and hasn't heard from him since. Now she knows, and can't have these illusions anymore. But that hurts her too.

Some children clearly wanted to deny their father's absence or indifference. One mother of a preteenaged son gave this example:

A [male] friend of mine was here—we were going to a movie together that evening. My son was trying to build a soapbox derby car and was fussing about it. I hadn't been any help; I'd been working, and I didn't know what kind of tools he needed. My friend said to him, "Gee, I have what you need. Maybe we could work on it tomorrow afternoon in my garage." My son glared at him and said, "Oh, my dad always helps me do these things. He's real good with tools." He hasn't seen his father in months, and they never do anything like that together. I don't know what happens to kids like that. I guess we'll all find out.

These mothers were not confident about being able to help their children deal with the neglect that prompted such fantasies. Their own anger at the father's rejection of his children, usually mixed with anger about his nonpayment of support, made it hard for them to think and plan rationally.

The custodial parent can't win. My daughter used to tell me her father wouldn't treat her like I was treating her. I used to get so frustrated. Where was he? Why wasn't he visiting? He didn't care, but she didn't know that. Or if she did, she couldn't accept it. At least if he had visited, she would have seen that he was a real person, and not perfect either. And she would have seen that he also has to make choices between working and seeing his kids, or going on dates and being with them. But my kids never got to see any of that. I wish my daughter could realize that she actually has it better living in a single-parent home than she would if her father were here. But there's that fantasy about the unknown, what could have been. I heard once, and I think it's true, that the expectation is greater than the realization. She only thinks about what could have been; she was too young to remember what things were really like. He was never home even when we were married. He didn't engage in conversations or activities with the kids—he was always lost in a magazine. But she's created vast dreams about him, and she lives with those.

Several mothers believed the pain their children felt over their father's abandonment was essentially irreparable, and they shared their children's sorrow:

> I'd love it if he would visit the children. I used to beg him to, for the kids' sake and for his. My older daughter, who's seventeen now, talks about her father a lot, and sometimes says she'd really like to see him. She's devised little fantasies about how she could trace and find him. She has fantasies about us reuniting and making up for all these lost years. If I have any regrets, it's about the girls—I'd want them to have a father. . . . Just for fun, one day last year we did a little psychological game from a magazine. Some of the questions in it were about your parents. And my daughters, each of them independently, came up to me with the question, "Who should I write for father?" Oh God, that hurt. And when I'd meet someone who was a real nice guy when the kids were younger, both would just glom on to him—and I'd feel really bad about that. They really want a father.

Absent Fathers and Serious Problems with Children

Although a large majority of these mothers said their children had experienced no major problems since the divorce and that they were generally enthusiastic about their children's positive adjustment, eight minor children and one young adult son had gone through periods of serious emotional or behavioral disturbance.* Significantly, all the major difficulties they described were related to the father's role after divorce: the child either felt rejected by the father or was distressed by his part in the continuing hostility between the parents.†

The mother who experienced the most wrenching crisis suffered

---

*The findings by Wallerstein and Kelly to the effect that the parents' postdivorce relationship affected children's overall well-being have been summed up as follows: "The most distressed children were found to be those who became the focus of their parents' conflicts; those whose custodial parents were themselves most distressed; and those whose parents received little emotional support from family and friends" (Levitan, 1979:8).

†Only 4 of these 8 children reported as having serious problems were among the 121 living with their mothers at the time of the interviews. Three others lived with relatives and one child had died.

the loss of her eleven-year-old son by hanging. Because he was playing in his own backyard with a younger friend present, the death was ruled accidental. But unanswered questions remained in her mind:

> At the time it happened, my kids really weren't adjusting very well. One of my three girls had been well adjusted, but the other two and my son had their problems. I don't know if that was related to the divorce—anything could relate to that. After their dad remarried, the kids didn't see much of him. My son was a real sensitive boy. He wasn't what his father figured a boy would be—or even what I figured a boy would be. He was creative inwardly. He liked computers and anything technical. He liked sports, too, but his father didn't know that. Actually, the girls were their father's favorites, and I know my son knew that. When his father called, he never asked to talk to him. And my son was the oldest, too. He was different from his sisters. He was hard to talk to, and wasn't real open about his feelings. Who knows what he felt?

Two other children, both teenaged girls, had attempted suicide— each while visiting her father. Both had taken an overdose of drugs and were saved when they were discovered by their fathers and stepmothers. One of them was living with her father for a year. The other was visiting her father during the summer, after having had no contact with him for four years; she had tracked him down and begged him to let her visit him. Her mother explained:

> The week before school started, she called me from her father's place: she was crying and asked me to talk to her father. I said no, I wanted to talk to her. But she cried and begged, so I talked to him first. He told me she'd gone out with her friends and had drunk alcohol and taken tranquilizers—too many of them. Her father found her very much asleep, called the doctor, and took her to the hospital, where they got her stomach cleared and got her walking. So when her father put her back on the phone, I said, "Are you all right?" And then she said, "Yes, don't blame dad." I told her I loved her and wanted her to come home. Then I wrote her a long letter. I told her again to come home and said that while suicide crosses our minds, it's not an answer and that things can be worked out. She did come home then, and things have gone very well. I think part of the reason she tried suicide is this: children need rules and supervision. I'm willing to negotiate the rules, and talk things over, but I tell her I need to know where she is and when she'll be back. But her father believes she's old enough to take care of herself. So maybe she thought I didn't trust her. That was

part of it. But part of it, I think, was that she thought if she went down there, she could break up that marriage and get dad to come home. I think she needed to know what was going on down there. There's been no communication between the two places. I don't know how it went for her, except for what she told me. I can be very vocal, and I know the children have wished I wouldn't express my anger at their father and our economic circumstances so much. But she's doing well in school now, and she even has a part-time job, which thrills her. This summer she went to her father's to visit and came home as planned. As you can imagine, I was very relieved.

Both of the girls who attempted suicide entered counseling with their mothers after returning home. According to the mothers, neither they nor their daughters fully understood the reasons for the suicide attempt. Both girls were happy and adjusting well, although one of them had not heard from her father again.

There were several common features in the lives of the two children who made suicide attempts and the one child who died. All three mothers had absolutely no association with their ex-husbands: two fathers and one mother refused to have any contact. All three children were aware of the bad feelings between their parents. Both girls' mothers had openly expressed anger over the behavior of their ex-husbands. One was angry because the father had disappeared from the children's lives and contributed no financial support, even though this meant that his children lived in poverty while he lived well. The other mother was angry at the divorce process: her husband had left her for another woman but had denied it for several months. He had arranged property matters to his advantage and then filed for divorce in another state. The mother of the boy who had died was not angry at her ex-husband; she had wanted the divorce. But her ex-husband remained angry, and on the few occasions when he did see his children, he kept them informed of his anger.

Two other teenaged girls of divorced parents had serious school problems: repeated truancy and failure in several courses. Their fathers had made no efforts to contact them and had discouraged their attempts to arrange visits. One of the girls had lived with her maternal grandmother, who drove her to and from school each day, which her mother was unable to do because of her employment. The mothers of these girls had no particular explanation for their daughters' behavior; their other children, all boys, showed no comparable behavioral problems. The children's fathers had paid no support, however, and both families' economic situations had grown worse over the years, as the children became teenagers and food prices rose.

Two other teenagers, a girl and a boy, had experienced school problems after their parents divorced. Unlike the other two teenaged girls with school problems, these two teenagers had some contact with their fathers. The girl had seen her father each summer. Her parents had gone through a comparatively stormy divorce and had continued their battle in court, where each had argued that the other was unfit to be a parent. The teenaged boy dropped out of his high school a year after his parents' divorce. He had deliberately limited his contacts with his father out of anger over his father's remarriage. His mother said:

> My son was really emotionally upset after the divorce. He might have dropped out [of school] sometime anyway, but he did it when he was a sophomore. All my kids have been in and out of college, but this is the first one to drop out of high school. He wanted to stay out for about six months. He was having a lot of repressed emotional things happening around the divorce, and he was having violent dreams. Once he woke up after one of those dreams with his hands stuck through the glass of the bedroom window right next to his bed. He couldn't remember the dream. His therapist said that he needed more time to do things that would release that unconscious material—that anger, really. So during those six months, he took yoga and creative writing and saw a woman who works through dreams and uses therapy methods. He's been seeing this woman for several years now, and they're real close friends. After six months, he was a lot more settled emotionally, but he didn't want to go back to school, so he took off and did some traveling. He came back and got a job. His boss loves him; he's really good there, and he's been made department manager. But it's such a shame; there's a whole period of his life that he'll never recapture. He hasn't taken the high school equivalency test yet. He's very smart, and I'm sure he could pass it. I'm sure all this is related to the way the divorce happened, the way his father just suddenly left. And his father still blames me for everything—for not loving him enough and for not being there to take care of his pain.

One of the women who had encountered serious parenting problems after divorce said she had been unable to control her oldest son and that after he moved in with his father, the other son began running away from her until he too was allowed to move. She said:

My children don't all live here now. Originally when we separated and were divorced, I was given custody of all three children. The two boys, who are the older ones, have since moved out to live with their father, who lives nearby. None of the kids had acted out when we were married, but I guess it wasn't such a great shock, though, when they did that after the divorce. They'd watched their father be abusive toward me; and their father would see them being abusive to me and condone it. So I've been alone in trying to set limits. I see the boys frequently, but the oldest one is not real welcome to come back here right now. I've had to set limits to his visiting here. The second son visits regularly, frequently. I meet with the older one and take him somewhere close to his home, say for an ice cream cone, so that if he misbehaves, he can walk home. I took him out to dinner for his birthday at a place just three blocks from his father's home. I told him that if he didn't behave, then he either would go or I would go, but I wasn't going to sit there and be abused. He's very verbally abusive and can be physically abusive, too.

Although both of these sons lived with their father, they continued to depend on their mother for certain kinds of parental care:

I'm still the parent in many ways. I take them to their appointments, shop with them for clothes. I'm trying to help my oldest son find a job, because he borrowed money from his grandfather to buy a computer. He tries and tests out a lot. He'll come around and ask me to do things for him. Like: "Will you take me to the dermatologist?" He won't ask his father to do that. Or when he broke his arm at school in P.E., his father was home, but my son called me and asked me to take him to the hospital. I do the mothering thing that he really wants from me. But I won't be abused either. I have to set limits.

Finally, one mother's young adult son had "fallen apart" since his parents' divorce:

I worry much more about my twenty-six-year-old son than about the younger ones. He seems to be destroyed by all of this. He desperately needs help. He's dropped out of school, and now he only waits tables some of the time. In my mind, this boy is the real tragedy. He's the one who discovered his father's affair in the first place and asked him to help him understand it. His father was incredibly angry and hasn't forgiven him.

These particular reports do not suggest that continued problems between the divorced parents or lack of parental involvement are sufficient in themselves to provoke a crisis in the lives of children. All nine of the children with serious problems had siblings, and none of their brothers or sisters had experienced serious problems. And the other families of the sixty women, some of which shared the same basic characteristics, reported no such crises. Nevertheless, in the major parenting problems just described, there was a common element: in each case, no positive or even emotionally neutral relationship had emerged between the divorced spouses. Three of the children felt abandoned by their fathers. Another three had some contact with their fathers, but their parents remained completely estranged, and the children were aware of the intensity of their anger and bitterness. One child, whose parents had an emotionally difficult relationship, generally refused contact with his father because of his own anger. Open hostility and acrimony between their parents was the situation for the other two children.

7

Social and Personal Life

When these sixty women had begun the process of getting a divorce, they had not thought much about how it might change their friendships and their daily social lives. They had not expected to be any more isolated than they had been as married women, as mothers concerned chiefly with parenting and running a household. And although they were aware of the social stereotypes about divorced women, they had not believed they would be affected by them. A few experienced some ambivalence and confusion about developing new relationships with men, but most had been so preoccupied with the immediate emotional effects of ending a marriage that they gave little consideration to the problem of developing new personal and intimate relationships.

In contrast to their expectations, most of these sixty women struggled for years to attain a satisfactory personal and social identity. In one sense, they were now single; divorce had ended their married status. In another sense, they were not single; they were mothers who were no longer married.* The cultural definitions of these two identities—single woman *and* primary parent—were often contradictory, and these women found no traditions to guide them in their efforts to integrate conflicting roles:

---

*Unfortunately, there has been little discussion or study of the resocialization of adult women who become single through divorce. Some discussion of divorced women's social lives is offered by Weiss (1975, 1979a).

I've had a lot of problems playing both roles. I've really struggled with whether to be a woman or a mommy.

The fact is that I still see myself as married. I live like a married woman in a lot of ways—I'm still cooking, still mothering, still grocery shopping. In that sense, I don't see myself as any different.

What we're struggling with is who we are as women, aside from being mommy and wife or ex-wife. We don't know how to feel—or who we are—separate from these roles, or how to get that sense of self. I've been working a lot on who I am as a person, and it's just recently that I've even begun to think of myself as a potential mate.

These women wanted adult contacts, friendships, and activities outside of work. Many wanted satisfying relationships with men, including sexual ones. But socially, where did they belong? With single adults? With married couples who were parents? With other divorced parents? Time constraints, general fatigue, and social isolation made it hard for them to pursue answers to basic questions about their personal and social lives. At the same time, these questions continued to press for resolution, especially since many former friendships and relationships had disintegrated. In fact, over *three-quarters* of the women told of losing former friends, usually during or immediately after divorce. This unexpected occurrence was painful and heightened their emotional confusion. By divorcing, they had lost their social as well as their economic moorings.

The women offered several explanations for the loss of friends. Most of their close friendships had been with other married people, and the friendships had involved them as couples. Friends withdrew for several reasons: They felt uncomfortable about how to respond to the changes prompted by divorce. They were reminded that their own marriages might be at risk. Their divorced friend's pinched financial circumstances limited the activities they might share. They kept up a close friendship with the friend's ex-husband. But eventually finding an explanation did little to ease the pain of abandonment:

It was really lonely to have your friends treat you like you're diseased. It didn't occur to me that maybe people were feeling self-conscious. I just felt that they were being judgmental, that maybe I wasn't acceptable to them in some way. Probably they were uncomfortable and didn't know what to say. A lot of people told me it was hard hearing about my divorce because it made them realize how shaky marriage can be. I tried to tell them that just because I made this decision doesn't mean I think they can't be dissatisfied with their marriages and still work on them—that for me [the need to divorce] was overwhelming, but for them it might not be. Do you find that most women lose friends? And do they ever get their friends back? It was such a loss for me.

Women who divorced after long-term marriages, during which most of their friends had belonged to other married couples, felt especially afflicted by old stereotypes of the "divorcée":

There's a stigma about being divorced, at least in my age group. Another thing was interesting: some married men can't handle single women. Some of the husbands I know aren't comfortable with me. I try to laugh it off, but I'd like to know why, and it hurts. I'm not interested in anybody else's husband—not a bit. I'm not looking at them. But there's one couple who never invites me to their house anymore. They see me at other places, not in their home. They still see my ex-husband regularly, and at their home.

Changed financial circumstances led some of the divorced women to limit their contacts with former friends. Lack of money to participate in formerly shared activities and embarrassment about the decline in their standard of living deterred them from actively maintaining friendships. Trying to hide the new situation was common:

I had some good friends then who are still friends. They're supportive of me as a person, but I don't think they've ever understood my financial situation. Lots of times they'll invite me to go places, and I can't go because I don't have the money. So I give other excuses, and usually I just avoid them. I keep thinking this may be a temporary inconvenience, and someday I'll be able to go again. But as it is, I don't have the money, and I can't go. If I did go, they'd probably think I'm chintzy now. They can eat at better restaurants, shop for nicer things, and so on. I think they're like I was before the divorce, and they can't really relate to this situation.

The women's emotional trauma was increased when close friends, instead of providing encouragement and support, backed off without explanation. Their children were also hurt by the disappearance of family friends who might have provided emotional support or shared activities to compensate for their father's absence; they asked their mothers, who did not yet understand this withdrawal themselves, to explain it. Although the twelve women who were employed at the time of their divorces also lost friends shared in the marriage, they were less isolated and lonely because of contacts at work. But like the others, they found that establishing solid new relationships was a slow process and did not ease the pain of losing old friends at a critical time.

Relationships with Men

Ambivalence and uncertainty characterized these women's feelings about relationships with men. They questioned not only their own personal involvement with men, but male-female relationships in general. Some of them described men and women as "two different species," and many said that men and women are experiencing personal and social growth at different rates, so that the distance between the sexes is widening. They mentioned broad social changes, such as increasing numbers of employed women and the high divorce rate, as causes of this, but their interest was not theoretical. They were talking about changes they had experienced personally, often profoundly, as a result of divorce. They had assumed the role of family provider, they had adapted to a considerable loss of financial resources, and they had learned to handle children alone. They had shared these experiences with many other women, but they knew of few comparable changes occurring among men.

More than 80 percent of the women interviewed said that differences in social and personal awareness between men and women were increasing, and that struggle between the sexes would become more common. Much of their pessimism seemed to come from their belief that men felt threatened by women who demonstrated independent competence. Because the responsibilities of being divorced mothers had forced them to become more independent and self-reliant, they favored major social changes—such as greater respect for women as individuals and as parents, greater equality in the labor market, and enforcement of child support orders—that were not likely to endear them to the men they knew. Only a few of them thought that relations between men and women might eventually become more harmonious. What little optimism they had was based on a belief that young men and women are now being raised with different values and expectations:

> I feel really sorry for men who are thirty-five or over—they're really caught. Things changed on them, and they weren't socialized to accept the change. That's one of the things that appeals to me about men under thirty: they don't have the same expectations about women. They weren't socialized into expecting to be waited on and taken care of all the time. I think most women are fed up with men who are over thirty-five or forty.

The anger these women expressed was both general and specific. It was directed at men generally, for ignoring the hardships caused by sexist policies and practices, and at the particular men who had oppressed them and their children. In content, this statement was typical of many:

> I want consideration from men, and they give so damned little that it enrages me. I asked my last boyfriend, "Hey, don't you guys have any feelings in there?" I don't expect anything anymore. I think if it weren't for the sexual thing, I wouldn't have anything to do with them. I'm tired of it. I'm tired of always being the one to give. I'm tired of them treating me like I'm sixteen. I may be blond, but I wasn't born yesterday. I know how to take care of myself. I know who I am, and I know what I like and don't like. I can be by myself, too—but that doesn't mean I'm a solitary person. Men are afraid of women who are outspoken and can take care of themselves. But what am I supposed to do? Am I supposed to wilt away waiting? I can't be somebody else. No one else is taking care of me—and I don't want to be taken care of *that* way anyway. I need to be a *person*. And men can't deal with angry women very well. It's not that we hate men. We're trying to say something to them about the treatment they've given us. But they can't hear it. I used to hope that would change. It still might, on an individual basis, when you get a man to talk and listen. But on a wider level, I think it's too ingrained.

Despite their generally pessimistic assessment of relations between the sexes, few of the women had rejected relationships with men altogether. Most either tried to meet men or were concerned because they were not trying. Six of the women had a fairly steady relationship with a man at the time of the interview, and a few said that they had had such a relationship at one time or another since divorce. Some women said they had had only one date, and a few had not dated at all. Nothing seemed to explain these variations, which revealed no pattern of age, length of time married or divorced, or number and ages of children. All of the women who had not dated even once had been physically battered during their marriages; but even this fact was not a reliable predictor, since some of the women who had been abused had done some dating.

Few of the women reported patterns of steady dating, and only eighteen said they had been involved at some time since their divorce in a fairly consistent relationship with one man.* In describing her steady relationship, this woman touched on several issues that confront divorced women with children:

> I've been involved with the same man for about three years now, not on a continuous basis, but off and on. In the last couple of years, I've gone out mostly with him because I don't care much anymore about dating a lot of different people. It's very difficult in this town to meet people—everyone is either married or connected in some other way. At first I did do a lot of hanging out at bars. That's how I got dates, by going to bars with my girlfriends. But I really burned out on that. There comes a time when you don't have the energy, money, or interest in continuing that kind of life. Now I'd rather be home with my son and working on my house and that sort of thing. It's very convenient to have just one relationship. And it's easy to work it out with him because he lives just one street over from me. I guess "convenient" isn't a very flattering way to refer to this relationship. But that's how I see it.

Almost a third of the women said they had dated only once in the previous three months, and nine reported having had several dates during that period. The reasons given for not dating included feeling depressed and overloaded, not being interested in any specific person, and not meeting any appealing men. Dating was seen as an activity that could be given up in order to conserve energy and accomplish the necessary tasks of parenting and earning a living. As one woman said:

*The term "dating" is used to refer to all social engagements, formal and informal, with adult men.

I go through periods. Sometimes I date, and other times I don't. At this point, I can't see myself falling in love with anybody. Partly that's because there's so much turmoil in my life right now. Bringing another person into it would require too much more energy. I don't have the energy to put into a serious relationship, and it's just not a high priority.

Although several women found their self-confidence enhanced by a particular relationship, positive experiences were uncommon. Most women found dating more trying than rewarding, and many said that dating produced anxieties reminiscent of adolescence—a particularly ironic experience for those who were mothers of teen-aged children, who were themselves already dating. Some found dating degrading; others found that it threatened to draw them back into the sort of dependent role behavior they had rejected:

I'm not dating. I'm finding out that men don't like women who are able to take care of themselves, women who are independent and don't want to play the games. I don't want to say I'm too independent, I'm not. It's just that I'm not going to play the game anymore—the game of being submissive, or playing the mother role, or whatever they're looking for. I come into contact with a lot of men who could take care of me financially. But I won't even go out to dinner with them if I'm not interested in them as people. Dating's like being in high school again. I still feel like that sometimes—except that when I was in high school, I wasn't beaten down.

Some women were reluctant to become seriously involved because of a general distrust of men, and knowledge of other women's negative experiences strengthened their reluctance. Seven of the women interviewed reported particularly troubling and frightening experiences with a man they had dated. One of them who had abandoned dating explained:

I guess the worst part of being divorced, besides the constant worry about money, has been the dating. Learning to say no and getting heard was the hardest part. I used to be easily intimidated by guys. I felt like I owed a guy something for the nice dinner, things like that. It was awful. Maybe it was just the kind of guys I went out with, or maybe that's the way it is today. I dated the first year [after divorcing], but it got to be just too hard to take. The last date I had was two Christmases ago. I was chaperoning a group of girls, and the guy who was driving seemed real nice. We talked the whole trip, and the girls sang Christmas carols. So we had a date; he took me to see a Christmas play, and we had dinner afterward. I thought, "Here's somebody with class and some sense," so later I invited him over—the girls were at their father's. I was wrapping presents and addressing cards. The next thing I knew he had a hammerlock on me and was trying to force me down. I jumped up and told him to leave, but the next thing I knew he had me pressed against the door—it was just horrible. I decided I just couldn't go through that again.

Meeting suitable and interesting men was a major difficulty, and not meeting such men was a common explanation for inactive social lives:

I've never been much of a joiner or club person. I'd rather go to a class. I've taken some interesting classes, like pottery and photography. If I met somebody that way, it would be okay. But who has time for classes? And how can you meet somebody in a bar? I've been through that, too. The older you get, there aren't that many places you can go to. And you wonder why are *those* particular men *there?*

There aren't that many good men out there. You know what I'm talking about—the really nice men are not available. They're already connected with somebody, or there's some reason why they don't want to be. So, you know, I feel kind of scared about that.

One inescapable difficulty in meeting interesting men was said to be the fact that men are generally attracted to younger women and to women less independent than divorce had taught these women to be:[1]

Men my age—forty-one—still prefer younger women. There's age discrimination, I'm sure. Men can say they admire independent and self-reliant women, but they marry the younger, dependent fluff. Now at forty-one, I'm no longer willing to be just someone on a man's arm. And it seems that men are no more mature in their fifties or sixties, either.

Many of those interviewed, and especially those whose marriages had been troubled by substance abuse, expressed unwillingness to become involved with men who used alcohol or drugs. Yet many of the best-known ways to meet men involved social drinking.

Another problem in meeting men was discovering whether or not they were married. A few of the women had knowingly dated married men. The more common story, however, was for a woman to learn later that the man with whom she was involved was married. Here is one example:

> This guy I went with for four years was a married man. Was it worth it? I don't know. I sure liked him, and he was well-to-do! Good to the kids too. I didn't know for three years that he was married, I swear to God. He had his own apartment and an answering service—a past master at juggling his two lives. When I broke off with him, I thought to myself, "Are you a loser? First an alcoholic husband and then you get mixed up with this!" So I'm taking time out and really trying to analyze it. It was the biggest blow I've had in years—maybe ever. He spent weekends here and even some holidays—not major ones, because he went out of town, or said he did. He had a wife and two little kids. It was an unusual thing. What fooled me was that I liked being free and yet having someone on the weekends and maybe on Wednesday or Thursday. We'd go out or he'd come over for dinner. It was just enough. Even after I found out, I stayed on for a while. I even met the kids. But it got worse and worse. I couldn't take being second; I just couldn't take it. It was hard on my kids, too. One of the boys still sees him.

About a fifth of the women had dated an "old flame" from school days. Going out with someone they already knew was less threatening than going out with new acquaintances. But difficulties soon emerged in these kinds of involvements, too. For example:

> I enjoyed dating two old boyfriends. I especially had a great time with the one I'd always sort of pined for. I'm sorry he's not living closer, we'd go out more. The other one was an old friend from high school. It was exciting and romantic with him. He'd been divorced for twelve years, and I think he figured he was going to marry me. I was divorced, so I needed somebody, and he was going to be the knight in shining armor! But the more time we spent together, the more he could see that I wasn't the same person I was twenty-four years ago. He wanted to see me as the helpless female. Then he began to see that although I welcomed his suggestions about what I should do, it didn't mean that I was going to take them.

This same woman continued by observing that her situation was much different than it had been twenty-four years earlier:

He wanted me to act all the time like I did when we were out together. He'd complain that I was different when we came back to my place. You bet I was different! This was home, and there were children here. Everybody gives you that old line: the children don't need you that much; you should do your own thing. But you're a family, and you really do need each other. In a nutshell, what they mean is that you're not giving them enough because you're giving your kids something. That's what my husband used to say: "You're spending too much time with the kids."

Groups organized for singles attracted some of the women, who specifically mentioned Parents Without Partners and church-sponsored singles' groups. Eight women were active members of such groups; another twenty had either gone only once or attended for a while and then stopped. Reactions to experiences with these groups tended to be either strongly positive or strongly negative. One woman, however, described how her initial enthusiasm was waning:

I met a man just last Saturday night at a singles' party. I'm very involved with a singles' group connected with the church—I'm one of the facilitators there. I've been in it about six months. We have groups that meet once a month on Friday nights and special groups that meet more often. They're real nice because they give us a chance to get to know each other before meeting on the dance floor, so to speak. And I love it—I just get real high, I feel really good. I can get to know so many people, and I'm asked to dance by more people than I have time to dance with. Actually, though, I've begun to get a little disillusioned with it. I'm realizing that there's a core group of people who are always alone—and I'm one of them. There are two couples who keep coming, but they're together, and everybody else is alone. There's a deep loneliness that just radiates through everything. The whole thing in these people's lives is to go to these social functions. It takes the place of staying at home alone at night. It's sad to see, and I don't want to get hooked into it.

Another woman voiced a common complaint: going to singles' groups made her feel even more adolescent than dating:

You know, I sure would like to meet somebody, but where? I go to these singles' places and think, "Oh my Lord, what am I doing here?" It feels like one of those popularity contests in high school. It's true. I feel like I've regressed. And I don't really have any girlfriends to go with. That probably would help.

One aspect of personal and social life that both aroused fears and created confusion was sexual relations. Many women said that their interest in having sexual relations both attracted them to men and kept them reluctant about becoming involved.

I've chosen not to abstain absolutely [from sexual relations]. What I did originally was to pick a man who was totally unmarriageable. At first I didn't go out for nearly two years. Finally I got myself to a dance—Parents Without Partners. I'd never gone to a dance before. I started out hating it—all those terrible, terrible husbands who obviously got kicked out by their wives! Then this very nice gentleman asked me to dance. He was very sweet and said he'd really like to see me again. He recognized my reluctance about giving an answer, and I gave him my telephone number. Later, when he called me, I went out with him, and I ended up going out with him for two years. He'd been married once and said he was never going to marry again. He was very nice, and I was very traumatized about men. So we'd see each other once a week. It quickly became a sexual relationship, and I paid a lot of attention to that because there'd been a lot of sexual dysfunction in my marriage. I've gradually regained sexual confidence.

The Role of Children

In all their social relations, and especially in their relations with men, these women were profoundly affected by their role as primary parents. When dating, they were not simply single women looking for a good time but mothers of dependent children; thus they were never truly single. The front-door confrontation was mentioned by many women. One said:

Some men the kids really like, but with some they groan and say, "Oh mom, oh mom." I'll never forget one time a guy came to the door. My son answered the door, came to the bedroom, and said, "Mom, you can do better than that!" But I fell in love with that man.

The fact that a woman had children reduced the pool of potential dates; many men would not date women with children, and some who did eventually drew back because of the children. There were also logistical problems: children needed to be cared for, and "mom had a curfew." The men these women met did not have custody of children themselves and therefore found it hard to appreciate the responsibilities of a divorced mother:

> I've been seeing this man off and on for almost two years now. If I want to go and do something, and I don't want to go alone, I call him. When he feels the same way, he calls me. He comes to the house, and I guess you could say we date—though the last time we did was about six months ago. But he gets irritated about the time I have to spend with the kids. When he's here and they're here, I still have to do things for them. I think he's finally beginning to understand it, or at least accept it. But I always have a curfew. I have children to pick up and get home to, and he still doesn't like that. It's too bad, but there's no getting around it.

Conflicts with men over the demands of children went deeper than caretaking and supervision problems. Women also felt emotionally torn between their children and their male companions, and they usually resolved this sort of conflict by ending their relationship with the man. Resentments about these experiences were keen.

> I've often felt torn in several directions. One man I had a long relationship with had trouble over the fact that I was so close to my daughters, especially my youngest one. He often said I was closer to her than I was to him and that he felt left out. Well, I did care more about her! There's a special bond there—maybe especially because I'm a single parent.

Ten of the women wondered if they used their parent status as an excuse for being socially inactive, and especially as an excuse for not dating, thereby leaving basic apprehensions about male-female relationships unresolved. A mother who had dated only once in four years put it clearly:

> It's a real issue for single women with children. Do I have no social life because I have a kid? Or is it because I'm dealing with my own inner things? My guess is that it has nothing to do with the child, that it has to do with relationships with men. I can't get away from the question—am I using my child as an excuse?

The actions, opinions, and demands of the children themselves further complicated dating. Many children at first opposed their mothers' dating, but in all families, their behavior toward adult male friends tended to improve over time, as they concluded that their parents were not going to resume family life together and found a sense of family stability in the changed circumstances. Still, none of the women would venture a prediction about how their children might behave in the future, as this comment suggests:

> When one of the first men I went out with came home with me, my son brought out the scrapbooks of family pictures. He said things like, "Here's daddy and here's mommy. We were all together before you showed up!" He's changed some by now, though. He'll ask if I wouldn't like to marry somebody he knows. He especially liked this guy who'd roughhouse with him and play sports—he thought that was wonderful. But I've never had an ongoing relationship that I thought might lead to marriage or something like that. So I don't know how he would react to someone I got serious about. We haven't faced that issue yet.

Some children became attached to their mothers' male friends and became active lobbying agents for them. In such cases, when the relationship ended, it involved the children as well as their mothers. For example:

> My daughter really loved one man I went out with, and she was very disappointed once when he canceled a date with us. She and I were to go to his place to do something, and when he canceled the date, the two of us sat here and cried. I saw him only once or twice after that. I think it made her a bit wary of the other men I've seen.

Major problems arose whenever a male friend of the mother's tried to exercise any authority over the children; they treated him as an outsider, cautiously and with suspicion, regardless of their mother's feelings for him. Unfortunately, according to these women, the men often reacted by trying to exercise even more authority, which set off a cycle of intense power struggles with the children. The women felt caught in the middle until they ended the relationships, which most of them did.

A few children, usually teenagers, urged their mothers to have more active dating lives:

> My sons decided I should have a lover! They were trying to solve mother's problems—my seventeen- and twenty-four-year-olds! They had psychoanalyzed it very neatly—how afraid I was—and they weren't wrong. I've talked to each of them about it, one to one. But I've also tried to show them that statistically it's not the easiest thing to

do. I feel like I'm in between the widows and the young singles and bachelors. Also I don't socialize that much. And I reminded them that they were very critical of the one person I ever got serious about for a short time. They could feel, I think, that a new partner could never quite match up to dad.

Another problem these women faced was the matter of sexual activity, and particularly whether to engage in sexual relations in the home. These two stories are representative:

My decision now, after some very painful experiences, is that mothers should keep all sexual activities away from the home. There's too much identification by the children if they are so aware of their mother's sexual behavior. But even if a mother has a relationship that she doesn't bring home, it still affects the children. They realize that she's not home because she's with some man. So I think single mothers are damned if they do and damned if they don't. I asked my daughter what she would recommend, what she thought a single mother should do. She said she didn't have an answer, but she thought mothers didn't have the right to affect their children's lives that way. I think this is one of the things mothers aren't aware of as they go through the singles situation while their children are growing up.

I don't think there's any way to successfully integrate being sexually active with being a single mother. I seem to go from one extreme to another—indiscriminate or abstaining. I wasn't doing it in the living room or anything, but the kids knew. Some mothers give it up totally—they can't acknowledge that they have sexual needs. One night my son broke through the bedroom door when I had a man there and we were making love. He just stood there shouting obscenities. It was terrible, a real horror scene.

Some women diligently refrained from any sexual activity in their homes in order to shield their children. Others, like this woman with a twelve-year-old son, said their children were not bothered when a man spent the night with them:

My son doesn't object to my having someone sleep over with me as long as we're here. He just wants me in the house. One night we slipped in, and we were in the bedroom when he pushed the door open. He said, "Going to bed, mom? A friend? Good! Good night." But then, I've had only one serious relationship [since the divorce], and my busiest times socially have been during the few times my son's been away seeing his father. I'm not seeing anybody now on a regular basis, so it isn't a pressing question for me.

All of the women said that the question of how to handle sexual activity as a single mother was complex. On the one hand, if they engaged in sexual activity in the home, even discreetly, they might arouse fear, hostility, and deep confusion in their children; on the other hand, if they engaged in sexual activity away from the home, they might deprive their children of the comfort of their presence and availability. Sexuality and appropriate sexual behavior for an unmarried woman, more general confusions about relationships with men, and lingering doubts about their marriages further complicated the problems these women had with their sexual lives after divorce. Only the women whose children were nearly grown, and likely to leave home soon, believed that the issue would become less complicated. But even they said that other questions about dating and being sexually active would probably remain unresolved.

Considering Remarriage

All of these women expressed great ambivalence about the idea of marrying again.* Their attitudes fell into no discernible patterns according to age, length of marriage, ages or number of dependent children, or length of time divorced. Some stated strongly that they would never marry again, but the majority said they were uncertain or doubtful about it, and some had already declined marriage proposals. Their ambivalence about remarriage seemed rooted in a new feeling of independence, a new sense of self that required protection: their hard-won gains might be lost in a new marriage. As one woman said:

I'd marry again if I found a man that was caring, self-sufficient, able to take care of himself, and willing to allow me to remain myself. I'd

---

*Census data show that men are more likely to remarry after divorce and tend to do so more quickly than women. Five out of six divorced men eventually remarry, but fewer than two out of three divorced women do (Norton and Glick, 1979; U.S. Bureau of the Census, 1983c). Furthermore, remarriage rates have not kept pace with the rise in divorce, and the remarriage rate for women has declined more rapidly than the rate for men (National Center for Health Statistics, 1984).

never be dependent like I was [in my first marriage]. I think that he would get a very good marriage, and that I would be a very good wife. But he would have to accept me for what I am, not some image of what a wife is supposed to be.

Remarriage seemed attractive to these women because it would provide a financial route back into their former middle-class lifestyles. But they had to weigh the economic advantages against other factors:

I haven't remarried, though I've had men I was very fond of. I'm happy, but something tells me—actually, society says—"You ought to be married." No doubt in most ways it would be easier. It's easier to be a cared-for housewife. But could I stand it? Maybe I could if I had something else too, like a wonderful hobby or something, or the money to travel. But I could never sit in a house and stare at a sink. Still, the question remains: should I get married for money? It's always an idea. I don't tell people, but *should I?*

Even when offered strong economic incentives to remarry, some women had chosen to remain single, as this woman's story indicates:

I almost got married last year. He was a millionaire. But the truth of it is that I never really loved him. Everybody thinks I was crazy not to marry him—even my mother. He was a gracious man, kind and generous. And I thought how easy it would have been for all of us. I could quit worrying; my kids could go to college. We had the wedding all planned, but I just couldn't do it. I broke it off two days before the wedding. It hadn't been a long-term relationship, so my kids took it fairly well. This man had a habit of embarrassing my son, and I was more and more afraid of what might happen if we all lived together. After I called it off, I was really happy just to be in my own house with the kids. It almost makes me laugh now, because it was almost like I was living in a dream, a fairy tale. We'd been so poor that to have had this change would have been like a fairy tale. As a matter of fact, I've been able to survive unemployed because I've been selling off the jewelry he gave me. I can't part with the watch, but I'll end up selling the rest this month if I don't get a job right away. It was bizarre.

Satisfaction with single parenting and a new family stability also diminished the attractiveness of remarriage, especially when it was considered primarily for economic reasons:

I had a boyfriend for a while who was really nice to me. He was so different from my husband. He wanted to marry me, but he never thought about my kids. He'd never been married and didn't have children. He didn't understand that my children go with me. A man would be marrying me *and* my children. I'm not interested in men who aren't nice to my children or who don't understand that they need me until they're grown up. When they're grown, then fine. But now I have to think of them.

Age was a recognized problem in regard to remarrying.[2] Only the women in their twenties and early thirties did not say that age was an important element in their thinking about remarriage.* Almost all of them agreed that men in general, and their ex-husbands in particular, would want to marry younger women. They believed that the longer they remained unmarried, the more unlikely it would be that they would ever marry again:

I know that at forty you're as young as you feel, but I don't feel as young as forty. And I know that men of my age want the younger girls. My ex-husband did. He almost married a twenty-two-year-old. I thought she was beautiful, but I wondered, "What does *she* see in him?" I thought, "What man wouldn't want that?" It really bothered me, and it still does to a certain degree.

These men all seem to be remarrying rapidly, but the women don't seem to be, whether by their own choice or because they're not asked. I believe men are marrying younger women because they think they can form and mold them the way they want to. My ex-husband thought he could mold and form his new wife and not have the problems he had with me. She was a sixteen-year-old girl when he married

---

*Age accounts for striking differences between the remarriage patterns of men and women. Whereas men tend to remarry regardless of age, women become less likely to remarry as they grow older. Younger women *are* likely to remarry; women over thirty-five are less likely to do so. In fact, the likelihood of remarriage begins to decline for women over the age of thirty (National Center for Health Statistics, 1984). After the age of forty, fewer than 28 percent of women remarry (Weitzman, 1985). On the other hand, divorce after forty is on the rise. Thus, in the total population over the age of thirty-five, there are 30 percent more divorced women than men. Because men more frequently remarry younger partners, this difference increases for older cohorts. Between the ages of twenty-five and forty-four, men remarry at a rate one and three-quarters times that of divorced women; between the ages of forty-five and sixty-four, men remarry two and a half times as frequently, and men over sixty-five remarry more than three times as often as women (Norton and Glick, 1976).

her, and he was thirty-six. She's twenty-one now and has two little boys. But she's strong-willed and independent, so it will be interesting to see what happens. Will she stay "in her place," so to speak?

Confusion about gender roles and conflicts in marriage added to the women's ambivalence about remarriage. Either remaining single or remarrying would involve sacrifices, and some of the conflicts seemed irreconcilable:

> In order to become a provider for my family as a single person, I had to become an assertive person. I had to take on other roles and learn how to be assertive and take control. I don't want to give up control of my life now. But I feel like I'm a misfit because I'm not the ideal woman. I scare men to death by being able to take care of myself. Do you know how rare it is to meet a man who doesn't want that wifely role in a woman? Do you know how rare it is to meet a man who is willing to have equality in a relationship? I find myself thinking that now that my kids are almost raised, I'll have to go back to being the submissive woman in order to relate to men. I want to look more "feminine." Part of me says that I'll have to learn to be quieter, more retiring, and more sensual. But can I do that again in this life? I realize I still have some guilt left over from my years of being a single parent. This society has roles for women, and being a single parent doesn't fit its expectations. I've gotten through the parenting of young children, but society is still telling me that in order to be okay, I have to be a coupled woman. So that's a part of what I've had to learn: the things that are supposed to make me successful as a woman would have made me unsuccessful as a single mother. It's not fair. There's a real need to belong. Being an individual who can achieve isn't enough for a woman.

Personal Growth

Some of the women's ambivalence about remarrying stemmed from a desire to protect the personal gains they had made since divorcing. Despite their experiences with financial and social deprivations, nearly all of them expressed satisfaction with the personal growth they had accomplished:

> The best part has been finding myself—finding out that I'm a human being and capable of taking care of myself in situations that aren't

pleasant. Sometimes I really have a fear of getting involved with a person and losing myself, so I hold back a lot. I don't want to go through it all over again. I like being independent, not having to rely on anyone else. It's emotionally gratifying. I feel like, coming from where I was, I've accomplished so much.

Even women who had not wanted to be divorced, like this one whose husband of twenty years had left her to marry another partner, were pleased with their personal growth.

The best thing that's happened out of this divorce experience is acquiring a sense of myself. I've learned that I have a lot of abilities and skills and that I can make it. It's still scary job-wise, but the kids and I will survive. I've done an awful lot of growing, and I feel really good about that. And I feel pretty good about who I am and where I am. I would have never gone through it if I hadn't been on my own. The last time I saw my ex-husband, just a few months ago, I said to myself, "Thank God I'm not married to that man." I'd been thinking that for quite a while, but that was the first time I could say it and really mean it. I still have some anger because I'd like to be able to spend more time with my children, but working full-time prevents it. But I've come so far!

In explaining how they could find such satisfaction despite their difficult situations, these women mentioned release from an unhappy marriage and its particular roles, new autonomy and independence, and success in managing to cope as a parent in changed circumstances. Of course, personal growth after divorce did not require harrowing experiences. Indeed, the women whose circumstances were relatively less difficult not only experienced personal development but also had the relative luxury to explore it and channel it in the directions they wanted. They simply had more options than most of the others.

Freedom from the dependency they had known in their former marriages was central to the experience of significant personal development. Almost all the women said that their identities had been defined in large part by their relationships with their husbands. Most said that their lack of a sense of self during marriage had come about partly because they felt they were providing emotional caretaking for their husbands but not receiving any nurturing themselves. After divorcing, they began to view themselves as separate persons, interpreting and defining their identities for themselves. Divorce "gave them life" and helped them mature:

> I don't always have to be ready to make good conversation and listen to him even if I don't want to or I'm tired. I don't have to be on display, and there's all kinds of freedom now. I realize now, at forty, that I've been a child all my adult life. I've been a doll and a child—taken care of while being the perfect hostess and wife. My husband shaped me in the ways he wanted, and I never even questioned it. Now I can be my own person with the right to feel, the right to have an opinion, the right to be. This has given me the opportunity to grow up, even when I didn't really want to!

"Being in control" and making independent decisions about how to approach situations built self-confidence. Psychological autonomy, initially frightening, came to be viewed as hard earned, deserved, and adultlike:

> I think the best thing about being divorced is being able to make some decisions by myself and be responsible for myself. I like that. The good things, for me, have been finding out that I can take care of myself, that I can make my own choices about what I want to do. It's really been the growth aspect, having room to grow. It's not just being able to have crackers in the bed—you know, crumbs—with nobody to complain about it. Like I went on a weekend by myself. And I've made these new friends. And I'm getting a new job! And I asked for a one-hundred-dollar raise. It's really been gradual, but everything has converged.

Dealing with the legal divorce process, redefining their relationships with the men who had been their husbands, finding a job and coping with a drastically reduced income, adapting to parenting alone, and coming to terms with a changed social and personal identity were all major adult tasks. In confronting them, these women discovered previously unknown capabilities and acted resourcefully. They assessed their situations, weighed their options, and acted. For many, learning to act independently as providers and family heads meant rejecting much of their earlier training, which had been directed toward marriage as a career.[3] This woman, for example, was certain that had she been born male instead of female, she would have been encouraged to develop her business talents during her twenties rather than marrying and putting her efforts into building her husband's career. Now a mother in her thirties, she was attempting to build a career of her own:

> I feel a lot happier than I ever have, since I was in high school maybe, except for the time when my son was born. I've gotten over being bitter. I know if I hadn't gotten married and had gone to work, or maybe on to graduate school, I'd be a vice-president of some big corporation by now. In the long run, that probably won't happen for me, and that's something that's bothered me a lot—for society to say, "You can't change that now." But I know that being bitter about it will only destroy what you're doing now. You don't think you've come very far because it happens so slowly. But I spent an evening with a neighbor recently who has just separated. And it was interesting to see where she is and realize that I've come a long way.

Many said that coping with changed circumstances had given them an increased awareness of the larger social picture and their place in it, as this woman's reflections suggest:

> I think that when you marry young and have children, it stunts your emotional growth. You get so tied up taking care of other people's needs that you don't have time to attend to your own. It took me a long time to realize that, to recognize that I had to pay attention to me too. When I go to night classes—which I've not been able to do for a while now because I can't afford the books or the gas to drive there and I'm too tired to deal with the bus at night—I sit there amazed at how much everybody else knows. And I think, "No wonder it's been so hard!"

The women also measured growth in terms of their increased ability to see what was really important to them now. Keeping their families going, surviving economically and emotionally, had become a fundamental measure of success.

> It's been a good experience. I'm stronger, and I know more about what it takes to live. I know that I can do it. I'm more realistic. When I hear people complain about little things, I realize they don't understand how easy they have it. I'm strong, and feel like this has been a victory.

To some extent, the positive assessment these women made of their struggles with hardship was an attempt to compensate emotionally for the things they had lost. Their claims to having achieved personal growth and "a new sense of self" were genuine enough; but the claims were also a kind of emotional labor made by the women to encourage themselves in the face of circumstances that showed no sign of changing. This could be seen from the notably comparative nature of their assessments. They compared their present state of adjustment to the worst emotional times they had endured—the unhappiness of the last months of marriage, the emotional chaos and identity crisis of the first months after divorce, the pain of losing friends and a life-style, the anxieties about how the divorce would affect their children, and the ongoing economic uncertainties.[4] Those experiences made the present look good:

> Time has been the key. I feel so much better now than I did. When I look back on it, I think I've been mentally ill for the last four years—I really think so. The stress before and the stress after [divorcing]—when you're in it, you don't realize how intense it is. It becomes a way of life. Not until you start feeling a little bit better do you realize how awful it was. I really am better off now. I have some idea of who I am.

The element of psychological compromise could also be seen in the ambivalence these women felt about remarriage, their fears that the new sense of self could be easily lost if they married again. They saw their gains in personal development as hard won but fragile and in need of constant protection. Because they were so isolated and received so little support, they understood growth and achievement in largely personal terms. Broader social validation for their successful efforts simply was not available. Meeting changed situations, learning new roles, and coming to terms with a different identity brought stress and emotional upheaval—but also, eventually, a heightened self-esteem.

8

Gender Bias in Divorce

The sixty women who participated in this study reported fundamentally similar experiences. Their accounts of hardship, injustice, and social and emotional isolation strongly suggest the damaging influence of many popular assumptions about divorce. Let us return to the seven assumptions stated in the first chapter and consider them in light of these women's experiences.

Divorce is equally hard on men and women.   These women said that recovery from divorce-related anxiety and emotional stress took much longer than the two years considered typical by researchers who have used psychological approaches. They were in agreement that the most difficult part of their experience was coping with the economic fall and financial insecurity prompted by divorce. For the large majority, the psychological consequences of marital disruption, in terms of personal loss and separation, paled in comparison to the emotional turmoil and stress caused by the economic effects of divorce—which for most of them proved nearly insurmountable. In this regard, their experiences differed notably from those of their former husbands: it was the women who lost their middle-class lifestyles and who were confronted after divorce with continuous economic hardship and uncertainty.

Constraints built into our society limited these women in their efforts to be successful providers for their families. Low-level jobs and the low wages typically paid to women employees kept them from earning incomes that would adequately support them and their children. Job discrimination against female workers had a powerful and direct impact on their lives. And because the wage-labor sector does little to facilitate the coordinating of employment with family responsibilities, they encountered frequent conflicts between the demands of their jobs and the needs of their children. Thus the stress of financial hardship was accompanied by the strain of being both the primary income provider and a single parent. For most of these sixty women, neither financial nor logistical help was available, and no relief was in sight. The impact of this situation—which none of their ex-husbands experienced—was far more significant for them than any purely personal suffering.

Children of divorced parents are likely to have serious problems. Many of the women complained bitterly about the prevalence of this stereotype and its possible effects on their children. They resented seeing their children stigmatized simply because their parents had divorced—especially since most self-appointed critics knew nothing about their circumstances and had no interest in helping them in any way. These women were committed mothers and careful observers of their children's development. They had been primary parents during their marriages, they had very definite ideas about parenting and its importance, and they had always expected to give priority to their parenting activities while their children were young. In short, they were anything but indifferent mothers. All of them shared a deep concern about the possible effects of divorce on their children.

These mothers had strong indications that their children had adjusted well to the family changes brought about by divorce, despite the widely held belief that divorce harms children psychologically. Most of their children were doing well in school, had good relations with peers and the primary adults in their lives, and were maturing at a normal rate both physically and emotionally.

A variety of situations faced these children. A few of them had fathers who participated actively as parents after divorce, but many more of them saw relatively little of their fathers, if they saw them at all; some of them had witnessed continued conflict between their divorced parents, and some had not. Each child had a unique way of understanding and coping with his or her situation; but regardless of their ages and particular family arrangements, a large majority seemed to find appropriate behavioral responses.

The children could not help being adversely affected by the reduced standard of living and new economic stresses that confronted their mothers. They were affected most directly by the conflict between their own needs and the demands of their mothers' new jobs. Being put into child care, being without supervision before and after school, having to remain home alone when ill, or having to deal with mothers who felt chronically fatigued and overburdened were all major adjustments for many of them. Most of them lost more than the daily presence of their fathers and the full-time parenting efforts of their mothers; they lost a way of family life. Finally, many of them were essentially abandoned by their fathers when the parents divorced. And yet, despite the many and varied adjustments required of them, these children were doing well. Most of the mothers said they were delighted with their children's progress and pleased with their own success as single mothers living in difficult circumstances. It is important to note that the women who were most satisfied were those who had experienced the least economic hardship and had the most logistical and parenting support from their ex-husbands.

These women's experiences strongly suggest the need for more caution in drawing generalizations about the effects of divorce on children. In every case, the effects of the sudden change in standard of living prompted by divorce, the role played by the divorced father in his child's life, and the particular mother-child relationship must be considered. It is both inadequate and misleading to draw conclusions from clinical populations without studying comparative groups or controlling for socioeconomic factors.

Reformed divorce laws have given equality to women. Both personal testimony and recent research suggest that any equality women have gained within divorce law is largely symbolic. The sixty women interviewed had been repeatedly penalized within the law for having been primarily wives and mothers and not wage earners. Although husbands and wives apparently have equal access to obtaining a legal divorce, in practice even that equality is mythical. In being treated by the law as if they were social and economic equals, these women were put at a profound disadvantage, and the inequities of the traditional marital arrangement were obscured. They lost their primary source of income and were given nearly total responsibility for their dependent children and themselves. The law's failure to recognize that these women confronted a gender-structured society which puts them at a disadvantage as single-parent providers contributed directly to the extent of the hardship they encountered.

In other words, our society's promise to honor the role of motherhood proved hollow in divorce; the law, which at least theoretically represents society's values, did not recognize these women's contributions to family life and gave them no protection for carrying on their mothering activities. It simply left them alone, to cope individually with increased responsibilities.

These women were also at a disadvantage in the practical process of divorcing legally. Lacking experience, social prestige, and large amounts of money, they found that lawyers frequently treated them as second-class citizens. Their frustration over the puzzles and inequities of divorce law was compounded by the treatment they received from certain legal professionals.

Community property laws treat wives and husbands equally. Because these women lived in California, a community property state, they were legally entitled to an equal share of the assets and belongings acquired during their marriages. However, as they learned at the time of divorce, the legal definitions of community property systematically denied them a share of the major assets thus acquired. Most important, their contributions to a husband's education and earning power were ignored in the divorce property settlement; the law simply did not recognize a husband's career development and professional attainments as jointly acquired and owned. Nor did the law recognize that many of these women, when married, had accepted a division of labor whereby they would put their primary efforts into parenting and maintaining the family's domestic life while their husbands would pursue income-earning and career enhancement activities. The law ignored the fact that during married life both spouses had viewed this arrangement as a reasonable, normal, and equal exchange. After divorce, the parenting and homemaking skills these women had learned did not help them find jobs. Instead, they found themselves severely and permanently penalized for having been economically dependent on their husbands, who were able to leave marriage with their jobs and their earning abilities intact.

Besides experiencing the immediate economic hardships brought on by narrow definitions of community property, these divorced women had to face highly uncertain futures. Legal definitions of the ownership of retirement funds and Social Security benefits, for example, discriminated against them; they would be penalized for life because they had spent their married years "unemployed," engaged in family activities. In other words, the penalties for accepting the traditional gender role assigned to women—the role of a wife and mother who is an economic dependent—are by no means short-term. Unless these women regain economic security through remarriage, most of them will face a dismal future as the very poorest of the elderly portion of our society. It may be true, as some researchers have concluded, that women who divorce in community property states are better off in certain ways than those in common-law states. But this does not mean that divorce settlements in those states treat men and women equally. As these women's experiences testify, they do not.

Divorced fathers pay heavily to support their ex-wives and their children. Census data and other research findings reveal a shocking pattern of failure by divorced fathers to comply with child support orders and to contribute to the economic support of their minor children. These data also show that there is no relationship between a father's financial ability to pay and his degree of compliance or noncompliance with child support orders. Further, until legislative actions taken in 1984, the task of seeking to enforce child support orders has fallen on divorced mothers themselves.

The experiences of the sixty women in this study are consistent with such findings. Only twenty-three of them received child support regularly; another thirteen received child support occasionally; and the remaining twenty-four received no financial support at all from the fathers of their children. Although child support payments were an important addition to their incomes, the amounts these women received were typically low and fell far short of an equitable contribution. Indeed, the average amount received per child by the mothers who *did* receive child support was only $112 per month. Among the mothers interviewed, those who sought legal enforcement of child support orders found only more legal expenses and increased frustration; none succeeded in obtaining monthly support contributions. There can be no doubt that these mothers carried the major financial responsibility for the support of their children, even though their earnings were significantly smaller than those of their former husbands. Only six of these sixty women received a spousal support award at the time of divorce, and only one of these awards was given for an indefinite period of time. None of the spousal support awards provided an adequate monthly income.

Therefore, these women were expected to become immediately self-supporting, regardless of their skills, age, and child-care responsibilities. As women who had shared economic security with their husbands during marriage and who were well established in a middle-class life-style, divorce led to a dramatic decline in the amount of income available to them and to their dependent children. As their accounts showed, once they divorced, many of them quickly entered the ranks of the poor. On the other hand, their former husbands, who retained their income-earning activities and who paid little or no child support or spousal support, actually gained economically.

Divorce affords great opportunities for personal growth and development. Most of these women were engaged in an ongoing struggle to make ends meet, to handle simultaneously the tasks of parenting and earning an income, and to cope with the stress brought on by the uncertainties of their lives. Rather than being liberated single women, they were socially and emotionally isolated, as well as overloaded with demands on their time and energy. Additionally, many mothers felt worry and guilt about how their children might be affected by the limited attention they were able to give them. And all agreed that there was a price to be paid for any freedom gained by leaving an unhappy marriage: each of them believed that the economic hardship prompted by divorce had reduced her opportunity to be the kind of mother she had hoped to be.

For these women, feelings of satisfaction and reward about having coped successfully were reached only by experiencing shaken self-esteem, social and emotional isolation, anxiety and stress, and doubts about their continued ability to manage all the tasks confronting them as single parents. Even the few women who had experienced some lessening of stress and some increased mastery of their situations faced uncertain futures. Many were convinced that their disappointment over not being able to provide for their children as they had anticipated during marriage would never fully be erased, no matter what gains they might eventually make. According to their own reports, many women also wondered occasionally about their personal identities: they had gained a new sense of self through divorcing and meeting the situations confronting them, but they had had little leisure time for reflection and the pursuit of self-knowledge. They identified themselves as single mothers and often took pride in what they had been able to accomplish in difficult circumstances, but they also wondered how they would feel about themselves when their children were grown.

These women were aware that their former husbands did not suffer the hardships that characterized their own lives: their husbands retained their comparatively high incomes, typically participated little (if at all) in parenting activities, and had the time, energy, and financial resources to pursue various personal interests and activities. Furthermore, the gap between the experiences of these women and their ex-husbands continued to widen as the years passed.

Postdivorce problems are only temporary, because most people remarry. Personal experience proved this assumption misleading in several ways. To begin with, these women were fully occupied in coping with circumstances of the moment; they were real people trying to manage their daily lives. In that sense, whether any of them eventually remarry is beside the point: the problems that confronted them, often unremittingly, were in no way diminished by the possibility of remarriage. Their experiences were real, and the psychological effects of the hardships they have known will never completely disappear. Likewise, many of the parenting opportunities lost to them because of the social and economic consequences of divorce will not be recovered: as children continue to grow and develop into adults, the time for parenting runs out. All of these women had already lived for several years in these uncertain conditions, some of them for seven or eight years—which is a long time in terms of childrearing. Their sense of regret over lost opportunities will linger on, whether they remarry or not.

Pragmatically, it is unlikely that any significant number of these women will remarry. Most of them said they did not expect to marry again, partly because they knew that as single mothers nearing middle age (or older), they were not the most desirable marriage candidates. Also, most of them simply had little time to put into meeting potential mates and little energy for working out their feelings about divorce or their inner conflicts about relations with adult men. And, of course, women who do remarry have no certain immunity from another divorce.

Gender—social identity based on biological sex—remains the central organizing principle in contemporary American family life. The experiences of divorce described in this book were shaped by the particular social, economic, and political context within which they occurred: a liberal democratic and capitalistic society with a patriarchal tradition.* In other words, divorce is a socially structured experience that reflects the gender-based organization of our society, with all its related inequities. In fact, because it exaggerates and increases these inequities, the experience of divorce has two distinct types: his and hers. The popular assumptions that obscure this truth, hiding the realities of divorce as experienced by the female half of the population, live on partly because of our unwillingness to confront the continued presence of gender stratification.

Just as gender politics continue to shape society, marriage, and family life, they continue to shape divorce. Pervasive gender inequities and discrimination place limits on the successful functioning of divorced mothers. The women we have studied were in situations that reflect their secondary status in a gender-stratified society: their low social, legal, and economic status shaped every aspect of their lives after divorce. Most of the claims that women have achieved equality with men look feeble in the light of one conclusion drawn by all the women in this study: in order to secure a decent standard of living, a reasonably comfortable and manageable life-style, and the respect to which a full citizen is entitled, a woman with children must be married.

The burdens that these divorced women carried after divorce were

---

*See Zillah Eisenstein's *The Radical Future of Liberal Feminism* for a thorough discussion of the intersections between liberal democracy, capitalism, and patriarchy in our society.

heavy: primary responsibility both for parenting and for the financial support of themselves and their children, unequal treatment under divorce law, and the need to compete in a wage-labor and occupational market that discriminates against them. Each of these inequities is itself a consequence of social practices based on particular ideas about gender. As the women in this study discovered, these practices came together with dramatic impact as soon as they divorced.

During marriage the economic dependency of these women was ignored, taken for granted as normal, or openly agreed to by both husband and wife as being in the best interests of the family. In this regard, both husband and wife were behaving according to cultural expectations for men and women who are married and have dependent children. The possible consequences of the wife's dependency were hidden by various beliefs—chiefly that the husband's gains in the employment sector were really family gains, not simply individual ones, and that the wife's contributions to family life were equally important. For these women, it took divorce to reveal the actual inequality of gender roles in the family, by demonstrating that their middle-class status (and that of their children) depended on the husband's wage-earning efforts and class position.

Our continued failure to recognize the social and economic plight of divorced mothers and their children is in itself a reflection of gender bias. The injustices that spring from a socially maintained gender hierarchy are numerous and far-reaching, yet they remain largely ignored by policy-makers and elected officials. The declassing and even the impoverishment of divorced women with children has increased steadily for more than a decade, yet little public attention has been directed to it, and there has been no collective definition of the phenomenon as a social problem. Unfortunately, it seems improbable that divorced mothers themselves will find the resources to publicize their situations and demand corrective action.

This study raises many important questions. They cannot appropriately be answered here, but perhaps simply acknowledging some of them, and stating them in a provocative way, will help point us toward the kind of thinking we need to do.

Do we really value women's activities as parents, or do we reward mothering only when it is done in the context of a marriage? Do we believe that all individuals—men and women alike—have the right to make personal choices about their family arrangements? If we do, why do we continue to penalize divorced women who accept the long-term responsibility for raising their children? Is our ideal of equal rights and equal opportunities for everyone still a philosopher's abstraction—a justification for individual choice that ignores the demands of all cooperative efforts, and especially the effort involved in raising children?

How much do we really care about the lives of children in our society? If divorce—which nationally is a 50 percent possibility—means that both mothers and children are likely to be declassed, impoverished, and confronted with lives of continuous uncertainty, how narrow is our concern? Do we care only for children whose parents are married? And what values are we teaching our children—not only the children directly affected by divorce but also those who benefit from the social system of gender stratification? Are we promoting a spirit of social and gender reconciliation and cooperation, or are we promoting divisiveness, the pursuit of self-interest, and social alienation?

Do we really appreciate social heterogeneity and pluralism, or do we actually want conformity and traditional arrangements? Will we allow reactionaries, those who oppose any change in the status quo, to dictate the terms of our social policies and programs, regardless of the effect on individuals and large groups, such as divorced mothers? Will we use our collective creativity to develop innovative programs and policies, or will we continue to accept piecemeal "fixes" for the problems faced by single-parent families?

Ultimately, the questions raised by this study point to basic ideas about human beings and the kind of group life we seek. Will we encourage *all* persons to be self-actualizing and committed citizens, regardless of gender or parental status? Will we recognize the extent of our social nature, the ways in which we are inescapably dependent upon each other? Will we learn how to value every person's access to a high quality of life? Will we move beyond word-battles about what defines a family, and begin to seek a more just and equitable society?

Questions like these point to the broad scope of the problem, and they bring into focus many of our basic assumptions about family life and social cooperation generally. Certainly they have complex sources, and answering them fully could take many years. But both practical and moral considerations call for corrective action now. Although the ultimate need is to end all systems of social stratification and address fundamental questions about group life, there are some things we can do now to give immediate help to divorced mothers and children. As we know from the successful efforts of other advanced industrial nations, programs and policies that further the following goals are neither mysterious nor impossible to implement:

1. A truly adequate and guaranteed minimum family income, to be obtained through a variety of sources, including reasonable child support payments, fair wages, and where necessary, supplementary grants.

2. Effective training programs and full employment opportunities for women reentering the job market.

3. Flexible work schedules that permit a reasonable coordination between the job and family life.

4. Affordable, high-quality child care programs.

5. Protected access to health care and to retirement pension coverage.

6. Adequate, affordable, and safe housing.

7. Centralized community resource offices that offer information on all social support programs available to families in transition.

Programs like these, aimed at easing the lives of divorced mothers and their children, can only enhance the health of our whole society.

Appendix A

Methods, Sources, and Research Needs

Because the methodological task of this study was to gain access to the personal experiences of divorced mothers, the primary research tool was the in-depth, open-ended interview. Data were obtained through direct and systematic discussions with sixty divorced women. Both my choice of the interview method and my use of the data it yielded reflect a basic assumption: that individuals actively interpret and construct their social and psychological lives. As Herbert Blumer has written: "The human being is not a mere responding organism, only responding to the play of factors from his world or from himself; he is an acting organism who has to cope with and handle such factors and who, in so doing, has to forge and direct his line of action" (1969:55). In-depth interviewing, which yielded partially structured personal conversations, allowed women to explain in their own words how they responded to changed circumstances and unexpected events and how they came to understand themselves and their relations to society.

Subjects

I began my effort to construct a random sample of divorced mothers by consulting the public records of the superior courts in two Bay Area counties. I collected the names of two hundred women who had received final decrees of divorce at least two years earlier and then sent each one a letter describing the project and inviting her participation. The response was poor, chiefly because so many of the recorded addresses were out of date; over half the letters were returned because the post office could find no forwarding address. From among the women I was able to make contact with, twenty ultimately met the criteria for being interviewed and were willing to participate in the study. In ideal circumstances (without constraints of time or money), all subjects would have been located through public records in order to avoid some of the dangers of self-selection by subjects. But after discussions with my dissertation committee and other researchers, I decided that other means of contacting divorced women could appropriately be used.

Subsequently, I contacted divorced women by leaving announcements of the project at various places: a child care center, a latchkey program, two workplaces that employed hundreds of persons in a wide variety of jobs, and two large urban churches that sponsored adult singles' groups. Unexpectedly, a newspaper story about the project encouraged interested persons to contact me, by telephone or through the mail, at my expense. The response became almost overwhelming, and I spent many hours on the telephone talking with women who were interested but did not meet the criteria for participation in the study.

I began formally interviewing women in 1983. I stopped interviewing after the sixtieth subject, because by then both the general and the particular aspects of the divorced women's accounts could be "more or less predicted," a strategy summed up by Jacqueline Wiseman (1979:282). The sixty women interviewed lived in six different Northern California counties in the San Francisco Bay Area and as far east as Sacramento. I found no substantial differences between the accounts of the women located through court records and through other means, and no differences that reflected county of residence.

Each interview subject met the following criteria: she was a legally divorced mother who had not remarried; she had been divorced for more than two years; she had custody of at least one minor child; and she viewed herself as having been "middle class" during marriage. I used two years as the minimum time since divorcing because other researchers have shown that it takes most family units of women and children approximately two years to regain some kind of equilibrium. Because I was interested mainly in examining how divorced mothers had made new arrangements and reached new understandings of their lives, I decided to avoid the complications of studying women who were still caught up in the direct emotional effects of separation. And because I wanted to discover what divorced women with children had to say about their lives as single heads-of-household, I decided not to interview women who shared a residence with an adult male. (According to data from the U.S. Bureau of the Census, the majority of divorced mothers do not pool resources with an adult male.)

I chose to study women who had been "middle class" during marriage because much divorce research has traditionally focused on persons of low-income and lower-class status, with the result that many of the stereotypes about divorce reflect an assumption that divorce is not common to the middle class. Recent studies using descriptive statistical data, such as the University of Michigan's longitudinal Panel Study of Income Dynamics, have shown that the dramatic increase in the divorce rate has involved persons of all status groups, and that persons belonging to the "middle class" have been particularly affected by it. Therefore the need to study divorced women of "middle class" status is acute.

My attempt to select women of "middle class" socioeconomic status requires more explanation, for it poses many conceptual and definitional difficulties. Family class status is typically measured by the educational and occupational position of the husband, not the wife; researchers have demonstrated that most people tend to rate their personal class status higher rather than lower; and patterns of occupational mobility and economic change tend to be obscured in personal reports. However, most wives—and even those who are employed—are economically dependent on their husbands (U.S. Bureau of the Census, 1985; Rainwater, 1984). People's tendency to rate their socioeconomic class status higher than statistical criteria would suggest can be minimized by asking particular questions. Variations in socioeconomic class status can also be discovered by asking the respondents specific questions about their reports on class status. The women interviewed for this study were well educated and had been married to highly educated men, had economically comfortable family life-styles, and shared an understanding of themselves as belonging to the middle class. I declined offers to interview several women who reported a primary reliance on welfare by more than one generation of women in the family; again, I did this as a precaution, for I had no sure knowledge that they were not in fact "middle-class" women living in unusual circumstances.

Clearly, I have not used a perfectly representative sample of all divorced women with children. I have studied the experiences after divorce of sixty individual women, each of whom was a custodial parent, considered herself to have been "middle class" during her marriage, and was a single head-of-household with no adult male in residence. It should be noted, however, that if the sample were truly representative of the general population, the portrayal of women's postdivorce experiences would probably be even more shocking. Census data and other statistics show clearly that divorce has the most devastating economic effects on lower-income and poverty-stricken families; and also that women deserted by husbands or separated without being divorced are the poorest of all categories of low-income women. By limiting my study to divorced women who had not remarried and were not living with an adult male, I have not taken account of all the ways in which women cope with the difficulties of being divorced with children. Divorced mothers living with an adult man, although they may well have other pressing problems in their lives, have more opportunities for relieving financial uncertainties and perhaps also for reducing stress overload, loneliness, and conflicts about "dating" and sexual activity.

Interviews

Early in my research, I also asked five attorneys who do divorce work (not all of them were specialists in family law) and ten public school teachers to give me their impressions of the effects of divorce on children and family life. These background interviews, which I did not include in the analysis, helped increase my sensitivity to some of the issues that emerged as I began interviewing the divorced mothers.

Before beginning the formal interviews, I developed an interview instrument, reviewed it with several qualitative researchers, and refined it. I pretested it by interviewing five divorced women acquaintances and then revised it again. The instrument listed all the basic questions I wanted to ask in the formal interviews; however, I quickly found that strict adherence to its structure tended to interfere with the interviewee's train of thought, and I soon accepted Norman Denzin's statement that "as a social process, the interview relationship assumes emergent and not wholly predictable dimensions" (1978:171). As a result, the interviews were largely open-ended but followed a general pattern of questioning. I sought consistency among the interviews by checking to see that each of the particular areas covered by the instrument were discussed at some point in each interview.

I developed questions for the following specific areas: general background information, which included age, level of education, number and ages of children, age at marriage, length of marriage, time divorced, and family socioeconomic status; description of the marriage; the legal aspects of divorce; economic effects of divorce; sources of income, income level, and employment; parenting; domestic activities; leisure activities and dating; relations with the ex-husband and his involvement with the children; kinds of support found available and used; and a personal expression of hopes and fears for the future. I learned from pretesting the interviews that the weakest area of questioning in my early interview instrument was the one concerned with the legal aspects of divorce. Because my assessment was confirmed in the first two formal interviews, I subsequently gave more attention to this facet of divorcing. The instrument otherwise proved to be more than adequate.

The interviews were long; most took more than three hours, and several lasted more than five hours. Follow-up interviews were done with five of the women. Fifty-one of the interviews were done in the women's homes, and nine were done either in my office or at the women's places of work. Each woman chose the site of the interview.

All of these women were volunteer subjects who came to the interview with some understanding of my research goals. They were informed that they could redirect the questioning at any point and even stop the conversation if they wanted. Anonymity was assured to the extent possible.

Children freely entered and left the interview situations in over two-thirds of the home interviews. I was usually introduced to them, frequently shown their bedrooms, and sometimes shown pictures of their fathers. Because of the limitations of this research project, I declined many invitations to interview children. However, their presence during parts of the interview sessions gave me an unexpected opportunity to observe parent-child interactions. My observations proved valuable in that they tended to support mothers' assertions about their children.

I tape-recorded the interviews (with the permission of the interviewees) and took some notes during the sessions. I asked questions and sought clarification when I did not understand what was being said, and I also tried to clarify apparent inconsistencies. However, I adopted the premise that the interviewee was the "only possible expert" regarding her own experiences (Schwartz and Jacobs, 1979:73). I actively sought to gain access to each woman's perspective and understanding—to each woman's picture of her own social reality. I recorded my own comments and observations immediately after leaving the interview, often while driving home or to my office.

The cooperation and interest I received from these women exceeded my earliest hopes. Although the subject of divorce and life after divorce was an emotionally painful one, many women told me they felt they had benefited from being able to talk about it with me.

As the interviews proceeded, I began to understand their eagerness and candor. In part, at least, they wanted to break through the sense of isolation they had felt as divorced mothers. The interview gave them an opportunity to express their frustration about social indifference to their situations; it gave them a ray of hope, however slight, that they "might be heard." Further, by sharing their experiences, they felt validated in them. I think this sense of validation was particularly important to most women in regard to their parenting. The desire to have some recognition for their parenting efforts and for their success at maintaining their families, even under adverse conditions, was what led them to invite me to interview their children and tour their homes.

Data Analysis

I transcribed the tape-recorded interviews in duplicate; one copy was left intact for ready reference to the total interview, and the other was cut apart and used for coding. I analyzed the data according to the procedures delineated by Barney Glaser and Anselm Strauss (1967) and further described by Howard Schwartz and Jerry Jacobs (1979) in their works on grounded theory. I found, as Schwartz and Jacobs have written, that "in grounded theory, data collection, observation, coding and categorizing the data, and developing theories all tend to go on simultaneously and to mutually support one another" (28).

As core variables were discerned, I recoded and organized data by the emergent categories. The major categories of these divorced women's experiences were as follows: married and family life; economics and income sources; single parenting; life as a single divorced woman; children; the legal experiences of divorce; relations with family; relations with the ex-husband; sources of logistical and emotional support; and personal assessment. Each of these categories was then broken down into subcategories. Both the categories and the subcategories were revised as coding of the data proceeded.

Research Needs

From my experience with this project, I believe that two kinds of academic studies are needed most urgently: first, sociological studies geared toward the practical development, implementation, and evaluation of programs aimed at meeting the greatest needs of today's divorced mothers; and second, empirical studies of divorced men.

The specific needs of divorced women that ought to be addressed are as follows: a decent and protected minimum income, to be made possible through a variety of sources (themselves open for evaluation and reform), including adequate child support payments and supplementary sources of income; reentry training programs; health insurance and retirement conversion plans; affordable and quality child care; improvement of the work-family relationship by modifications of the workday and work structure; adequate housing; and community and social support programs. Ideally, this type of research will be augmented by continuing longitudinal studies of diverse groups of divorced women: only by following the experiences of women over several years will we be able to discern the short-term and long-term needs that require political action.

The second area in which research is most obviously needed concerns the lives of divorced men. Except for a few studies, which have used predominately psychological approaches to explore attitudes toward intimate relationships and remarriage, men have been ignored in divorce research. We need empirical data on the social and economic factors in men's lives after divorce. We also need to know how they interpret their own experiences of divorce, for many questions remain unanswered. For example, what have been the principal events and influences in divorced men's lives? How has divorce affected their sense of self, their objectives and priorities, their spending patterns? I believe that the actual choices divorced men make about social activity, living arrangements, and spending priorities deserve as much attention as the ways in which they think and feel. We also need more research on how divorced men relate to their children. How do they deal with the fact that their children, in most cases, are living with their former wives? Discovering the factors that contribute to satisfactory or unsatisfactory relations between divorced men and their children could be of great help in planning how to help families make the transitions required by divorce. We also need to know why some men pay child support even while most do not. What kinds of events or understandings alter men's payment patterns? And what kinds of family support resources and services would divorced fathers use if they were available?

Ideally, academic studies of family life and divorce will analyze data on both men's and women's experiences, so that they can be contrasted and understood in relation to each other. Specifically, we need studies of divorced men and women who are parents of minor children, and studies of men and women who divorce after long-term marriages. And of course, the effects of the social definition of gender on the experiences of family life and intimate relationships require continued analysis.

Appendix B

Tables

Table 1   *Divorced Persons per 1,000 Persons Living With Spouse,*
by Sex, Race, Age, 1960–1982

Year	Total	Male	Female
1960	35	28	42
1965	41	34	49
1970	47	35	60
1975	69	54	84
1978	90	71	110
1980	100	79	120
1982	114	92	137

Year	Race		Age			
	White	Black	15–29	30–44	45–64	65–over
Males						
1960	27	45	16	25	39	24
1970	32	62	28	33	40	42
1975	51	96	51	61	57	32
1980	74	149	78	104	70	48
1982	86	176	91	125	83	41
Females						
1960	38	78	28	41	53	44
1970	56	104	46	61	66	69
1975	77	178	75	93	86	69
1980	110	258	108	147	112	89
1982	128	265	117	171	129	99

Source: U.S. Bureau of the Census, *Statistical Abstract of the United States, 1984,*
p. 45.

Table 2   Marital Status of the Population, by Sex and Age, 1982 (Percent Distribution)

Sex and Age	Single	Married	Widowed	Divorced
Male				
Total	24.5	67.2	2.4	5.9
18–19 years	94.9	4.9	—	.1
20–24 years	72.0	26.7	—	1.3
25–29 years	36.1	57.9	—	6.0
30–34 years	17.3	73.4	.1	9.2
35–44 years	8.8	81.4	.3	9.4
45–54 years	5.4	84.9	1.5	8.2
55–64 years	4.6	86.5	3.5	5.4
65–74 years	4.9	84.0	7.5	3.6
75 and over	3.3	72.5	21.8	2.4
Female				
Total	17.6	61.9	12.5	8.0
18–19 years	84.9	14.4	—	.7
20–24 years	53.4	42.9	.1	3.5
25–29 years	23.4	67.4	.5	8.8
30–34 years	21.6	75.6	.7	12.1
35–44 years	5.6	79.4	2.4	12.6
45–54 years	4.1	78.5	6.8	10.6
55–64 years	4.2	70.9	17.3	7.7
65–74 years	5.3	51.3	38.3	5.1
75 and over	6.1	23.6	68.5	1.8

Source: U.S. Bureau of the Census, *Statistical Abstract, 1984*, p. 46.

Table 3   Female Family Householders With Children Under 18 and No Spouse Present, 1960–1982 (in Thousands)

Unit	1960	1970	1980	1982
Total families in census	25,661	28,812	31,022	31,012
Female family householders	1,891	2,926	5,445	5,868
Percent of all families	7.4	10.2	17.6	18.9
Percent under 35 years old	35.0	43.1	52.4	51.4

Source: U.S. Bureau of the Census, *Statistical Abstract, 1984*, p. 54.

Table 4   Living Arrangements of Children Under 18 Years Old, by Marital Status of Parents (in Percentages)

Children Living With	1970	1980	1982
Both parents	84.9	76.7	75.0
Mother only	10.7	18.0	20.0
Divorced	3.3	7.5	8.2
Married, spouse absent	4.7	5.7	5.6
Single	.8	2.8	4.4
Widowed	2.0	2.0	1.8
Father only	1.1	1.7	1.9
Neither parent	3.3	3.7	3.1
Number of children (in millions)	69.5	63.4	62.4

Source: U.S. Bureau of the Census, *Statistical Abstract, 1984*, p. 53.
Note: Percentages may not add up to 100 because of rounding.

Table 5   Persons Below Poverty Level and Below 125 Percent of Poverty Level by Family Status, 1959–1982

Family Status	Percentage Below Poverty Level[a]			
	1959	1969	1979	1982
Female householder,				
no husband present	50.2	38.4	32.0	36.2
Related children under 18	72.2	54.4	48.6	56.0
All other families	18.7	8.0	7.0	9.8
Related children under 18	22.4	8.6	8.5	13.0

Family Status	Percentage Below 125 Percent of Poverty Level			
	1959	1969	1979	1982
Female householder,				
no husband present	57.1	47.8	41.3	44.9
Related children under 18	79.4	66.2	58.0	64.0
All other families	27.7	12.6	10.6	14.2
Related children under 18	33.8	14.4	13.0	18.6

Source: U.S. Bureau of the Census, *Statistical Abstract, 1985*, p. 455.

Note: Percentages may not add up to 100 because of rounding.

[a]For 1982, the government defined a poverty income as $10,178 for a family of 4 persons, as $7,938 for a family of 3 persons, and as $6,483 for a family of two persons.

Table 6   Percentage of Children in Poverty, by Family Structure

Children From	1969	1979	1983
All families	13.8	16.0	21.3
Two-parent and male- headed families	8.6	8.5	13.4
Female-headed families	54.4	48.6	56.0

Source: U.S. Bureau of the Census, *Statistical Abstract, 1985*, p. 455.
Note: Percentages may not add up to 100 because of rounding.

Table 7   Study Sample: Race and Age (N = 60)

Age	Caucasian	Black	Hispanic	Asian
25–29	4			
30–34	8	1	1	
35–39	18	1		1
40–44	11	1		
45–49	10			1
50–54	2			
55–59	1			
Total	54	3	1	2

Table 8 Study Sample: Years Married and Length of Time Divorced (N = 60)

Years Divorced	3	5	6	7	8	9	10	11	12	13	14	15	16	17	18	20	21	22	23	24	25	26	34
2											1												
3		1	2				2		1	1			2		2				1	1	1		
4			1	2	1	1	1	1	1	1	2	1	1	3			1	1		1		1	1
5	1				3	1	1	2	1		1	1				1	1		1				
6				1	1	1		2					1					1					
7						1				1													
8		1																					
9								1															

Table 9   Study Sample: Educational Achievement (N = 60)

Education	Number
High school diploma	25
Some college education	18
College degree	17
Some graduate education, specialized credential, license	5

Table 10   Study Sample: Family Incomes Before and After Divorce, 1982 (in 1982 dollars)[a]

Family Income	Year Before Divorce	1982
Under $9,999	0	4
10,000–12,499	0	21
12,500–14,999	1	22
15,000–19,999	2	8
20,000–24,999	5	3
25,000–29,999	23	2
30,000–34,999	11	
35,000–39,999	8	
40,000–49,999	4	
50,000–99,999	3	
Over 100,000	3	

[a] Because the rates of inflation were different in the various years that these women divorced, it was necessary to convert all incomes prior to divorce to 1982 dollars.

Table 11   Study Sample: Employment Histories During Marriage, Before Divorce Anticipated (N = 60)

Employment	Before Birth of First Child	After Birth of First Child
Full-time, regularly	37	3
Full-time, intermittently	2	3
Part-time, regularly	4	4
Part-time, intermittently	0	13
Worked for husbands, no wages	2	4
No employment	15	33

Table 12   Study Sample: Sources of Income in 1983

| Secondary Sources | Primary Sources | | |
	Employment	Unemployment Ins.	Welfare
Child support, regularly[a]	23		
Child support, some[b]	12	1	
Family aid	5		1
None	15	1	2

[a] Three of these women also received aid from their families (in the form of monetary assistance); one woman also received temporary spousal support; two received temporary spousal support and had some savings from the divorce settlement; one had temporary spousal support, savings, and family aid; and one had temporary spousal support and family aid.

[b] Seven of these women also received aid from their families (in the form of monetary assistance); one woman received temporary spousal support and had savings from the divorce settlement.

Table 13   Median Usual Weekly Earnings,
Family Type, 1980 and 1982

Family Type and Number of Workers	Median Usual Weekly Earnings	
	1980	*1982*
Married couple families	$436	$496
One worker	312	343
Two workers or more	536	619
Families headed by women		
no husband present	227	253
One worker	188	211
Two workers or more	373	420
Families headed by men		
no wife present	365	403
One worker	289	311
Two workers or more	500	558
All families	405	452

Source: U.S. Bureau of the Census, *Statistical Abstract, 1984,* p. 435.

Table 14   Married, Separated, and Divorced Women:
Labor Force Participation, by Presence and Age of Children,
1960–1982 (in Percentages)

Marital Status	1960	1970	1980	1982
Married, husband present, total	30.5	40.8	50.1	51.2
No children under 18	34.7	42.2	46.0	46.2
Children 6–17 yrs. only	39.0	49.2	61.7	63.2
Children under 6	30.3	45.1	48.7	48.7
Separated, total		52.1	59.4	60.0
No children under 18		52.3	58.9	57.5
Children 6–17 yrs. only		60.6	66.3	68.4
Children under 6		45.4	52.2	55.2
Divorced, total		71.5	74.5	74.9
No children under 18		67.7	71.4	71.6
Children 6–17 yrs. only		82.4	82.3	83.6
Children under 6		63.3	68.3	67.2

Source: U.S. Bureau of the Census, *Statistical Abstract, 1984,* p. 414.

Notes

Chapter 1

1. Glick (1983); data from U.S. Bureau of the Census (1980).
2. Duncan and Morgan (1974, 1976, 1978, 1979); M. Hill (1981).
3. U.S. Bureau of the Census (1985). There has been no significant change in the proportion of children living with a single-parent father since 1960 (U.S. Bureau of the Census, 1983c, 1985).
4. National Advisory Council on Economic Opportunity (1981:46).
5. U.S. Bureau of the Census (1985). In fact, more than half of all families in poverty are headed by women, even though female-headed households make up only about 20 percent of all households; and 55.4 percent of all children in female-headed households live in poverty; children in two-parent and male-headed families who live in poverty total 13.4 percent (U.S. Bureau of the Census, 1985).
6. McCarthy (1985).
7. Weitzman (1981a, 1981b, 1985); Duncan and Morgan (1974, 1976, 1978, 1979); M. Hill (1981); Wattenberg and Reinhardt (1979); Chambers (1979).
8. Weitzman (1981a). Among the research findings that support Weitzman's figures are University of Michigan's Panel Study of Income Dynamics and Chambers's 1979 Michigan study.
9. Johnson and Minton (1982); Duncan and Morgan (1979); Weitzman (1985).
10. Wallerstein and Kelly (1980); Hetherington, Cox, and Cox (1976).
11. Wallerstein and Kelly (1980:4).
12. Holmes and Rahe (1967).
13. Kitson, Lopata, Holmes, and Meyering (1980:299).
14. For example, see Glueck and Glueck (1968); "Children of Divorce" (1978).

15. See Weitzman (1985); Fineman (1983); and Halem (1980). According to Fineman (1980:883), divorce reform has been "the triumph of rule equality . . . at the sacrifice of equity" and has therefore been "symbolic rather than real."

16. Fisher (1974:194–196).

17. Schechter (1982).

Chapter 2

1. One of the goals of the highly publicized 1970 California divorce law reforms was to abolish the legal inequalities of divorce. Discarded was the need for judges to make moral judgments about guilt or innocence of the marriage partners in adhering to marriage law and social expectations. In other words, the court no longer had to rule on the guilt of one spouse and the innocence of the other in order to legally allow divorce. "Irremediable breakdown of the marriage" or "incurable insanity" replaced the previous grounds for divorce, which were fault-based. For discussions of these legal reforms, see Halem (1980); Weitzman (1981a, 1981b, 1985); Fineman (1983); Bruch (1982).

2. Legal aid, a program funded and regulated largely by the federal Legal Services Corporation, was specifically aimed at providing legal services to the poor. Some counties' legal aid programs received additional funding from nonprofit organizations, such as the United Way. The Reagan administration has proposed dismantling the Legal Services Corporation, and although Congress has opposed a complete dismantling, the program's funding has been substantially reduced. Legal aid, in the counties where it remains today, is able to offer only a fraction of the services that it offered in 1980. See Villers Advocacy Associates (1985).

3. This pattern has been noted by others. See Bernard (1972, 1975); Pleck (1979); Vanek (1980); Hoffnung (1984); Weitzman (1981b).

4. Halem (1980:246–247). Goldstein, Freud, and Solnit (1979) argue persuasively that children's interests, especially in continuity of family relationships, "should be the paramount consideration" in placement decisions. They believe that legal recognition of a child's right to such continuity would vastly reduce the number of court challenges to custody and attempts to modify it.

5. In 1981, 53 percent of women with custody of children and court-ordered support awards did not receive the child support payments due them (U.S. Bureau of the Census, 1984). The government estimates that approximately $4 billion in child support goes unpaid each year (U.S. Department of Health and Human Services, 1984). Weitzman reports three consistent findings about compliance with child support. "First, fewer than half of the

fathers comply more or less regularly with court orders to pay child support. . . . Second, it is evident that a majority of fathers who comply do so irregularly and are often in arrears (perhaps as many as 89 percent). . . . Third, all the research indicates that a very sizeable minority of fathers—a hefty 47 percent—never make a single payment." The higher rate of child support payments to women in the group I interviewed might be explained by two facts: the ex-husbands were relatively stable income earners, and most of them kept their jobs and remained in their communities after divorce. The threat of garnisheeing salaries in order to collect support may have been more effective because the ex-husbands lived nearby. For discussions of the effects of wage garnishment on divorced fathers for payment of child support, see Chambers (1979); Weitzman (1981a, 1981b); Weitzman and Dixon (1979).

6. Data for the nation show that women with court-ordered payments received only about 55 percent of the amount they were owed in 1981 and that child support payments made up "only about 13 percent of the average male income" (U.S. Bureau of the Census, 1983c:2).

7. This situation has changed since the time of the interviews. Effective July 1, 1984, the California legislature directed that "the court shall take into consideration the age increase factor developed by the judicial council" in modifying a child support order (California Civil Code, sec. 4700.3, in *West's California Code,* 1985). Further, on July 1, 1984, a simplified procedure for requesting the modification of a child support order by a custodial parent became effective. An increase of 10 percent of the current award can be requested every twelve months without requiring legal assistance or representation (California Civil Code, sec. 4700.1, in *West's California Code,* 1985).

8. For thorough discussions of divorce law reforms, see Fineman (1983); Bruch (1982, 1983); Weitzman (1985). All argue that women have gained not real but only symbolic equality under the law.

9. Bruch (1982:821).

10. Weitzman (1981a, 1981b, 1985) and Halem (1980).

11. For discussions of the development of community property laws in the United States, see Babcock et al. (1975); Golden (1983); Fineman (1983); Harwood (1985); Weitzman (1981a, 1981b).

12. Babcock et al. (1975:613).

13. Weitzman (1981a, 1981b); Babcock et al. (1975); Halem (1980).

14. Golden (1983:5).

15. Harwood (1985:67).

16. Also, according to Golden (1983:4), more predictable and less costly settlements will emerge when more common-law states adopt the Unified Marital Property Act of 1981, proposed by the National Conference of

Commissioners on Uniform State Laws. This act created two classes of property: individual and marital. Individual property is all property acquired prior to marriage and certain kinds of property acquired thereafter—personal injury awards, property received in exchange for individual property, and some kinds of gifts. All other property is assumed to belong to the marriage; each spouse is said to have "a present undivided one-half interest in marital property," which is to be divided equally at divorce.

17. Harwood (1985:67).

18. The California Supreme Court ruled in January 1985, in the *Sullivan* re *Sullivan* divorce case, that a spouse *may* have a right to the other spouse's career earnings and returned the case to the lower court for further action. As yet, no precedent governs the division of career and education as community property. For a discussion of educations and careers as community property, see Raggio (1982); Kennedy and Thomas (1979); Weitzman (1985).

19. Raggio (1982:160).

20. Among the federal pensions and insurance policies not viewed as community property are railroad retirement pensions and Social Security Old Age Insurance. Federal mandates override state definitions of community property. In 1982, Congress passed legislation that gave states the right to define military retirement pay as community or separate property, reversing the Court's decision in the *McCarty* case of 1981, which ruled military retirement to be separate property. However, cases decided in the nineteen-month interim between the Supreme Court's ruling and the congressional action were allowed to stand, so that spouses, mostly wives, of military personnel who divorced during that period had no rights to the military retirement funds accrued during the marriage. The ruling that some federal pensions, including railroad retirement pensions, are sole property, regardless of whether a state has community property laws, remains valid. Further, because they are strictly *separate* property, there can be no offsetting of these pension funds with other assets. Cohen (1982:326) notes: "In many marriages the pension is the most valuable asset earned during the marriage. Yet one spouse, usually the wife, has no right or only limited right to future pension benefits and may have no right to benefits already received from that source." See Cohen (1982) for further discussion of recent Supreme Court and congressional actions regarding military and federal pensions and retirement funds and Social Security benefits.

21. Factors to be taken into account in determining a spousal support award, specified by California law (California Civil Code, sec. 4801a) are "(1) The earning capacity of each spouse, taking into account the extent to which the supported spouse's present and future earning capacity is impaired by periods of unemployment that were incurred during the marriage to permit the supported spouse to devote time to domestic duties; (2) the needs of

each party; (3) the obligations and assets, including the separate property, of each; (4) the duration of the marriage; (5) the ability of the supported spouse to engage in gainful employment without interfering with the interests of dependent children in the custody of the spouse; (6) the time required for the supported spouse to acquire appropriate education, training, and employment; (7) the age and health of the parties; (8) the standard of living of the parties; and (9) any other factors which it deems just and equitable" (*West's California Code*, 1983b:713–714.)

22. Since 1970, reforms of California spousal support mandates have been intended to aid mothers with young children, women needing transitional support to become self-supporting, and women who have been married for a long time or can be considered too old to become self-supporting. Weitzman (1981b:46–47), among others, concludes that in practice none of these women has been protected. In 1977, only 12 percent of mothers with preschoolers and only 46 percent of women married fifteen years or longer were awarded spousal support. After divorce, women from long-term marriages received only 24 percent of the previous family income, whereas their ex-husbands' incomes were 87 percent of the previous family income. And Bruch (1982:774) concludes: "Changes in support law have been interpreted as reducing the justification for spousal support. The impact has been dramatic. Although spousal support seems rarely to have been awarded to more than 15 percent of divorcing women, those few who receive awards under the new law are receiving smaller amounts for a shorter period."

23. The earnings gap between men and women increases with age: by the time women are forty-five years of age, they earn less than half of what their male counterparts earn. In fact, 35 percent of working women fifty-five or older fall below the poverty line (McCarthy, 1985). Homemakers divorced after long marriages are likely to receive little or none of their husbands' pensions, so the economic hardship following divorce is likely to continue throughout these women's lives. King and Marvel (1982:44) conclude: "The dramatic increase in divorce, especially in the marriages of long duration, predicts an increase in the number of older women living alone and in poverty in the next generation."

Chapter 3

1. Some other studies that show the adverse economic impacts of divorce on women are Duncan and Morgan (1979); Weitzman (1981b, 1985); Spanier and Casto (1979); Eisler (1977); Espenshade (1979); Levitan and Belous (1981); U.S. Commission on Civil Rights (1983); McCarthy (1985). An analysis of the University of Michigan's Panel Study of Income Dynamics, a nationally representative and longitudinal study of five thousand families,

concludes: "Former husbands are better off than their wives. . . . even after adjusting for these transfers [child support and alimony], husbands are still better off than their wives" (Hampton 1974:169). Another major study found: "It is only the women and children whose standards of living decline even when the father is making payments. . . . Four in five fathers can live at or above the Intermediate Standard Budget" (Chambers, 1979:48).

2. The University of Michigan Panel Study of Income Dynamics found that the economic decline experienced by women after divorce is not temporary (Duncan and Morgan, 1974, 1976, 1978, 1979; Hill, 1981). Saul Hoffman and James Holmes (1974:24) state: "Even after adjusting for demographic and environmental variables, female-headed families with children were shown to be two and one-half times as likely to be temporarily poor and twice as likely to be persistently poor as similar families headed by married couples." See also Rainwater (1984); Kamerman (1984); Corcoran, Duncan, and Hill (1984); McCarthy (1985).

3. Various studies have found that reduced consumption of both goods and services is a major response by divorced mothers to economic decline; for example, see Hampton (1976); Espenshade (1979); Masnick and Bane (1980). They spend much less than divorced men do on food, recreation, clothing, and discretionary items (Masnick and Bane, 1980). According to McCubbin et al. (1980:866), a 1979 General Mills study reports: "in order to cope with inflation, 75 percent of the single-parent families were cutting back on health-related items (medical care, dental care, etc.)."

4. George Masnick and Mary Jo Bane (1980) note that many single-parent families move several times in two or three years. Buehler and Hogan (1980) note that women and their children frequently move to poorer housing in order to economize following divorce.

5. Michael Smith (1980:80) concludes from his analysis of the Panel Study of Income Dynamics that no emotional recovery period is evident: regardless of the number of years since their divorce, divorced women had lower community participation and efficacy, as well as a greater sense of alienation and loss of control over their lives. He states that powerlessness and limited community participation may be viewed as important indicators of the societal conditions with which single parents must cope.

Chapter 4

1. A government study concludes: "Even when female householders were employed, their families were nearly four times as likely as other families with employed householders to have annual incomes below the officially estimated poverty threshold. Consistently, about one-third of all families maintained by women have incomes below the poverty level" (U.S. Bureau of the Census, 1982:3, 5).

2. Public assistance (welfare) to families eligible for Aid to Families with Dependent Children serves only as a "mop-up" program, assisting those in the most dire economic circumstances. It provides less than supplementary assistance programs operating in other nations (Kamerman, 1978, 1984; Keniston, 1978; Adams and Winston, 1980). Millions of persons who need cash assistance do not receive it; indeed, only 53 percent of the nation's poor children receive any federal assistance (Children's Defense Fund, 1985).

3. "Earnings of single mothers are the most important source of income for their households, providing on the average between 60 and 70 percent of family income" (Masnick and Bane, 1980:81). Specifically, divorced mothers with no children under eighteen had employment rates of 72.4 percent; those with children between ages six and seventeen, an employment rate of 83.4 percent; and those with children under age six, a 65.4 percent employment rate (U.S. Bureau of the Census, 1984). Divorced and separated mothers are more likely to work than to depend on welfare or other forms of assistance as the major adjustment to the loss of a male wage earner: "the fact is that the majority of mothers who are solo parents are in the labor force" (Rainwater, 1977:1). See also U.S. Bureau of the Census (1985); Corcoran, Duncan, and Hill (1984); Diamond (1983).

4. See Cook (1979) for a discussion of problems of reentry for women who have invested time in family responsibilities. Only Sweden has long-term programs aimed at meeting women's reentry needs and getting women back to work. See also Shields (1981); Rix (1984); King and Marvel (1982); Baruch et al. (1983).

5. Weitzman and Dixon (1980:165) found that: "When asked whether they expected mothers of preschool children to stay home with the children, or to go back to work to earn money, only a third of the Superior Court judges who hear family law cases in Los Angeles said they preferred to have her stay home to care for the children." They found four key themes in the judges' responses: It is "good" to earn money and better than being dependent on a former husband. Work is "healthy" and a form of rehabilitation to build a new life. The combination of motherhood and work is "normal." Work is simply an economic necessity (the most frequently cited reason).

6. Howe (1977). "A high proportion of the jobs that are open to women are in the marginal low-paid, low-status areas generally lacking in opportunities for advancement" (Pifer 1979:23). Nationally, "nearly half of the forty-three million women working in the first quarter were in 'technical, sales and administrative support' jobs, where they represented two-thirds of all workers in those fields. More than one-fifth of all employed women worked in 'managerial and professional specialty' occupations, accounting for two-fifths of all workers in those jobs" (U.S. Bureau of the Census, 1983c:1). In 1980, 37.6 percent of fully employed women earned less than $10,000; 12.1 percent of employed men did so. Only 3.4 percent of fully

employed women but 27.4 percent of men earned over $25,000 (U.S. Department of Labor, 1982). For additional discussions of women's participation in the labor force, see Blau (1984); Glenn and Feldberg (1984); Kanter (1977).

7. Being overeducated for their work is not unusual for women workers. A government study concludes: "More than 26 percent of Black, 23 percent of Hispanic, and 20 percent of White women are overeducated for their jobs. This means they may have a college education, but work in jobs only requiring a high school diploma, or have a high school diploma, but work in jobs requiring an elementary school education" (U.S. Commission on Civil Rights, 1983:19).

8. U.S. Bureau of the Census (1985).

9. Women are more vulnerable than men to unemployment (U.S. Department of Labor, 1983). In December 1983, the unemployment rate of women who maintain families was 10.9 percent; that for male household heads was 5.2 percent (U.S. House Budget Committee, 1984). In 1970, the unemployment rate for divorced women was 5.4 percent (U.S. Bureau of the Census, 1984).

10. "Discrimination against women in the form of low pay is well documented. While men tend to obtain good jobs with rapid advancement, women receive unequal pay for equal work and are assigned to low-level jobs without promotion potential" (U.S. Commission on Civil Rights, 1983:24). "Women in general earn less than men today . . . much of the difference is because the jobs that women hold are generally paid at lower rates than the jobs held by men" (U.S. Bureau of the Census, 1982:3, 5).

11. For discussions of ageism, see Sommers and Shields (1984); Estes, Gerard, and Clarke (1984); Block, Davidson, and Grambs (1981).

12. See MacKinnon (1979:1): "Sexual harassment, most broadly defined, refers to the unwanted imposition of sexual requirements in the context of a relationship of unequal power. Central to the concept is the use of power derived from one social sphere to lever benefits or impose deprivations in another. . . . American society legitimizes male sexual dominance of women."

13. For a discussion of flexible working hours, see Kanter (1977b) and Adams and Winston (1980).

14. According to a *Region V Child Care Study Report* cited in McCarthy (1985), child care costs in the San Francisco Bay Area averaged $225 a month for a preschool child and $310 a month for an infant in 1983, and these costs have continued to rise. For discussions of child care in contemporary America, see U.S. Bureau of the Census (1983a, 1983b); Norgren (1984); Grossman (1982); Children's Defense Fund (1985); McCarthy (1985).

15. Among 1981 AFDC recipient mothers, 36.5 percent had children

under age six, 33.0 percent had children between six and eleven, 27.1 percent had children between twelve and seventeen, and 2.7 percent had children between eighteen and twenty (U.S. Bureau of the Census, 1984). In 1983, only 53.3 of every 100 poor children received AFDC; in 1973, the figure per 100 was 83.6; in 1978, it was 76.1 (Children's Defense Fund, 1985). Some 38 percent of women without child support, but only 13 percent with child support, received AFDC in 1978 (U.S. Bureau of the Census, 1979). In 1981, 20 percent of those eligible for AFDC were families in which the father was absent due to divorce, and 24.4 percent were families from which one parent had separated (U.S. Bureau of the Census, 1984).

16. For a discussion of the adverse effects on mother-headed families of the 1981 Omnibus Budget Reconciliation Act (welfare reforms), see U.S. Commission on Civil Rights (1983); Zinn and Sarre (1984); Children's Defense Fund (1985); U.S. House Budget Committee (1984). "Between 60 and 70 percent of the [governmental] 'savings' were made at the expense of the poor. Because women and children constitute 60 to 80 percent of the consumers of this assistance, these cuts directly influenced the economic status of poor American women and their children" (Diamond 1983:95).

17. "Private sources contribute about 9 percent of total income" (Masnick and Bane, 1980:88). Of the three sources of income to divorced mothers—earnings, public transfers, and child support—child support falls in "a poor third place" (Cassetty, 1978:135).

Chapter 5

1. Agreement that the first year of divorce is felt to be the most difficult has been confirmed by Weiss (1979a). Despite the great number of single-parent families, few studies have examined mother-child relations in the family headed by a single mother. And the significant exceptions—Wallerstein and Kelly (1979, 1980); Hetherington, Cox, and Cox (1979); Weiss (1979a, 1979b)—have used primarily psychological approaches.

2. Weiss's (1979b:98) findings are similar: "A general impression from talking with single parents and with children who live in single-parent households is that children have developed capabilities for independent functioning and for the assumption of responsibility, as well as some specific skills, unusual among their peers from two-parent households."

3. On this point, see also Wallerstein and Kelly (1979, 1980).

4. Middle-class female-headed families, unlike those in lower-income groups that have "extended kin networks," typically have little family support available to them.

5. The negative stereotypes remain strong: "Evidence still exists that for female-headed households, the community traditionally values the widow

most highly, the divorced or separated woman with less regard, the never-married mother as immoral, and the lesbian mother with contempt" (Wattenberg and Reinhardt, 1979:465).

Chapter 6

1. A theoretical perspective on the development of the postdivorce relationship between former spouses, such as Berger and Kellner's "Marriage and the Construction of Reality," would help illuminate this area (Berger and Kellner, 1974).

2. Surprisingly little research exists regarding the postdivorce relationship between the noncustodial divorced parent and the children. Hetherington, Cox, and Cox (1976, 1979) and Wallerstein and Kelly (1979, 1980) are among the few who have given this relationship some attention.

3. Wallerstein and Kelly (1980:122) found: "The greatest change in postdivorce parent-child relationships is precisely that which takes place between the visiting parent and the visited child. At eighteen months post-separation there was no correlation whatsoever between the visiting patterns that had emerged by that time and the predivorce father-child relationship." Further, they found no relationship between sex of child or the custodial parent's attitude about the visitation and the visiting parent's involvement with his children.

4. In their study of forty-eight families of divorce, in which "fathers were probably more interested since they were willing to participate," Hetherington, Cox, and Cox (1976:421) found that father involvement with children steadily decreased over time. "By two years after divorce, 19 of the divorced fathers were seeing their children once a week or more, 14 fathers saw them every two weeks, 7 every three weeks, and 8 once a month or less." An Oxford Centre study, cited by Bruch (1978), found that fewer than 50 percent of noncustodial parents in England and Wales were visiting their children; only seventeen out of two hundred and ninety were not visiting because of the custodial parent's refusal to allow it.

Chapter 7

1. See Bell (1984) and Berkun (1983) for brief discussions on the double standard of aging.

2. See Hess and Waring (1984) and King and Marvel (1982) for discussions of the effects of different rates of remarriage between men and women.

3. "Traditional female socialization does not prepare women never to marry, or for the loss of their role as wife, the demands of raising children alone, or the stress of 'single again' identities. When women separate, they

show classic symptoms of distress compounded by economic helplessness. Women are slowly adapting to this reality, however. There is a new woman emerging on the social landscape. Encouraged by the egalitarian ideology of the women's movement, having realistic expectations of themselves, and valuing their own independence, single mothers may live with confidence and even zest" (Wattenberg and Reinhardt, 1979:465).

4. Jessie Bernard's (1972) argument that married women "may be interpreting happiness in terms of adjustment" despite the evidence that a "wife's marriage is pathogenic" lends some support to understanding these divorced women's personal satisfactions as a form of compensation.

Bibliography

Abarbanel, A. 1979. "Shared Parenting After Separation and Divorce." *American Journal of Orthopsychiatry* 49:320–329.

Adams, C., and K. Winston. 1980. *Mothers at Work: Public Policies in the United States, Sweden, and China.* New York: Longman.

Albrecht, S. 1980. "Reactions and Adjustments to Divorce: Differences in the Experiences of Males and Females." *Family Relations* 29:59–68.

Aldous, J. 1981. "Second Guessing the Experts: Thoughts on Family Agendas for the Eighties." *Journal of Marriage and the Family* 43(2):267–270.

Aldous, J., M. Osmond, and M. Hicks. 1979. "Men's Work and Men's Families." In W. Burr, R. Hill, I. Nye, and I. Reiss (eds.), *Contemporary Theories About the Family.* New York: Free Press.

Allen, C. 1979. "Defining the Family for Post-Industrial Public Policy." In D. Snyder (ed.), *The Family in Post-Industrial America.* Boulder, Colo.: Westview Press.

American Women Workers in a Full Employment Economy. 1977. "A Compendium of Papers Submitted to the Subcommittee on Economic Growth and Stabilization of the Joint Economic Congress of the United States." Washington, D.C.: U.S. Government Printing Office.

Aslin, A. 1978. "Counseling 'Single-Again' (Divorced and Widowed) Women." In L. Harmon, J. Berk, L. Fitzgerald, and M. Tanny (eds.), *Counseling Women.* Monterey, Calif.: Brooks/Cole.

Babcock, B., A. Freedman, E. Norton, and S. Ross. 1975. *Sex Discrimination and the Law: Causes and Remedies.* Boston: Little, Brown.

Bahr, S. 1979. *Economics and the Family.* Lexington, Mass.: D. C. Heath.

Baker, D., and S. Allen (eds.). 1976. *Dependence and Exploitation in Work and Marriage.* New York: Longman.

Bandler, J. 1975. "Family Issues in Social Policy: An Analysis of Social Security." Unpublished doctoral dissertation. Ann Arbor, Mich.: University Microfilms.

Bane, M. 1976. *Here to Stay: American Families in the Twentieth Century.* New York: Basic Books.

————. 1978. "The American Divorce Rate: What Does It Mean?" *Family Policy Note: 10.* Cambridge, Mass.: Joint Center for Urban Studies of MIT and Harvard.

————. 1979. "Marital Disruption and the Lives of Children." In G. Levinger and O. Moles (eds.), *Divorce and Separation: Context, Causes, and Consequences.* New York: Basic Books.

Bane, M., and R. Weiss. 1980. "Alone Together: The World of Single-Parent Families." *American Demographics* (May) 1–7.

Barrett, N. 1979. "Women in the Job Market: Occupations and Career Opportunities." In R. Smith (ed.), *The Subtle Revolution.* Washington, D.C.: Urban Institute.

Barron, R., and G. Norris. 1976. "Sexual Division and the Dual Labour Market." In D. Barker and S. Allen (eds.), *Dependence and Exploitation in Work and Marriage.* New York: Longman.

Baruch, G. 1984. "The Psychological Well-Being of Women in the Middle Years." In G. Baruch (ed.), *Women in Midlife.* New York: Plenum.

Baruch, G., R. Barnett, and C. Rivers. 1983. *Life Prints: New Patterns of Love and Work for Today's Women.* New York: McGraw-Hill.

Baxandall, R., E. Ewen, and L. Gordon. 1976. "The Working Class Has Two Sexes." *Monthly Review* 28(2): 1–9.

Beal, E. 1979. "Children of Divorce: A Family Systems Perspective." *Journal of Social Issues* 35(4): 140–154.

Bell, C., and H. Newby. 1976. "Husbands and Wives: The Dynamics of the Deferential Dialectic." In D. Barker and S. Allen (eds.), *Dependence and Exploitation in Work and Marriage.* New York: Longman.

Bell, I. 1984. "The Double Standard: Age." In J. Freeman (ed.), *Women: A Feminist Perspective.* Palo Alto, Calif.: Mayfield.

Beller, H. 1970. "Father Absence and the Personality Development of the Male Child." *Developmental Psychology* 2(2): 181–201.

Benston, M. 1969. "The Political Economy of Women's Liberation." *Monthly Review* 21(4): 13–27.

Berardo, F. 1981. "Family Research and Theory: Emergent Topics in the 1970s and the Prospects for the 1980s." *Journal of Marriage and the Family* 43(2): 251–257.

Berch, B. 1982. *The Endless Day: The Political Economy of Women and Work.* New York: Harcourt Brace Jovanovich.

Berger, P., and H. Kellner. 1974. "Marriage and the Construction of Reality." In R. Coser (ed.), *The Family.* New York: St. Martin's Press.

Berk, M., and A. Taylor. 1983. "National Health Care Expenditures Study. Women and Divorce: Health Insurance Coverage, Utilization, and Health

Care Expenditures." Paper presented at the annual meeting of the American Public Health Association.

Berk, R., and S. Berk. 1979. *Labor and Leisure at Home: Content and Organization of the Household Day.* Beverly Hills, Calif.: Sage.

Berk, S. 1979. "Husbands at Home: Organization of the Husband's Household Day." In K. Feinstein (ed.), *Working Women and Families.* Beverly Hills, Calif.: Sage.

———— (ed.). 1980. *Women and Household Labor. Sage Yearbooks in Women's Policy Studies,* vol. 5. Beverly Hills, Calif.: Sage.

Berkun, C. 1983. "Changing Appearance for Women in the Middle Years of Life: Trauma?" In E. Marksun (ed.), *Older Women.* Lexington, Mass.: Lexington Books.

Bernard, J. 1972. *The Future of Marriage.* New York: Bantam Books.

————. 1974. *The Future of Motherhood.* New York: Penguin.

————. 1975. *Women, Wives, Mothers.* Chicago: Aldine.

————. 1981. "The Good Provider Role." *American Psychologist* 36(1): 1–12.

Blau, F. 1984. "Women in the Labor Force: An Overview." In J. Freeman (ed.), *Women: A Feminist Perspective.* Palo Alto, Calif.: Mayfield.

Blaxall, M., and B. Reagan (eds.). 1976. *Women and the Workplace.* Chicago: University of Chicago Press.

Bloch, J. 1978. "Another Look at Sex Differentiation in the Socialization Behaviors of Mothers and Fathers." *Psychology of Women: Future Directions of Research.* New York: Psychological Dimensions.

Block, M. (ed.). 1982. *The Direction of Federal Legislation Affecting Women Over Forty.* College Park, Md.: National Policy Center on Women and Aging.

Block, M., J. Davidson, and J. Grambs. 1981. *Women Over Forty: Visions and Realities.* New York: Springer.

Blood, R., and M. Blood. 1979. "Amicable Divorce: A New Lifestyle." *Alternative Lifestyles* 2:483–498.

Bloom, B., S. White, and S. Asher. 1979. "Marital Disruption as a Stressful Life Event." In G. Levinger and O. Moles (eds.), *Divorce and Separation.* New York: Basic Books.

Blumer, H. 1969. *Symbolic Interactionism: Perspective and Method.* Englewood Cliffs, N.J.: Prentice-Hall.

————. 1971. "Social Problems as Collective Behavior." *Social Problems* 18:298–306.

Bodenheimer, B. 1978. "Equal Rights, Visitation and the Right to Move." *Family Advocate* 1(1):22–26.

Bohannon, P. (ed.). 1970. *Divorce and After.* New York: Doubleday.

Bohen, H., and A. Viveros-Long. 1981. *Balancing Jobs and Family Life:*

Do Flexible Work Schedules Help? Philadelphia: Temple University Press.

Bohmer, C., and R. Lebow. 1978. "Divorce Comparative Style: A Paradigm of Divorce Patterns." *Journal of Divorce* 2(2):157–173.

Boss, P. 1980. "The Relationship of Psychological Father Presence, Wife's Personal Qualities and Wife/Family Dysfunction in Families of Missing Fathers." *Journal of Marriage and the Family* 42:541–549.

Bould, S. 1977. "Female-Headed Families: Personal Fate Control and the Provider Role." *Journal of Marriage and the Family* 39(2):309–349.

Boulding, E. 1979. "Family Wholeness: New Conceptions of Family Roles." In K. Feinstein (ed.), *Working Women and Families*. Beverly Hills, Calif.: Sage.

Bradbury, K., S. Daziger, E. Smolensky, and P. Smolensky. 1979. "Public Assistance, Female Headship, and Economic Well-Being." *Journal of Marriage and the Family* 41:519–533.

Brandwein, R., C. Brown, and E. Fox. 1974. "Women and Children Last: The Social Situation of Divorced Mothers and Their Families." *Journal of Marriage and the Family* 35:498–514.

Bridenthal, R. 1982. "The Family: The View from a Room of Her Own." In B. Thorne and M. Yalom (eds.), *Rethinking the Family: Some Feminist Questions*. New York: Longman.

Briggs, N. 1977. "Apprenticeship." *American Women Workers in a Full Employment Economy*. Washington, D.C.: U.S. Government Printing Office.

Brody, E. 1981. "Women in the Middle." *The Gerontologist* 21(5).

Brown, Carol. 1981. "Mothers, Fathers, and Children: From Private to Public Patriarchy." In L. Sargent (ed.), *Women and Revolution*. Boston: South End Press.

Brown, Carol, R. Feldberg, E. Fox, and J. Kohen. 1976. "Divorce: Chance of a New Lifetime." *Journal of Social Issues* 32:119–132.

Brown, Claire. 1982. "Home Production for Use in a Market Economy." In B. Thorne and M. Yalom (eds.), *Rethinking the Family: Some Feminist Questions*. New York: Longman.

Brown, P. 1976. "Psychological Distress and Personal Growth Among Women Coping with Marital Dissolution." Unpublished doctoral dissertation. Ann Arbor, Mich.: University Microfilms.

Brown, P., B. Felton, V. Whiteman, and R. Manela. 1980. "Attachment and Distress Following Marital Separation." *Journal of Divorce* 3(4):303–318.

Brown, P., and R. Manela. 1976. "Changing Family Roles: Women and Divorce." Paper prepared for the American Jewish Committee. Ann Arbor, Mich.: Program for Urban Health Research.

————. 1978. "Changing Family Roles: Women and Divorce." *Journal of Divorce* 1(4):315–328.

Bruch, C. 1978. "Making Visitation Work: Dual Parenting Orders." *Family Advocate* 41:1–44.

————. 1982. "Management Powers and Duties Under California's Community Property Laws: Recommended for Reform." *Hastings Law Journal* 34(2):229–291.

————. 1983. "Developing Normative Standards for Child-Support Payments: A Critique of Current Practice." In J. Cassetty (ed.), *The Parental Child-Support Obligation*. Lexington, Mass.: Lexington Books.

Buehler, C., and J. Hogan. 1980. "Managerial Behavior and Stress in Families Headed by Divorced Women: A Proposed Framework." *Family Relations* 29(4):525–532.

Burgess, J. 1978. "The Single-Parent Family: A Social and Sociological Problem." *The Family Coordinator* 9:132–144.

Burr, W. 1973. *Theory Construction and the Sociology of the Family*. New York: Wiley.

Cahalan, D., R. Roizen, and R. Room. 1976. "Alcohol Problems and Their Prevention: Public Attitudes in California." In R. Room and S. Sheffield (eds.), *The Prevention of Alcohol Problems*. Sacramento, Calif.: State Office of Alcoholism.

Carter, H., and P. Glick. 1976. *Marriage and Divorce: A Social and Economic Study*. Cambridge, Mass.: Harvard University Press.

Cassetty, J. 1978. *Child Support and Public Policy: Securing Support from Absent Fathers*. Lexington, Mass.: Lexington Books.

————. 1983a. "Emerging Issues in Child-Support Policy and Practice." In J. Cassetty (ed.), *The Parental Child-Support Obligation*. Lexington, Mass.: Lexington Books.

———— (ed.). 1983b. *The Parental Child-Support Obligation*. Lexington, Mass.: Lexington Books.

Cauhape, E. 1983. *Fresh Starts*. New York: Basic Books.

Chambers, D. 1979. *Making Fathers Pay: The Enforcement of Child Support*. Chicago: University of Chicago Press.

Chapman, J. (ed.). 1976. *Economic Independence for Women*. Beverly Hills, Calif.: Sage.

Chapman, J., and M. Gates (eds.). 1977. *Women into Wives: The Legal and Economic Impact of Marriage*. Beverly Hills, Calif.: Sage.

Cherlin, A. 1978. "Remarriage as an Incomplete Institution." *American Journal of Sociology* 84(3):643–650.

————. 1981. *Marriage, Divorce, Remarriage*. Cambridge, Mass.: Harvard University Press.

————. 1983. "A Sense of History: Recent Research on Aging and the Family." In M. Riley, B. Hess, and K. Bond (eds.), *Aging in Society: Selected Reviews of Recent Research.* London: Lawrence Erlbaum Associates.

"Children of Divorce: A Review of the Psychological Literature." 1978. *Law and Human Behavior* 2(2):167.

Children's Defense Fund. 1985. *Children and Federal Health Care Cuts.* Washington, D.C.: Children's Defense Fund.

Chiriboga, D., A. Coho, J. Stein, and J. Roberts. 1979. "Divorce, Stress, and Social Supports: A Study in Helpseeking Behavior." *Journal of Divorce* 3(2):120–135.

Clarke-Stewart, A. 1971. *Child Care in the Family: A Review of Research and Some Propositions for Policy.* New York: Academic Press.

Coalition on Women and the Budget. 1984. *Inequality of Sacrifice: The Impact of the Reagan Budget on Women.* Washington, D.C.: National Women's Law Center.

Coe, R., and J. Holmes. 1976. "Unmarried Heads of Household." In G. Duncan and J. Morgan (eds.), *Five Thousand Families,* vol. 3. Ann Arbor: University of Michigan Prss.

Cohen, M. 1982. "Federal Pension Benefits: The Reach of Preemption." *Hastings Law Journal* 34(2):293–328.

Colletta, N. 1979a. "The Impact of Divorce: Father Absence or Poverty?" *Journal of Divorce* 3(1):27–36.

———. 1979b. "Support Systems After Divorce: Incidence and Impact." *Journal of Marriage and the Family* 41:837–843.

Cook, A. 1977. "Working Women: European Experience and American Need." In *American Women Workers in a Full Employment Economy.* Washington, D.C.: U.S. Government Printing Office.

———. 1979. *The Working Mother: A Survey of Problems and Programs in Nine Countries.* New York: Cornell University Press.

Corcoran, M., G. Duncan, and M. Hill. 1984. "The Economic Fortunes of Women and Children: Lessons from the Panel Study of Income Dynamics." *Signs* 10(2):232–248.

Cox, M. 1983. "Economic Support of Children by Fathers Following Divorce: Some Theoretical and Empirical Considerations." In J. Cassetty (ed.), *The Parental Child-Support Obligation.* Lexington, Mass.: Lexington Books.

Crossman, S., and G. Adams. 1980. "Divorce, Single Parenting, and Child Development." *Journal of Psychology* 106:205–217.

Cutright, P. 1974. "Components of Change in the Number of Female Household Heads Aged 15–44: United States 1940–1970." *Journal of Marriage and the Family* 36:714–721.

Dalla Costa, M. 1975. "A General Strike." In W. Edmond and S. Fleming (eds.), *All Work and No Pay: Women, Housework, and the Wages Due.* Bristol, England: Falling Wall Press.

Daniels, P., and K. Weingarten. 1982. *Sooner or Later: The Timing of Parenthood in Adult Lives.* New York: W. W. Norton.

Davie, R., N. Butler, and H. Goldstein. 1972. *From Birth to Seven.* London: Longman.

Davis, K., and Rowland, D. 1983. "Uninsured and Underserved: Inequities in Health Care in the United States." In Presidential Commission for the Study of Ethical Problems in Medicine and Biomedical and Behavior Research, *Securing Access to Health Care,* vol. 3. Washington, D.C.: U.S. Government Printing Office.

DeFrain, J., and R. Eirick. 1981. "Coping as Divorced Single Parents: A Comparative Study of Fathers and Mothers." *Family Relations* 30(2):265–274.

Denzin, N. (ed.). 1978. *Studies in Symbolic Interaction,* vol. 1. Greenwich, Conn.: JAI Press.

Desimone-Luis, J., K. O'Mahoney, and D. Hunt. 1979. "Children of Separation and Divorce." *Journal of Divorce* 3(1):37–42.

Diamond, I. (ed.). 1983. *Families, Policies, and Public Policy: A Feminist Dialogue on Women and the State.* New York: Longman.

Duncan, G. 1974. "Unmarried Heads of Household and Marriage." In G. Duncan and J. Morgan (eds.), *Five Thousand Families,* vol. 4. Ann Arbor: University of Michigan Press.

Duncan, G., and J. Morgan (eds.). 1974. *Five Thousand Families,* vol. 4. Ann Arbor: University of Michigan Press.

————. 1976. *Five Thousand Families,* vol. 5. Ann Arbor: University of Michigan Press.

————. 1978. *Five Thousand Families,* vol. 6. Ann Arbor: University of Michigan Press.

————. 1979. *Five Thousand Families,* vol. 7. Ann Arbor: University of Michigan Press.

Dzodin, H. 1980. "In What Form Will the American Family Survive?" *Family Advocate* 3(2):16–27.

Easterlin, J. 1980. *Birth and Fortune.* New York: Basic Books.

Economics of Divorce. A Collection of Papers. 1978. Chicago: American Bar Association.

Eden, P. 1979. "How Inflation Flaunts the Court's Order." *Family Advocate* 1(4):2–6.

Ehrenreich, B., and D. English. 1978. *For Her Own Good: 150 Years of the Experts' Advice to Women.* New York: Anchor Books.

Eiduson, B. 1979. "Emergent Families of the 1970s: Values, Practices, and Impact on Children." In D. Reiss and H. Hoffman (eds.), *The American Family: Dying or Developing.* New York: Plenum.

Eisenstein, Z. 1981. *The Radical Future of Liberal Feminism.* New York: Longman.

Eisler, R. 1977. *Dissolution: No-Fault Divorce, Marriage, and the Future of Women.* New York: McGraw-Hill.

Espenshade, T. 1979. "The Economic Consequences of Divorce." *Journal of Marriage and the Family* 41(3):615–625.

Estes, C., L. Gerard, and A. Clarke. 1984. "Women and the Economics of Aging." In M. Minkler and C. Estes (eds.), *Readings in the Political Economy of Aging.* Farmingdale, N.Y.: Baywood.

Feagin, J. 1975. *Subordinating the Poor: Welfare and American Beliefs.* Englewood Cliffs, N.J.: Prentice-Hall.

Feiner, R., A. Stolberg, and E. Cowen. 1975. "Crisis Events and School Mental Health Referral Patterns of Young Children." *Journal of Consulting and Clinical Psychology* 43:305–310.

Feinstein, K. (ed.). 1979. *Working Women and Families. Sage Yearbooks in Women's Policy Studies,* vol. 4. Beverly Hills, Calif.: Sage.

———. 1984. "Directions for Day Care." In P. Voydanoff (ed.), *Work and Family.* Palo Alto, Calif.: Mayfield.

Feldman, H. 1979. "Why We Need a Family Policy." *Journal of Marriage and the Family* 41(3):453–455.

Ferri, E. 1976. *Growing Up in a One-Parent Family: A Long-Term Study of Child Development.* Berkshire, England: NFER Publishing Company.

Ferri, E., and H. Robinson. 1976. *Coping Alone.* London: NFER Publishing Company.

Fineman, M. 1983. "Implementing Equality: Ideology, Contradiction, and Social Change. A Study of Rhetoric and Results in the Regulation of the Consequences of Divorce." *Wisconsin Law Review* 4:789–886.

Fisher, E. 1974. *Divorce: The New Freedom.* New York: Harper & Row.

Foote, C., R. Levy, and F. Sander. 1966. *Cases and Materials on Family Law.* Boston: Little, Brown.

Fowlkes, M. 1980. *Behind Every Successful Man: Wives of Medicine and Academe.* New York: Columbia University Press.

Fox, G. 1981. "Family Research, Theory, and Politics: Challenges of the Eighties." *Journal of Marriage and the Family* 43(2):259–261.

Fox, W. 1978. "The Uniform Reciprocal Enforcement of Support Act." *Family Law Quarterly* 12(2):113–133.

Freed, D., and H. Foster, Jr. 1978. "Divorce in the Fifty States: An Outline." In *The Economics of Divorce.* Chicago: American Bar Association.

———. 1983. "Family Law in the Fifty States." *Family Law Quarterly* 16(4):289–383.

Freeman, J. (ed.). 1984. *Women: A Feminist Perspective.* Palo Alto, Calif.: Mayfield.

Friedan, B. 1963. *The Feminine Mystique.* New York: W. W. Norton.

Friedman, L., and R. Percival. 1976. "Who Sues for Divorce? From Fault Through Fiction to Freedom." *Journal of Legal Studies* 5(1):61–82.

————. 1977. "A Tale of Two Courts: Litigation in Alameda and San Benito Counties." *Law and Society Review* 10(2):267–303.

Fulton, J. 1979. "Parental Reports of Children's Post-Divorce Adjustment." *Journal of Social Issues* 35(4):126–139.

Furstenberg, F. 1979. "Recycling the Family: Perspectives for a Neglected Family Form." *Marriage and Family Review* 2(3):1–7.

Garfinkel, I., and A. Sorensen. 1982. "Sweden's Child Support System: Lessons for the United States." *Social Work* 207:509–515.

Garfinkel, I., D. Betson, T. Corbett, and S. Zink. 1983. "A Proposal for Comprehensive Reform of the Child-Support System in Wisconsin." In J. Cassetty (ed.), *The Parental Child-Support Obligation*. Lexington, Mass.: Lexington Books.

Gasser, R., and C. Taylor. 1976. "Role Adjustment of Single Parent Fathers with Dependent Children." *The Family Coordinator* 225:397–402.

Gatley, R., and D. Koulack. 1979. *Single Father's Handbook: A Guide for Separated and Divorced Fathers*. New York: Anchor Books.

General Mills. 1979. *The American Family Report, 1978–79: Family Health in an Era of Stress*. Minneapolis: General Mills.

Glaser, B. 1978. *Theoretical Sensitivity: Advances in the Methodology of Grounded Theory*. San Francisco: Sociology Press.

Glaser, B., and A. Strauss. 1967. *The Discovery of Grounded Theory*. Chicago: Aldine.

Glaser, N. 1980. "Everyone Needs Three Hands: Doing Unpaid and Paid Work." In S. Berk (ed.), *Women and Household Labor*. Beverly Hills, Calif.: Sage.

Glen, E., and R. Feldberg. 1984. "Clerical Work: The Female Occupation." In J. Freeman (ed.), *Women: A Feminist Perspective*. Palo Alto, Calif.: Mayfield.

Glendon, M. 1977. *State, Law, and Family*. New York: North-Holland.

Glick, P. 1977. "Updating the Life and Cycle of the Family." *Journal of Marriage and the Family* 39:3–15.

————. 1979a. "Children of Divorced Parents in Demographic Perspective." *Journal of Social Issues* 35(4):180–192.

————. 1979b. "The Future of the American Family." *Current Population Reports*. Washington, D.C.: U.S. Government Printing Office.

————. 1983. "Marital Status and Living Arrangements: March 1982." *Current Population Bulletin*. Washington, D.C.: U.S. Government Printing Office.

Glick, P., and A. Norton. 1977. "Marrying, Divorcing, and Living Together in the United States Today." *Population Bulletin*. Washington, D.C.: U.S. Government Printing Office.

Glueck, S., and E. Glueck. 1968. *Delinquents and Nondelinquents in Perspective*. Cambridge, Mass.: Harvard University Press.

Goetting, A. 1980. "Former Spouse-Current Spouse Relationships." *Journal of Family Issues* 1(1):58–80.

———. 1981. "Divorce Outcome Research: Issues and Perspectives." *Journal of Family Issues* 2(3):350–369.

Golden, L. 1983. *Equitable Distribution of Property*. New York: McGraw-Hill.

Goldstein, J., A. Freud, and A. Solnit. 1979. *Beyond the Best Interests of the Child*. New York: Free Press.

Goode, W. 1956. *After Divorce*. Glencoe, Ill.: Free Press.

———. 1974. "The Theoretical Importance of Love." In R. Coser (ed.), *The Family: Its Structure and Functions*. New York: St. Martin's Press.

———. 1982. "Why Men Resist." In B. Thorne and M. Yalom (eds.), *Rethinking the Family: Some Feminist Questions*. New York: Longman.

Gorden, R. 1975. *Interviewing: Strategy, Techniques, and Tactics*. Homewood, Ill.: Dorsey Press.

Gottman, J., H. Markham, and C. Notarius. 1978. "The Typography of Marital Conflict." *Journal of Marriage and the Family* 29:461–477.

Gove, W., and C. Peterson. 1980. "An Update of the Literature on Personal and Marital Adjustment: The Effect of Children and the Employment of Wives." *Marriage and Family Review* 3:63–96.

Granvold, D., L. Pedler, and S. Schellie. 1979. "A Study of Sex Role Expectancy and Female Postdivorce Adjustment." *Journal of Divorce* 2(4):383–393.

Green, M. 1976. *Fathering*. New York: McGraw-Hill.

Greenberg, J. 1972. "Single-Parenting and Intimacy." *Alternative Lifestyles* 2(3):308–333.

Greenwood-Audant, L. 1984. "The Internalization of Powerlessness: A Case Study of the Displaced Homemaker." In J. Freeman (ed.), *Women: A Feminist Perspective*. Palo Alto, Calif.: Mayfield.

Grossman, A. 1977. "The Labor Force Patterns of Divorced and Separated Women." *Monthly Labor Review* 100:48–53.

———. 1979. *Divorced and Separated Women in the Labor Force*. Washington, D.C.: U.S. Department of Labor.

———. 1982. "More Than Half of All Children Having Working Mothers." *Monthly Labor Review* 41.

Hahlo, H. 1983. "Child Support: A Global View." In J. Cassetty (ed.), *The Parental Child-Support Obligation*. Lexington, Mass.: Lexington Books.

Halem, L. 1980. *Divorce Reform: Changed Legal and Social Perspectives*. New York: Free Press.

Hamptom, R. 1974. "Marital Disruption: Some Social and Economic Consequences." In G. Duncan and J. Morgan (eds.), *Five Thousand Families*, vol. 4. Ann Arbor, Mich.: University of Michigan Press.

Hartmann, H. 1976. "Capitalism, Patriarchy, and Job Segregation by Sex." *Signs* 1(3):137–169.

————. 1981a. "The Family as Locus of Gender, Class, and Political Struggle: The Example of Housework." *Signs* 6(3):143–169.

————. 1981b. "The Unhappy Marriage of Marxism and Feminism: Towards a More Progressive Union." In L. Sargent (ed.), *Women and Revolution*. Boston: South End Press.

Harwood, N. 1985. *A Woman's Legal Guide to Separation and Divorce in All Fifty States*. New York: Scribner's.

Hayden, D. 1984. *Redesigning the American Dream: The Future of Housing, Work, and Family Life*. New York: W. W. Norton.

Hennessey, E. 1980. "Explosion in Family Law Litigation: Challenges and Opportunities for the Bar." *Family Law Quarterly* 14(3):187–201.

Hess, B., and J. Waring. 1984. "Family Relationships of Older Women: A Women's Issue." In E. Marksun (ed.), *Older Women: Issues and Prospects*. Lexington, Mass.: Lexington Books.

Hess, R., and K. Camara. 1979. "Post-Divorce Family Relationships as Mediating Factors in the Consequences of Divorce for Children." *Journal of Social Issues* 35(4):79–96.

Hetherington, E., M. Cox, and R. Cox. 1976. "Divorced Fathers." *The Family Coordinator* 25:417–428.

————. 1979. "The Development of Children in Mother-Headed Families." In D. Reiss and H. Hoffman (eds.), *The American Family: Dying or Developing*. New York: Plenum.

Hill, M. 1981. "Some Dynamic Aspects of Poverty." In G. Duncan and J. Morgan (eds.), *Five Thousand Families*, vol. 9. Ann Arbor: University of Michigan Press.

Hill, R. 1981. "Whither Family Research in the 1980s: Continuities, Emergents, Constraints, and New Horizons." *Journal of Marriage and the Family* 43(2):255–257.

Hochschild, A. 1973. "A Review of Sex Role Research." *American Journal of Sociology* 78:1011–1029.

————. 1979. "Emotion Work, Feeling Rules and Social Structure." *American Journal of Sociology* 85:551–575.

————. 1984. *The Managed Heart: Commercialization of Human Feeling*. Berkeley and Los Angeles: University of California Press.

Hofferth, S., and K. Moore. 1979. "Women's Employment and Marriage." In R. Smith (ed.), *The Subtle Revolution*. Washington, D.C.: Urban Institute.

Hoffman, L., and F. Nye. 1974. *Working Mothers*. San Francisco: Jossey-Bass.

Hoffman, S., and J. Holmes. 1974. "Husbands, Wives, and Divorce." In

G. Duncan and J. Morgan (eds.), *Five Thousand Families,* vol. 4. Ann Arbor: University of Michigan Press.

Hoffnung, M. 1984. "Motherhood: Contemporary Conflict for Women." In J. Freeman (ed.), *Women: A Feminist Perspective.* Palo Alto, Calif.: Mayfield.

Holmes, T., and R. Rahe. 1967. "The Social Readjustment Rating Scale." *Journal of Psychosomatic Research* 2:213–218.

Hood, J., and S. Golden. 1979. "Beating Time/Making Time: The Impact of Work Scheduling on Men's Family Roles." *The Family Coordinator* 28:575–582.

Howe, L. 1977. *Pink Collar Workers: Inside the World of Women's Work.* New York: Avon Books.

Hunter, J., and N. Schuman. 1980. "Chronic Reconstitution as a Family Style." *Social Work* 14:446–451.

Huston-Stein, A., and A. Higgins-Trenk. 1978. "Development of Females from Childhood Through Adulthood: Careers and Feminine Role Orientations." In P. Baltes (ed.), *Life-Span Development and Behavior.* New York: Academic Press.

Inker, M., J. Walsh, and P. Perocchi. 1978. "Alimony Orders Following Short-Term Marriages." *Family Law Quarterly* 12:91–112.

Johnson, R. 1978. "Visitation: When Access Becomes Excess." *Family Advocate* 1(1):14–18.

Johnson, W., and M. Minton. 1982. "The Economic Choice in Divorce: Extended or Blended Family?" *Journal of Divorce* 5(1–2):101–113.

Jones, C., N. Gordon, and I. Sawhill. 1976. *Child Support Payments in the United States.* Washington, D.C.: Urban Institute.

Kahn, A., and S. Kamerman. 1975. *Not for the Poor Alone: European Social Services.* New York: Harper & Row.

Kahn-Hut, R., A. Daniels, and R. Colvard. 1982. *Women and Work: Problems and Perspectives.* New York: Oxford University Press.

Kalter, N. 1977. "Children of Divorce in an Outpatient Psychiatric Population." *American Journal of Orthopsychiatry* 47:40–51.

Kamerman, S. 1978. "To Consider Planning for the White House Conference on Families." *U.S. Congressional Report,* February 2.

———. 1984. "Women, Children, and Poverty: Public Policies and Female-Headed Families in Industrial Countries." *Signs* 10(2):249–271.

Kamerman, S., and A. Kahn. 1983. "Child Support: Some International Developments." In J. Cassetty (ed.), *The Parental Child-Support Obligation.* Lexington, Mass.: Lexington Books.

Kanowitz, L. 1969. *Women and the Law: The Unfinished Revolution.* Albuquerque: University of New Mexico Press.

Kanter, R. 1977a. *Men and Women of the Corporation.* New York: Basic Books.

————. 1977b. *Work and Family in the United States: A Critical Review and Agenda for Research and Policy.* New York: Russell Sage Foundation.

————. 1978. "Jobs and Families: Impact of Working Roles on Family Life." *Children Today* 3:11–16.

Kantor, D., and W. Lehr. 1975. *Inside the Family.* San Francisco: Jossey-Bass.

Kauffman, L., and B. Bycel. 1980. "Divorce—American Style." *Center Magazine* 32:3–18.

Kay, H. 1974. *Sex Based Discrimination Text, Cases and Materials.* St. Paul, Minn.: West.

Keith, P., and R. Schafer. 1982. "Correlates of Depression Among Single Parent, Employed Women." *Journal of Divorce* 5(3):49–59.

Keniston, K. 1978. "Testimony of Dr. Kenneth Keniston, Chairman, Carnegie Council on Children." *U.S. Congressional Report,* February 3.

Keniston, K., and Carnegie Council on Children. 1977. *All Our Children.* New York: Harcourt Brace Jovanovich.

Kennedy, F., and B. Thomas. 1979. "Education and Professional Goodwill." *Family Advocate* 2(1):39–52.

Keyserling, M. 1977. "Women's Stake in Full Employment: Their Disadvantaged Role in the Economy: Challenges to Action." In *American Women Workers in a Full Employment Economy.* Washington, D.C.: U.S. Government Printing Office.

King, N., and M. Marvel. 1982. *Issues, Policies, and Programs for Midlife and Older Women.* Washington, D.C.: Center for Women Policy Studies.

Kitson, G., and H. Raschke. 1981. "Divorce Research: What We Know; What We Need to Know." *Journal of Divorce* 4(3):1–37.

Kitson, G., H. Lopata, W. Holmes, and S. Meyering. 1980. "Divorcees and Widows: Similarities and Differences." *American Journal of Orthopsychiatry* 50(2):291–301.

Kohn, M. 1969. *Class and Conformity.* Homewood, Ill.: Dorsey Press.

————. 1979. "The Effects of Social Class on Parental Values and Practices." In D. Reiss and H. Hoffman (eds.), *The American Family: Dying or Developing.* New York: Plenum.

Kreps, J. (ed.). 1976. *Women and the American Economy: A Look to the 1980s.* Englewood Cliffs, N.J.: Prentice-Hall.

Kreps, J., and R. Clark. 1975. *Sex, Age, and Work: The Changing Composition of the Labor Force.* Baltimore, Md.: Johns Hopkins University Press.

Kriesberg, L. 1970. *Mothers in Poverty.* Chicago: Aldine.

Kulzer, B. 1975. "Law and the Housewife: Property, Divorce and Death." *University of Florida Law Review* 28:1–56.

Kurdeck, L. 1981. "An Integrative Perspective on Children's Divorce Adjustment." *American Psychologist* 36(8):856–866.

Kurdeck, L., and A. Siesky. 1979. "An Interview Study of Parents' Perceptions of Their Children's Reactions and Adjustments to Divorce." *Journal of Divorce* 3(1):5–18.

————. 1980. "Children's Perceptions of Their Parents' Divorce." *Journal of Divorce* 3(4):339–378.

Landes, J. 1977. "Women, Labor, and Family Life: A Theoretical Perspective." *Science and Society* 41:386–409.

Leon, C., and R. Bedmarzik. 1978. "A Profile of Women on Part-Time Schedules." *Monthly Labor Review* 43:3–12.

Levine, J. 1976. *Who Will Raise the Children? New Options for Fathers (and Mothers)*. New York: J.B. Lippincott.

Levinger, G. 1966. "Sources of Marital Dissatisfaction Among Applicants for Divorce." *American Journal of Orthopsychiatry* 36:803–807.

Levinger, G., and O. Moles (eds.). 1976. "In Conclusion: Threads in the Fabric." *Journal of Social Issues* 32(1):193–207.

————. 1979. *Divorce and Separation: Context, Causes, and Consequences*. New York: Basic Books.

Levitan, S., and R. Belous. 1981. *What's Happening to the American Family?* Baltimore, Md.: Johns Hopkins University Press.

Levitan, T. 1979. "Children of Divorce: An Introduction." *Journal of Social Issues* 35(4):1–25.

Lewis, R., and J. Pleck (eds.). 1979. "Special Issue: Men's Role in the Family." *The Family Coordinator* 28(4).

Luepnitz, D. 1979. "Which Aspects of Divorce Affect Children?" *The Family Coordinator* 28:79–85.

McCarthy, L. 1985. *The Feminization of Poverty: Report of the Lieutenant Governor's Task Force on the Feminization of Poverty*. Sacramento: State of California.

Maccoby, E., and C. Jacklin. 1974. *The Psychology of Sex Differences*. Stanford, Calif.: Stanford University Press.

McCubbin, H., C. Joy, A. Couble, J. Comeau, J. Patterson, and R. Neidlee. 1980. "Family Stress and Coping: A Decade Review." *Journal of Marriage and the Family* 42:855–871.

McEaddy, B. 1976. "Women Who Head Families: A Socioeconomic Analysis." *Monthly Labor Review* 6.

MacKinnon, C. 1979. *Sexual Harassment of Working Women*. New Haven, Conn.: Yale University Press.

McLanahan, S. 1981. *Family Structure and Stress: A Longitudinal Comparison of Male and Female-Headed Families*. University of Wisconsin, Institute for Research on Poverty.

McLanahan, S., N. Wedemeyer, and T. Adelberg. 1981. "Network Structure, Social Support and Psychological Well-Being in the Single-Parent Family." *Journal of Marriage and the Family* 43(3):601–612.

Markey, C., Jr. 1983. *California Family Law: Practice and Procedure.* San Francisco: Matthew Bender.

Masnick, G., and M. Bane. 1980. *The Nation's Families: 1960–1990.* New York: Auburn House.

Minton, M., and M. Elia. 1981. "Jarrett v. Jarrett: The Custody Crossroads." *Journal of Divorce* 4(4):1–30.

Moles, O., and G. Levinger. 1976. "Introduction." *Journal of Social Issues* 32(1):1–4.

Moore, K., and S. Hofferth. 1979. "Women and Their Children." In R. Smith (ed.), *The Subtle Revolution.* Washington, D.C.: Urban Institute.

Moore, K., and I. Sawhill. 1976. "Implications of Women's Employment for Home and Family Life." In J. Kreps (ed.), *Women and the American Economy.* Englewood Cliffs, N.J.: Prentice-Hall.

Morgan, D. 1975. *Social Theory and the Family.* London: Routledge and Kegan Paul.

Mott, F. 1979. *The Socioeconomic Status of Households Headed by Women.* Washington, D.C.: U.S. Department of Labor.

Nagel, S., and L. Weitzman. 1971. "Women as Litigants." *Hastings Law Journal* 23:171.

Nakagawa, M. 1979. "Termination of Parental Rights and the Child Support Obligation—In Re Marriage of O'Connell." *University of California Davis Law Review* 12(2):632–645.

National Advisory Council on Economic Opportunity (NACEO). 1981. *The American Promise: Equal Justice and Economic Opportunity.* Washington, D.C.: NACEO.

National Center for Health Statistics. 1979. *Monthly Vital Statistics Report: Marriage and Divorce,* vol. 3. Washington, D.C.: U.S. Department of Health and Human Services.

———. 1984. *Monthly Vital Statistics Report. Supplement,* vol. 32(3). Washington, D.C.: U.S. Department of Health and Human Services.

———. 1985. *Monthly Vital Statistics Report.* February. Washington, D.C.: U.S. Department of Health and Human Services.

National Health Care Expenditures Study. 1982. "Out-of-Pocket Expenditures for Personal Health Services." Data Preview 13. U.S. Department of Health and Human Services.

National Research Council. 1976. *Toward a National Policy for Children and Families.* Washington, D.C.: National Research Council.

Norgren, J. 1984. "Child Care." In J. Freeman (ed.), *Women: A Feminist Perspective.* Palo Alto, Calif.: Mayfield.

Norton, A., and P. Glick. 1976. "Marital Instability: Past, Present and Future." *Journal of Social Issues* 32:5–20.

———. 1979. "Marital Instability: Past, Present and Future." In G. Levinger and O. Moles (eds.), *Divorce and Separation.* New York: Basic Books.

Nye, I. 1982. *Family Relationships.* Beverly Hills, Calif.: Sage.

Oakley, A. 1980. "Reflections on the Study of Household Labor." In S. Berk (ed.), *Women and Household Labor.* Beverly Hills, Calif.: Sage.

————. 1981. *Subject Women.* New York: Pantheon.

O'Rand, A. 1983. "Women." In E. Palmore (ed.), *Handbook of the Aged in the United States.* New York: Greenwood Press.

Orthner, D., T. Brown, and D. Ferguson. 1976. "Single Parent Fatherhood: An Emerging Lifestyle." *The Family Coordinator* 25:429–437.

O'Toole, J. (ed.). 1974. *Work and the Quality of Life: Resource Reports for 'Work in America.'* Cambridge, Mass.: MIT Press.

Palmer, J., and I. Sawhill (eds.). 1982. *The Reagan Experiment.* Washington, D.C.: Urban Institute.

Pearce, D. 1979. "Women, Work, and Welfare: The Feminization of Poverty." In K. Feinstein (ed.), *Working Women and Families.* Beverly Hills, Calif.: Sage.

————. 1984. "Farewell to Alms: Women's Fare Under Welfare." In J. Freeman (ed.), *Women: A Feminist Perspective.* Palo Alto, Calif.: Mayfield.

Pearlin, L., and C. Schooler. 1978. "The Structure of Coping." *Journal of Health and Social Behavior* 19:2–21.

Pett, M. 1982. "Predictors of Satisfactory Social Adjustment of Divorced Single Parents." *Journal of Divorce* 5(3):1–17.

Pifer, A. 1979. "Women Working: Toward a New Society." In K. Feinstein (ed.), *Working Women and Families.* Beverly Hills, Calif.: Sage.

Piotrkowski, C. 1979. *Work and the Family System: A Naturalistic Study of Working-Class and Lower-Middle-Class Families.* New York: Free Press.

Piven, F., and R. Cloward. 1971. *Regulating the Poor.* New York: Pantheon.

————. 1982. *The New Class War.* New York: Pantheon.

Pleck, E. 1976. "Two Worlds in One: Work and Family." *Journal of Social History* 10(2):178–195.

Pleck, J. 1979. "Men's Family Work: Three Perspectives and Some New Data." *The Family Coordinator* 28:481–488.

Polit, D. 1979. "Nontraditional Work Schedules for Women." In K. Feinstein (ed.), *Working Women and Families.* Beverly Hills, Calif.: Sage.

Prager, S. 1982. "Shifting Perspectives on Marital Property Laws." In B. Thorne with M. Yalom, *Rethinking the Family: Some Feminist Questions.* New York: Longman.

Price-Bonham, S., and J. Balswick. 1980. "The Noninstitutions: Divorce, Desertion, and Remarriage." *Journal of Marriage and the Family* 42:959–972.

Pringle, M., N. Butler, and R. Dave. 1966. *11,000 Seven Year Olds.* London: Longman.

Raggio, G. 1982. "Professional Goodwill and Professional Licenses as Property Subject to Distribution Upon Dissolution of Marriage." *Family Law Quarterly* 16(2): 147–160.

Rainwater, L. 1974. "Work, Well-Being, and Family Life." In J. O'Toole (ed.), *Work and the Quality of Life*. Cambridge, Mass.: MIT Press.

———. 1977. *Welfare and Working Mothers*. Cambridge, Mass.: Joint Center for Urban Studies.

———. 1984. "Mothers' Contributions to the Family Money Economy in Europe and the United States." In P. Voydanoff (ed.), *Work and Family*. Palo Alto, Calif.: Mayfield.

Rapoport, R., and R. Rapoport. 1975. "Men, Women and Equity." *Family Coordinator* 24(4): 421–432.

———. 1978. *Working Couples*. New York: Harper & Row.

Rapoport, R., R. Rapoport, and Z. Strelitz. 1977. *Fathers, Mothers, and Society: Toward a New Alliance*. New York: Basic Books.

Rapp, R. 1978. "Family and Class in Contemporary America: Notes Toward an Understanding of Ideology." *Science and Society* 42: 278–300.

Raschke, H., and V. Raschke. 1979. "Family Conflict and Children's Self-Concepts: A Comparison of Intact and Single-Parent Families." *Journal of Marriage and the Family* 41(2): 367–386.

Rawlings, S. 1980. "Families Maintained by Female Householders: 1970–1979." In *Current Population Reports*. Washington, D.C.: U.S. Government Printing Office.

Rein, M., and L. Rainwater. 1977. *The Welfare Class and Welfare Reform*. Cambridge, Mass.: MIT Press.

Reiss, D., and H. Hoffman (eds.). *The American Family: Dying or Developing*. New York: Plenum.

Repper, W, Jr., and C. Samuel. 1982. *Community Property in the United States*, 2nd ed. Charlottesville, Va.: Michie Contemporary Legal Education Series.

Richman, N. 1976. "Depression in Mothers of Preschool Children." *Journal of Child Psychology and Psychiatry* 17: 75–78.

Rix, S. 1984. *Older Women: The Economics of Aging*. Washington, D.C.: Women's Research and Education Institute of the Congressional Caucus for Women's Issues.

Roncek, D., R. Bell, and H. Choldin. 1980. "Female-Headed Families: An Ecological Model of Residential Concentration in a Small City." *Journal of Marriage and the Family* 42(1): 157–169.

Room, R. 1983. "Sociological Aspects of the Disease Concept of Alcoholism." In R. Smart, S. Glaser, J. Israel, D. Kalant, L. Popham, and T. Schmidt (eds.), *Research Advances in Alcohol and Drug Problems*, vol. 7. New York: Plenum.

Roper Organization. 1981. *The Virginia Slims American Women's Opinion Poll: A Survey of Contemporary Attitudes.* Storrs, Conn.: Roper Organization.

Ross, H., and I. Sawhill. 1975. *Time of Transition: The Growth of Families Headed by Women.* Washington, D.C.: Urban Institute.

Ross, S. 1979. "Social Security: A Worldwide Issue." *Social Security Bulletin* 42(8).

Rossi, A. 1968. "Transition to Parenting." *Journal of Marriage and the Family* 30:26–39.

Roth, A. 1976. "The Tender Years Presumption in Child Custody Disputes." *Journal of Family Law* 15:423–462.

Rubin, L. 1976. *Worlds of Pain: Life in the Working-Class Family.* New York: Basic Books.

———. 1979. *Women of a Certain Age: The Mid-Life Search for Self.* New York: Harper & Row.

Rubin, Z. 1973. "The Americanization of the Romantic Ideal." In Z. Rubin, *Liking and Loving: An Invitation to Social Psychology.* New York: Holt, Rinehart and Winston.

Sardoff, R. 1975. *Forensic Psychiatry: A Practical Guide for Lawyers and Psychiatrists.* Springfield, Ill.: Thomas.

Sargent, L. (ed.). 1981. *Women and Revolution: A Discussion of the Unhappy Marriage of Marxism and Feminism.* Boston: South End Press.

Sawhill, I. 1976a. "Discrimination and Poverty Among Women Who Head Families." *Signs* 1:201–221.

———. 1976b. "Women with Low Incomes." In M. Blaxall and B. Reagan (eds.), *Women and the Workplace.* Chicago: University of Chicago Press.

Sawhill, I., G. Peabody, C. Jones, and S. Caldwell. 1975. *Income Transfers and Family Structure.* Washington, D.C.: Urban Institute.

Scarf, M. 1980. *Unfinished Business: Pressure Points in the Lives of Women.* Garden City, N.Y.: Doubleday.

Schaffer, K. 1981. *Sex Roles and Human Behavior.* Cambridge, Mass.: Winthrop.

Schechter, S. 1982. *Women and Male Violence: The Visions and Struggles of the Battered Women's Movement.* Boston: South End Press.

Schleisinger, B. 1975. *The One-Parent Family: Perspectives and Annotated Bibliography.* Toronto: University of Toronto Press.

———. 1977. "One Parent Families in Great Britain." *The Family Coordinator* 26:139–141.

Schorr, A. 1981. "Single Parent Women and Public Policy." *Journal of the Institute for Socioeconomic Studies* 6(4):100–113.

Schorr, A., and P. Moen. 1979. "The Single Parent and Public Policy." *Social Policy* 3:15–21.

Schwartz, H., and J. Jacobs. 1979. *Qualitative Sociology*. New York: The Free Press.

Shields, L. 1981. *Displaced Homemakers: Organizing for a New Life*. New York: McGraw-Hill.

Skolnick, A., and J. Skolnick (eds.). 1983. *Family in Transition*. Boston: Little, Brown.

Slater, C. 1984. "Concepts of Poverty." *Journal of the Institute for Socio-economic Studies* 9(3): 1–12.

Smelser, N., and E. Erikson. 1980. *Themes of Love and Work in Adulthood*. Cambridge, Mass.: Harvard University Press.

Smith, M. 1980. "The Social Consequences of Single Parenthood: A Longitudinal Perspective." *Family Relations* 29(1): 75–81.

Smith, R. 1979a. "Hours Rigidity: Effects on the Labor-Market Status of Women." In K. Feinstein (ed.), *Working Women and Families*. Beverly Hills, Calif.: Sage.

———. 1979b. *The Subtle Revolution: Women at Work*. Washington, D.C.: Urban Institute.

Snyder, D. (ed.). 1979. *The Family in Post-Industrial America. Some Fundamental Perceptions for Public Policy Development*. Boulder, Colo.: Westview Press.

Sommers, T., and L. Shields. 1984. *Gray Paper: Issues for Action*, nos. 1–8. Oakland, Calif.: Older Women's League.

Spanier, G., and E. Anderson. 1979. "The Impact of the Legal System on Adjustment to Marital Separation." *Journal of Marriage and the Family* 41: 605–613.

Spanier, G., and R. Casto. 1979. "Adjustment to Separation and Divorce: An Analysis of Fifty Case Studies." *Journal of Divorce* 2(3): 241–253.

Spanier, G., and P. Glick. 1981. "Marital Instability in the United States: Some Correlates and Recent Changes." *Family Relations* 30(3): 329–338.

Spiegel, D. 1982. "Mothering, Fathering, and Mental Illness." In B. Thorne with M. Yalom (eds.), *Rethinking the Family: Some Feminist Questions*. New York: Longman.

Stack, C. 1974. *All Our Kin: Strategies for Survival in a Black Community*. New York: Harper & Row.

———. 1979. "Extended Familial Networks: An Emerging Model for the 21st Century Family." In D. Snyder (ed.), *The Family in Post-Industrial Society*. Boulder, Colo.: Westview Press.

Staples, R., and A. Mirande. 1980. "Racial and Cultural Variations Among American Families: A Decennial Review of the Literature on Minority Families." *Journal of Marriage and the Family* 42(4): 157–173.

Statsky, W. 1984. *Family Law*. St. Paul, Minn.: West.

Steil, J. 1984. "Marital Relationships and Mental Health: The Psychic Costs of Inequality." In J. Freeman (ed.), *Women: A Feminist Perspective*. Palo Alto, Calif.: Mayfield.

Stevens, J., Jr., and M. Matthews (eds.). 1977. *Mother-Child, Father-Child Relations*. Washington, D.C.: National Association for Education of Young Children.

Strauss, A. 1978. "A Social World Perspective." In N. Denzin (ed.), *Studies in Symbolic Interaction*. Greenwich, Conn.: JAI Press.

Strober, M. 1977. "Economic Aspects of Child Care." In *American Women Workers in a Full Employment Economy*. Washington, D.C.: U.S. Government Printing Office.

Strober, M., and C. Weinberg. 1977. "Working Wives and Female Employment." *Journal of Marriage and the Family* 39:781–791.

Stryker, S. 1959. "Symbolic Interaction as an Approach to Family Research." *Marriage and Family Living* 21:111–119.

Sussman, M. 1979. "Actions and Sources for the New Family." In D. Reiss and H. Hoffman (eds.), *The American Family: Dying or Developing*. New York: Plenum.

Swidler, A. 1980. "Love and Adulthood in American Culture." In N. Smelser and E. Erikson (eds.), *Themes of Work and Love in Adulthood*. Cambridge, Mass.: Harvard University Press.

Tavris, C., and C. Wade. 1984. *The Longest War: Sex Differences in Perspective*. San Diego, Calif.: Harcourt Brace Jovanovich.

Thorne, B. 1982. "Feminist Rethinking of the Family: An Overview." In B. Thorne with M. Yalom (eds.), *Rethinking the Family: Some Feminist Questions*. New York: Longman.

Turner, J., and D. Musick. 1985. *American Dilemmas: A Sociological Interpretation of Enduring Social Issues*. New York: Columbia University Press.

U.S. Bureau of the Census. 1979. "Divorce, Child Custody, and Child Support." In *Current Population Reports*, series P-23, no. 84. Washington, D.C.: U.S. Government Printing Office.

———. 1980. "Child Support and Alimony: 1978." In *Current Population Reports*, series P-23, no. 106. Washington, D.C.: U.S. Government Printing Office.

———. 1981. "Money Income and Poverty Status of Families and Persons in the United States: 1981." In *Current Population Reports*, series P-60, no. 134. Washington, D.C.: U.S. Government Printing Office.

———. 1982. "Trends in Child Care Arrangements of Working Mothers." In *Current Population Reports*, series P-23, no. 117. Washington, D.C.: U.S. Government Printing Office.

———. 1983a. "Child Care Arrangements of Working Mothers: June

1982." In *Current Population Reports,* series P-23, no. 129. Washington, D.C.: U.S. Government Printing Office.

———. 1983b. "Child Support and Alimony: 1981. Advance Report." In *Current Population Reports,* series P-23, no. 124. Washington, D.C.: U.S. Government Printing Office.

———. 1983c. "Households, Families, Marital Status, and Living Arrangements." *Current Population Reports,* series P-20, no. 382. Washington, D.C.: U.S. Government Printing Office.

———. 1983d. "Money, Income, and Poverty Status of Families and Persons in the United States: 1983." In *Current Population Reports,* series P-60, no. 140. Washington, D.C.: U.S. Government Printing Office.

———. 1984. *Statistical Abstract of the United States, 1984. National Data Book and Guide to Sources.* Washington, D.C.: U.S. Government Printing Office.

———. 1985. *Statistical Abstract of the United States, 1985. National Data Book and Guide to Sources.* Washington, D.C.: U.S. Government Printing Office.

U.S. Commission on Civil Rights. 1974. *Women and Poverty.* Washington, D.C.: U.S. Government Printing Office.

———. 1983. *A Growing Crisis: Disadvantaged Women and Their Children.* Washington, D.C.: U.S. Government Printing Office.

U.S. Department of Health and Human Services. 1984. *Child Support: An Agenda for Action.* Washington, D.C.: Office of Child Support Enforcement.

U.S. Department of Labor. 1982. *The Female-Male Earnings Gap: A Review of Employment and Earnings Issues,* report 673. Washington, D.C.: Bureau of Labor Statistics.

———. 1983. *Employment in Perspective: Working Women,* first quarter, report 683. Washington, D.C.: Bureau of Labor Statistics.

U.S. House Budget Committee. 1984. *A Review of President Reagan's Budget Recommendations, 1981–85.* Washington, D.C.: U.S. Government Printing Office.

U.S. House Select Committee on Aging. 1980. *The Status of Mid-Life Women and Options for Their Future.* Washington, D.C.: U.S. Government Printing Office.

U.S.A. Today. 1984. "Kids and Divorce: No Long-Term Harm." Thursday, December 20.

University of California Davis Law Review. 1972. "Symposium on Children and the Law." 12(2).

Vanek, J. 1974. "Time Spent in Housework." *Scientific American* 231: 116–120.

————. 1980. "Household Work, Wage Work, and Sexual Equality." In S. Berk (ed.), *Women and Household Labor*. Beverly Hills, Calif.: Sage.

Verbrugge, L. 1979. "Marital Status and Health." *Journal of Marriage and the Family* 41:267–285.

Victor, I., and W. A. Winkler. 1977. *Fathers and Custody*. New York: Hawthorn Books.

Villers Advocacy Associates. 1985. *Draft Analysis of President's FY 1986 Budget*. Washington, D.C.: Villers Advocacy Associates.

Voydanoff, P. 1984. *Work and Family. Changing Roles of Men and Women*. Palo Alto, Calif.: Mayfield.

Walker, K. 1973. "Household Work Time: Its Implications for Family Decisions." *Journal of Home Economics* 65:7–11.

Walker, K., and M. Woods. 1976. *Time Use: A Measure of Household Production of Family Goods and Services*. Washington, D.C.: American Home Economics Association.

Wallerstein, J., and D. Huntington. 1983. "Bread and Roses: Nonfinancial Issues Related to Fathers' Economic Support of Their Children Following Divorce." In J. Cassetty (ed.), *The Parental Child-Support Obligation*. Lexington, Mass.: Lexington Books.

Wallerstein, J., and J. Kelly. 1979. "Children and Divorce: A Review." *Social Work* (November): 468–475.

Walshok, M. 1979. "Occupational Values and Family Roles: Women in Blue-Collar and Service Occupations." In K. Feinstein (ed.), *Working Women and Families*. Beverly Hills, Calif.: Sage.

Walters, J., and L. Walters. 1980. "Parent-Child Relationships: A Review." *Journal of Marriage and the Family* 42:807–822.

Ware, C. 1982. *Sharing Parenthood After Divorce*. New York: Viking Press.

Wattenberg, E., and H. Reinhardt. 1979. "Female-Headed Families: Trends and Implications." *Social Work* 24:460–467.

Weiss, R. 1975. *Marital Separation*. New York: Basic Books.

————. 1979a. *Going It Alone: The Family Life and Social Situation of the Single Parent*. New York: Basic Books.

————. 1979b. "Growing Up a Little Faster: The Experience of Growing Up in a Single-Parent Household." *Journal of Social Issues* 35(4):97–111.

Weitzman, L. 1974. "Legal Regulation of Marriage: Tradition and Change." *California Law Review* 62:1169.

————. 1975. "To Love, Honor, Obey: Traditional Legal Marriage and Alternative Family Forms." *The Family Coordinator* 24:531–548.

————. 1979. *Sex Role Socialization*. Palo Alto, Calif.: Mayfield.

————. 1981a. "Economics of Divorce: Social and Economic Consequences of Property, Alimony and Child Support Awards." *UCLA Law Review* 28:1181–1268.

———. 1981b. *The Marriage Contract: Spouses, Lovers, and the Law.* New York: Free Press.

———. 1984. "Sex Role Socialization: A Focus on Women." In J. Freeman (ed.), *Women: A Feminist Perspective.* Palo Alto, Calif.: Mayfield.

———. 1985. *The Divorce Revolution: The Unexpected Social and Economic Consequences for Women and Children in America.* New York: Free Press.

Weitzman, L., and R. Dixon. 1976. "Alimony: A Quest for Justice in Changing Times." Paper presented at the annual meeting of the American Sociological Association, New York.

———. 1979. "Child Custody Awards: Legal Standards and Empirical Patterns for Child Custody, Support and Visitation After Divorce." *UC Davis Law Review* 12:473–521.

———. 1980. "The Alimony Myth: Does No-Fault Divorce Make a Difference?" *Family Law Quarterly* 14(3):141–185.

———. 1983. "The Transformation of Legal Marriage Through No-Fault Divorce." In A. Skolnick and J. Skolnick (eds.), *Family in Transition.* Boston: Little, Brown.

West's California Code. 1985. St. Paul, Minn.: West.

West's California Annotated Codes. 1983a. Sections 4000–5099. St. Paul, Minn.: West.

West's California Code, Compact Edition. 1983b. St. Paul, Minn.: West.

Wheeler, M. 1974. *No-Fault Divorce.* Boston: Beacon Press.

Williams, W. 1978. "1978 Supplement." In B. Babcock, A. Freedman, E. Norton, and S. Ross (eds.), *Sex Discrimination and the Law.* Boston: Little, Brown.

Wiseman, J. 1979. *Stations of the Lost: The Treatment of Skid Row Alcoholics.* Chicago: University of Chicago Press.

———. 1981. "The Family and Its Researchers in the Eighties: Retrenching, Renewing, and Revitalizing." *Journal of Marriage and the Family* 43(2):263–266.

Yankelovich, D. 1981. *New Rules: Search for Fulfillment in a World Turned Upside Down.* New York: Random House.

Yoder, J., and R. Nichols. 1980. "A Life Perspective Comparison of Married and Divorced Persons." *Journal of Marriage and the Family* 42:411–419.

Younger, J. 1973. "Community Property, Women, and the Law School Curriculum." *New York University Law Review* 48:230–240.

Zaretsky, E. 1976. *Capitalism, the Family, and Personal Life.* New York: Harper & Row.

Zinn, D., and R. Sarre. 1984. "Turning Back the Clock on Public Welfare." *Signs* 10(4).

Index

Adams, C., on effects of divorce on children, 4–5n
Age, and likelihood of remarriage, 144–145
Age discrimination, 59–60, 135
Agnos Child Support Standards Acts of 1984, 22n
Aid to Families with Dependent Children, 70, 185n.2; California standards for, 23n; recipients of, by age of children, 186–187n.15. *See also* Welfare
Alimony, 9; as percentage of income for mother-headed families, 53n. *See also* Spousal support
Anger: at loss of family support for children, 63; at low levels of child and spousal support received, 24–25, 76; in relations with ex-husbands, 106–108; at treatment by legal system, 12
Anxiety: counseling for, 49; in dealings with ex-husbands, 23, 102–103, 114–115; depression caused by, 43–44; divorce as cause of, 3–4; and economic loss, 46–52; and finding employment, 55; legal delays as cause of, 11–12; after paternal visits, 114–115; and sale of family home, 30; and single-parent situation, 80–81
Arizona, as community property state, 26n
Assumptions about divorce, 3–7, 9, 36, 80–81, 128–129, 150–160

Austria, collection of child support in, 20n

Bane, Mary Jo: on effects of divorce on children, 5n; on housing and consumer habits of single-parent families, 184nn.3, 4; on share of income provided by welfare, 71n
Bernard, Jessie, on personal growth in divorce, 189n.4
Blumer, Herbert, 161
Bruch, Carol: on "dual parenting," 115n; on equal distribution of community property, 26; on fathers' responsibility for children, 109n; on spousal support reform, 183n.22; on visitation by noncustodial parents in England and Wales, 188n.4
Buehler, C., on anxiety caused by financial distress, 47n

California: child support guidelines in, 22–23n, 181n.7; community property laws, 26, 153; divorce rate in, 159; and divorce under "no fault" system, 5, 9, 180n.1; spousal support standards in, 182–183n.21; study of impoverishment of women in, 2; Supreme Court, 182n.18
Chambers, David: on child support compliance, 22n; on income needs of custodial head of family, 38n; on relation between child support and visitation, 107–108n

215

Compositor: G & S Typesetters, Inc.
Printer: Murray Printing Company
Binder: Murray Printing Company
Text: 10/12 Times Roman
Display: Goudy Bold